PRAISE FOR
DICK VITALE AND **TIME OUT, BABY!**

"VITALE'S ENTHUSIASM JUMPS OFF EACH PAGE . . . *Time Out, Baby!*, filled with colorful anecdotes and Vitale's distinctive vocabulary, is a book for all basketball fans. Dick Vitale is truly the modern day ambassador of college basketball."
—*Athletics Administration* magazine

"VITALE IS EVER ON THE GO . . . will mesmerize students of perpetual motion!"
—*Publishers Weekly*

"HIS ENTHUSIASM FOR THE GAME IS CONTAGIOUS . . . Dick Vitale has done more to involve the general public in college basketball than any man alive."
—Lute Olson

"AMERICA'S MOST TALKED-ABOUT SPORTS ANNOUNCER."
—*Chicago Sun-Times*

"TAKE 'TIME' TO READ VITALE'S BOOK . . . It's called *Time Out, Baby!* And yes, it's by the always colorful and often controversial Dick Vitale . . . plenty of Vitale's best anecdotes . . . ENTERTAINING . . . FUN TO READ!"
—*Lexington Advocate-Messenger*

"HE HAS A HUGE AND LOYAL FOLLOWING and no one doubts his thorough knowledge of the game . . . INSIGHTFUL READING."
—*The Sports Final* (NY)

"DICK'S INVOLVEMENT IN COLLEGE BASKETBALL HAS BEEN LIKE A THREE-POINT SHOT AT THE BUZZER."
—Lou Carnesecca

About the Authors
DICK VITALE is a commentator for ESPN and ABC. His first book, *Vitale*, was a national bestseller. DICK WEISS has covered college basketball for the past twenty years, including seventeen for the *Philadelphia Daily News*.

TIME OUT, BABY!

DICK VITALE
With Dick Weiss
Introduction by Mike Krzyzewski

BERKLEY BOOKS, NEW YORK

This Berkley book contains the complete text
of the original hardcover edition. It has been
completely reset in a typeface designed
for easy reading and was printed from new film.

TIME OUT, BABY!

A Berkley Book/published by arrangement with
G. P. Putnam's Sons

PRINTING HISTORY
G. P. Putnam's Sons edition/November 1991
Published simultaneously in Canada
Berkley edition/December 1992

ISBN: 0-425-13534-9

A BERKLEY BOOK® TM 757,375
Berkley Books are published by The Berkley Publishing Group,
200 Madison Avenue, New York, New York 10016.
The name "BERKLEY" and the "B" logo
are trademarks belonging to Berkley Publishing Corporation.

PRINTED IN THE UNITED STATES OF AMERICA

10 9 8 7 6 5 4 3 2 1

I want to dedicate this book to my late mom, who I know is in heaven; and my dad, John, who is living in Elmwood Park, N.J., plus my brother John, sister Terry, and certainly my Vitale clan, Lorraine, Terri, and Sherri, for all of their support in good times and bad and their genuine compassion.

This book would not have been possible without all the beautiful people in TV land who helped me, including the Steve Bornstein family at ESPN and the Dennis Swanson family at ABC, all the producers, directors, play-by-play announcers, technicians, camera people, and all those who worked tirelessly behind the scenes.

I also want to acknowledge Dick Weiss, Gene Brissie of Putnam Publishing, Jeff Samuels of the *Philadelphia Daily News,* Joan Williamson, Karen Conway, and all the fans, players, coaches, and media who make up this one beautiful fantasyland known as college basketball.

A word about Dick Vitale from Mike Krzyzewski, coach of Duke University's 1991 NCAA championship team

Dick Vitale has been on the same upward spiral as college basketball has been on over the last five years. Somehow, the two are related. It's not just luck that it happened. Dick's a part of what's happened. His love for the game comes through so easily. People just see it. They may love what he says. They may hate it. But all of them marvel at his enthusiasm and passion for the sport. I think college basketball needed it. I think it still needs it. That's why he's been a main ingredient in how big the sport has become.

His feelings are genuine. Jusk ask our students. The students like him because there's no b.s. I think he wants to be like them and they accept him right away. The players do, too, but I think the student acceptance is even better. Sometimes, people accept him because they see him as a vehicle to their own success. With the students, you have to have your stuff together or they're going to boo you.

I don't agree with everything he says. He just puts it out there. He's not like the guy in the big corporation who doesn't talk and you don't know what he's thinking. Dick speaks his mind. He might say fifteen things, and five you don't like, but ten you do.

When I arrived at Duke nine years ago, my initial impression of Dick was that he was kind of crazy. I figured he was wacky. What I've found since is the complete opposite. He's a great family man who has deep, solid roots. He's sensitive. A good guy. I really like a lot of his old-fashioned values.

He has developed a forum and, with that forum, he expresses ideas I think are good for the game, be it in recruiting, rules of the game, or caring about coaches. He's shown he can make an impact, and he's been willing to do that. I just hope, for him and for basketball, that he always takes the time, as he's done in the past, to do the research so when he does make a statement, that statement is what's best for the game.

I think Dick has great sensitivity for coaches because he was a coach. When you get into your tunnel—the NCAA Tournament—he doesn't want to take up a lot of your time, but you get the feeling he almost wants to be there with you, not so much as a broadcaster, but as a person. I think he'd almost like to suit up and experience it with you.

A lot of guys want the exclusive. The main thing Dick wants is for your team to do well. I think he felt genuinely pleased when we won the national championship this spring. I really felt Dick had empathy for the fact we had been to the Final Four several times without winning, and I think he ached for us. It's not that he didn't want other people to win, but it was almost like, "They've been there five of the last six years. They've got to do it. The timing is right." I think he would have been depressed if we lost. That shows how much he puts into it. Dick's not anybody's fan. He's a fan of the game. To say he pumps one school or another is ridiculous. Dick Vitale pumps basketball.

In coaching, you want your players to play with passion. If you have people who play with passion, you have a good chance of reaching your potential. Dick has done that in his profession.

TIME OUT, BABY!

CHAPTER 1

FRIDAY, NOVEMBER 23, 1990—

I can't believe it. Two days ago, I was on ESPN saying that it's too early to be playing college basketball. But tonight is a big, big night: Arkansas and Arizona in the Big Apple NIT final at the Mecca, Madison Square Garden. A real marquee game, a real heavyweight battle. I mean, this is Evander Holyfield going against Mike Tyson.

As much as it tears my insides to say this, I don't believe practice should start until November 1, and the games shouldn't start until December 1, one week after Thanksgiving. Time for fans to get all that football out of their systems. Myself, I can see basketball every day of the week, twelve months a year. I mean, I eat it, I sleep it, I drink it, I love it, I need it, I want it.

And broadcasting a game like this has been a good way for a basketball junkie to get through a Thanksgiving without his family. I've been on the go since November 14, when I did Duke's opening-round tournament game against Marquette at Durham.

This is only the beginning of a real wacky journey. I'm gonna spend the next four months going from Chapel Hill to Vegas to the Carrier Dome to Cameron Indoor Stadium to Buckeye land at Ohio State to Bloomington to see the General. And to think I'm getting paid for this.

This is my twelfth year on ESPN, my fourth at ABC, and what better way to start off the year than visiting the Big Apple. I can still remember, as a little kid, standing outside the old Garden, dreaming of seeing my favorite Knicks players like Dick McGuire or Harry Gallatin, or sitting up in the third tier,

1

watching the late Joe Lapchick coach St. John's against Fordham. Now, here I am, courtside for a big doubleheader and it's not costing me a dime. So, let's get ready to tip it off, shoot the rock, rip it off the glass, run the lane, rock and roll.

The thing I love about these big preseason tournaments like the Big Apple NIT is that they create some real surf 'n' turf matchups. Games like Temple–Iowa, Vanderbilt–Arkansas, Arizona–East Tennessee State, Duke–Arkansas, and Arizona–Notre Dame get my juices flowing.

It's like taking a sneak preview into the Top 20, and it certainly beats taking the easy way out and scheduling cupcakes. Do you hear me, Ohio State coach Randy Ayers? You get my award this year for playing the No. 1 early-season cupcake schedule in America. Chicago State, Youngstown State, Wright State, American University, Delaware State, Bethune Cookman, Tennessee State. Seven quick W's before you hook up with the Hoyas of Georgetown. I could put together a team of Keith Jackson, Billy Packer, Jim Valvano, Brent Musburger, and yours truly and we'd probably go 7–0 against that kind of competition.

But a championship game between Arkansas and Arizona brings out all the big names in the media. I walked into the Garden tonight and ran into Roy Johnson and Billy Reed of *Sports Illustrated,* Lesley Visser of CBS, John Feinstein of *The National,* Gary McCann of Greensboro, and Jim O'Connell of AP.

They were all here to watch Lute-mania running wild. Lute Olson of Arizona—the Cary Grant of college coaching—told us in our pregame production meeting he felt his team could get the ball inside against Arkansas and get their big center, Oliver Miller, in foul trouble. Lute, you're a prophet, baby. You called it like it is. In the game, Miller got frustrated, picked up a technical foul with Arkansas up by six, and it turned the whole game around. Psychologically, that T just destroyed that team. Within four minutes, they went from six up to seven down—a 13-point turnaround. The final was Arizona 89, Arkansas 77. A victory of this magnitude and three more quality wins over Austin Peay, East Tennessee State, and Notre Dame in this tournament should go a long way toward establishing national credibility.

Sean Rooks, the big center, went wild inside for Arizona, got

31 points. And Chris Mills, you'd never know this guy has just started playing again after leaving Kentucky in the wake of all the NCAA violations and sitting out last season. In April 1989, a story broke concerning a package shipped from the Kentucky basketball office, via Emery Air Freight, to Mills's home in Los Angeles. Reportedly, the package broke open at the Emery warehouse in Los Angeles and $1,000 in cash and a videotape fell out.

Both Mills and the Kentucky staff denied any knowledge of the cash, but it wasn't long before the story was picked up nationwide. The package was one of several problems Kentucky had to deal with that year, and eventually the school went on probation.

Twenty-nine points and 13 rebounds for Mills tonight. They've got to be eating their hearts out down in Bluegrass country.

This was definitely a March game, and it's only November. It was a chance to watch six future pros—guys like forward Brian Williams, Rooks and Mills of Arizona, and forward Todd Day, Miller, and guard Lee Mayberry of Arkansas—on the floor at one time.

A victory of this magnitude should go a long way toward lending credibility to Lute's theory that the balance of power is starting to shift back toward the West, with teams like Vegas, UCLA, and Arizona rising to the top. Lute is always politicking for his region, even though the numbers say otherwise, even though I think the majority of teams are still located east of the Mississippi. But, it has to be a great confidence builder, beating Arkansas, which is definitely a Top 5 team.

Nolan Richardson has built Arkansas into a national power down there in the Southwest Conference. Arkansas is moving to the Southeastern Conference next year, but Richardson doesn't seem concerned. I can see why, too, after his team put away Duke in the semifinals.

Nolan's finally getting some of the respect he deserves, and he wants to make sure his players do, too, both on and off the court. Today, at our production meeting, he jumped in my face.

"Dick," he said, "you always talk about Duke and Notre Dame and their great graduation rates. I don't want to hear it. They get kids who should graduate.

"Let me tell you the Paul Pressey story. Paul didn't graduate from high school, came to the junior college in West Texas where I was coaching with a general equivalency degree. He not only graduated from junior college, but then he goes to Tulsa with me and he ultimately gets his degree.

"What you have to understand is that the North Carolinas, Indianas, and Notre Dames are getting the cream of the crop that a lot of us can't recruit. So the graduation rates aren't always legitimate. They're working a whole different ball game from the rest of us. The most a lot of us can hope for is to give a kid a chance."

Nolan has a pretty good point. There are usually only about twenty kids a year who combine superior athletics and academics. The rest have question marks.

Richardson has always cared about his kids, even the ones who get into trouble. Take Ron Huery, his sixth man, for example. He was suspended for a semester and had drinking-related problems. But Nolan told me he's turned the corner. "Dick," he said, "this is not a bad kid. When I went through my pain and suffering with the death of my daughter Yvonne and she was at the Mayo Clinic, Ron spent more time with my wife and family than anyone, including relatives."

I spent some time with Ron in the lobby of the Marriott Marquis, telling him I hoped his troubles were behind him. I love holding court in the lobby of the hotel after dinner during these big events. I was All-Lobby again this week, rapping with Lute and his wife Bobbi, Ed Janka of Nike, Nolan Richardson, recruiting guru Howard Garfinkel, players, fans, and celebrities like Calvin Hill until two in the morning.

That's right, I said Calvin Hill, the big-time running back with the Dallas Cowboys who's a vice president with the Baltimore Orioles. He and his wife are here to watch their son Grant, who is a freshman forward at Duke and should be a pro someday.

His son's team looks like it's a year away from making another run at the Final Four to me. But they intrigue me. So does their young sophomore lead guard, Bobby Hurley, Jr. I'm good friends with his father, Bob Hurley, Sr., who coaches St. Anthony's of Jersey City and has produced teams that have constantly been ranked in the Top 10 by *USA Today*.

I went over to the Garden earlier today to watch the shootarounds, and when I arrived, Bob Hurley, Bobby, and Danny, their youngest son, were the only ones in the gym. Danny, who's a senior at St. Anthony's and has just signed with Seton Hall, got a ball and was shooting around by himself. And suddenly, there was Bob Hurley, Sr., working with him. "Square up, follow through . . ." I can see why Bobby Hurley, Jr., has been able to make the transition to college ball so quickly. He and Christian Laettner, their junior center, will have to step it up a notch if they want to challenge North Carolina.

Laettner looked like he had already arrived against Notre Dame in the consolation game. Digger Phelps asked me to speak to the Notre Dame players prior to the game, but there was nothing I could tell them to stop Laettner in the post.

I spent a little time with Christian and his parents after the game. Boy, is he an improved player. His dad is a printer at the *Buffalo News,* and, according to his wife, he coached Christian in junior high school. Do you hear that, Mike Krzyzewski? He learned all those drop-step moves from his dad.

I told him, "Mr. Laettner, believe me, you will own the print shop when your son becomes a pro. You're talking millions, baby, millions."

Calvin Hill attracted that kind of attention too, when he came out of Yale. He was an All-America football player in the Ivy League, but he told me he also received a scholarship offer in basketball—from Lefty Driesell at Davidson, of all people. Lefty could spot 'em, even back then.

I was talking with Arkansas guard Arlyn Bowers, who's on my All-Rambo team, and Ernie Murray, another of Richardson's players. Murray told me was a big Dallas Cowboys fan, so I asked him to name the top four running backs in Cowboys history. He had no idea I was setting him up because Calvin was standing right next to me.

He started ticking them off. "Tony Dorsett, Robert Newhouse, Emmitt Smith . . ."

"What about Calvin Hill?" I said.

"Calvin Hill?" he said. "Yeah, he was good, too."

"Say hello to Calvin," I said.

He couldn't believe it. He kept shaking his head. "Is that really Calvin Hill?" he kept repeating over and over.

SATURDAY, NOVEMBER 24—

Ah, home. Bradenton, Florida. I couldn't wait to get back. This makes about twelve years in a row I haven't had Thanksgiving dinner at home, but that's the price you pay for the fame and the bucks we make in the entertainment world. Wonder if there's any leftover turkey in the fridge?

Once I settled in, I spent the afternoon watching Villanova beat LSU in the Hall of Fame Classic from Springfield, Massachusetts. As I sat there, I couldn't help but think about the late Eddie Steitz, the former athletic director at Springfield College and longtime head of the NCAA Rules Committee who died earlier this year of a heart attack. Steitz was the guy who instituted the three-point goal in college basketball, and what I kept thinking about was the way he used to take me out to the middle of the court when I was doing a game and challenge me in front of the fans.

"Come on," he would say. "Try to shoot the three. They tell me you're a great shooter, Vitale. You say this is an easy shot and should be moved back. Come on, Dickie, try to shoot the three with me right up in your face, playing perimeter defense." I couldn't get it over my man, Eddie, but then again I don't have the greatest quickness in the world. I need some screens. I've got to play in a system like the Knight system. I need to come off the screen and shoot my J, à la Steve Alford, who was the best ever in college at moving without the ball and utilizing a screen.

I went out to dinner with my wife, Lorraine, and daughters, Terri and Sherri, and when we came home we turned on the Notre Dame–Southern Cal football game. I've been an unabashed screamer for the Irish ever since Terri enrolled there. She's on the tennis team. I didn't realize it, but they tell me I gave a little rendition of the Fighting Irish fight song during the NIT. Anyway, the Irish pulled out a tough defensive battle, 13–10, and that made our day.

At least the football team is winning. It looks like it's going to be a long year for Digger Phelps after two straight blowouts in the NIT. Digger's supporters are diminishing, and there are already rumors out there this may be his last year. When I spoke with Lesley Visser in New York, she told me, "Dick, you and I are the only ones out there still defending him." Eddie

Broderick, a big Notre Dame alum who got both his under-graduate and law degrees at South Bend, came up to me the same night and told me Digger was through. No way, baby. The guy may be struggling, but he's been to the tournament six straight times, doesn't cheat, and graduates his players.

I went upstairs, and when I got into bed my wife was looking as pretty as can be, as charming as can be, and I guess she wanted to be as romantic as can be. But I said, "Uh-uh, it's the debut of The Diamond, Damon Bailey. I've got a chance to watch him on the tube. I have Indiana coming up at the end of the week against Louisville on ABC, and I've got to see the Hoosiers."

And there I was at midnight, watching the Hoosiers play Santa Clara.

SUNDAY, NOVEMBER 25—

I got a chance to watch some football today. Do I know how to pick those upsets or what?

The other day in New York, I was on WFAN and I told Bill Mazur the Giants would take their first L today against the Eagles. "It's over for the Giants, baby," I said. "Ten and zip is history. They'll be ten and one. They can't beat the Eagles, baby."

Well, the Eagles did it to them, 31–13, just as I said. Check it out. It's on tape.

I'll tell you what else is on tape. My feelings about foreign players. I did a bit for ESPN on that subject this weekend, and I said, basically, I have no problem with players like Luc Long-ley of Australia, who plays for New Mexico, Rick Fox of the Bahamas, who plays for North Carolina, and Dikembe Mutombo of Zaire, the big shot blocker at Georgetown. As long as they're not hired guns.

If they're mercenaries who only stay a year and then go back, I don't buy that. I don't like that siren. I had a problem with Andrew Gaze (Australia) from my alma mater a few years ago. Gaze showed up at Seton Hall immediately after the Olympics, helped lead the Pirates to the Final Four, then left right after the championship game in March.

MONDAY, NOVEMBER 26—

It was eighty degrees today and the sun was shining, so I just relaxed by the pool and took life easy. But I'll tell you what: I got up real early and threw a tape on the VCR of Syracuse beating Indiana last night in the Maui Classic. The game started at 1 A.M., which is why I didn't stay up to see it live.

I'm sorry, General. Not even for you, Bobby Knight, am I going to sit up at one in the morning and watch you and my man Jimmy Boeheim, one of the all-time crybabies on the sidelines, go at it.

As it turns out, Knight tried to play the percentages and put Syracuse freshman point guard Adrian Autry on the line late in the game, then tried to ice the shooter. But Autry, who played with North Carolina freshman Brian Reese at Tolentine in the tough New York Catholic League last year, is no ordinary freshman. He made both, and the General went down.

TUESDAY, NOVEMBER 27—

This was going to be another easy day. Or so I thought.

I was supposed to take my wife out to dinner, but my buddy Mike Mersch called—he's the editor of the *Bradenton Herald*— and we ended up going to Manatee Junior College to watch eight high school teams in something they call a jamboree.

I was kidding Mike on the way over, telling him this was football country, where guys like Joe Kinnan of Manatee High are king. But how could I pass up a chance to see eight teams in action? I also wanted to see Howard Porter, Jr. Remember that famous name? That's right, the same Howard Porter who took Villanova to the NCAA finals in 1971. Well, his son is a big star down here in Bradenton at Manatee High School. He's a 6-4 runner, jumper, and shooter who's going to the University of Central Florida in Orlando.

WEDNESDAY, NOVEMBER 28—

Phil Mushnick, the TV critic from the *New York Post,* called me yesterday to get on my case.

Dr. Mushnick, a man who battles issues like you can't believe, has been all over the sneaker people—Nike, Reebok, you name it—because he feels a lot of young kids out there, especially inner-city kids, are stealing, even killing, to get their hands on the shoes and the jackets. Mushnick's argument is that the shoe companies are manufacturing high-priced stuff and targeting the inner-city kids for their sales.

Mushnick is also really critical of the fact that Sonny Vaccaro, the national sales representative for Nike, is paying coaches big money to be part of his advisory staff. He feels Vaccaro has bought these coaches to control the college game, and feels I'm part of the whole scenario because he saw me doing an interview wearing Nike clothing and he also saw me on a Nike show.

Mushnick was in my ear like you couldn't believe. He ripped me from top to bottom. He accused me of defending Jim Valvano when he was at North Carolina State and Jerry Tarkanian at Nevada–Las Vegas because they're part of the Nike family. He said he doesn't want to hear about my praising Duke coach Mike Krzyzewski, because Duke did not graduate any of its three seniors last year and because the school was so afraid of agents writing to the kids that it started screening the players' mail.

I tell you, by the time he was finished, he had me feeling guilty. "Phil, Phil," I said, "you've got me feeling like a sinner tonight. I'm going to go see my pastor immediately and go to confession."

But that only lasted a few seconds—until I was able to collect my thoughts.

"Phil," I said. "I'm under contract to Nike and I'm not ashamed about it at all. I have never promoted Nike on the air, never promoted a player or a coach because they wore Nike shoes or were involved with Nike. They have never forced an issue on me. Sonny Vaccaro has never picked up the phone and said, 'Dick Vitale, you'd better sell one of our coaches or promote our coaches.' "

I'm honest on the air. Krzyzewski was my coach of the year one year, and he doesn't wear Nikes. Temple's John Chaney was my coach of the year one year—he didn't wear Nikes. One time at a Nike Q-and-A I was asked who I thought was the greatest all-around player in the game. I said Magic Johnson—and they had posters of Michael Jordan hanging all over the place. OK, so I might have made a mistake.

One of Nike's biggest representatives is a guy by the name of Eddie Sutton, who used to coach at Kentucky before the school went on NCAA probation and who is now at Oklahoma State. Now, just think about it. Who was that bald-headed, one-eyed guy who came on the air in Kentucky's opening game with Duke in 1988 and said that Mr. Sutton and his staff should step down immediately because of all the controversy stemming from the Emery Air Freight fiasco that led to the sanctions? Eddie worked as a consultant for Nike, but never once did they call me and say, "Oh, Dickie, you can't do that. He's a Nike guy."

Nike pays me a fee for doing five speeches a year. I get one half of the normal fee I receive from the Washington Speakers' Bureau to speak to high school prospects at the Nike camp about drugs and then address hundreds of coaches at clinics around the country.

As for the other stuff Mushnick said, it was so far from the truth. There is no way Michael Jordan or David Robinson, who advertise for the company, would ever condone any sort of violence by kids who want to get their hands on Nike products. As for me, I've jumped all over Valvano for his recruitment of players I felt didn't belong in college. I've jumped on Tarkanian for going after kids like Lloyd Daniels. And are you really going to blame Krzyzewski, as I said to Mushnick, for the fact that Alaa Abdelnaby, Phil Henderson, and Robert Brickey didn't graduate? Mike is such a highly principled guy and was so upset over those three that he wouldn't even hang a Final Four banner in Cameron Indoor Stadium. You don't think Krzyzewski did everything in his power to see that those kids graduated? And besides, Abdelnaby and Brickey both will have graduated by the time this book comes out.

I don't feel guilty at all. But Mushnick did one hell of a job making his points. He is a guy who believes in what he's doing and he is entitled to his opinion, and I respect him for that.

THURSDAY, NOVEMBER 29—

This must be the week for getting all over my case. Chip Brooks, a big basketball fan who works at the Nick Bollettieri Tennis Academy in Bradenton, was all over my case about this wacky promo where I'm talking about the games coming up

Saturday on ABC and they've got me in a cage. Outside the cage they've got Marvelous Marv, a wrestler dressed up in a security-guard uniform, and, like, I'm pounding on the cage, trying to get out of there, baby, so I can get down to the Hoosier Dome for the big doubleheader—Indiana against Louisville and Kentucky against Notre Dame. Brooks was saying he couldn't believe that I was out of the cage. He thought I should have been locked up forever.

We broke the big news of the day on ESPN. Got a scoop from one of my sources—you know I can't say who—that the NCAA had reversed itself and given UNLV the right to defend its championship. Jerry Tarkanian, whose team had been banned last summer from participating in the 1991 NCAA Tournament, went to the Infractions Committee last month and essentially plea-bargained his way back in, offering to sit out the tournament the following year and limit his team's TV appearances in the 1991–1992 season.

For Tarkanian, it was the end of a long struggle that began in 1977 when the NCAA put the school on probation for two years and attempted to impose a two-year suspension on the coach. UNLV served the probation but Tarkanian went to court, obtained an injunction against the NCAA and the university, and continued coaching. Tarkanian blocked the suspension in state court and the case was in the courts until December 1988, when the U.S. Supreme Court ruled in the NCAA's favor. Tarkanian finally signed papers ending the feud in March of 1990. Tarkanian agreed to pay $20,004 in court costs and legal fees incurred by the NCAA. He also agreed to pay nearly $350,000 in his own legal fees.

Last summer, though, the NCAA went a step further and banned the current UNLV team from postseason play this season. Tarkanian and university officials were outraged. "No American citizen can be punished for the same offense twice," Tarkanian said. "Players on this year's team, as well as students attending UNLV, were six or seven years old when this began. They are paying the price of the NCAA's vindictive decision."

Tarkanian, to say the least, was ecstatic when I spoke to him over the phone from Vancouver. He was happy that he would be coaching this year and that his players would be getting a chance to defend the title.

How do I feel about it? I thought the NCAA showed compassion. It's the first time in an appeal process that they've really bent. They didn't bend for Maryland. They didn't bend for Kansas. But I guess this is a different scenario. Why penalize kids like Larry Johnson and Stacey Augmon, who both passed up chances to go pro this year? They were six years old when the violations supposedly happened. We're talking 1977. I think common sense was called for in this case. And the school still is getting a penalty, big-time, next year.

You have to wonder about the future, though. Vegas already has been to the guillotine. Think about it. Once the initial ruling came down last summer, they lost both Ed O'Bannon and Sean Tarver, a pair of Southern California supers who had verbally committed to UNLV, to UCLA. You recruit kids like that for three, four years, you invest all kinds of time, money, phone conversations, you get them to the point where they say yes to you, and then, all of a sudden, that ruling comes down. It really blew the minds of both kids. You can't blame them for deciding to go elsewhere. I've always felt that, even if a kid signs a national letter of intent, he should have the freedom to change his mind if there is a coaching change or the school goes on probation.

Once the story broke, my phone started ringing. Lots of writers called, including His Eminence, Rudy Martzke of *USA Today*. Guys can say what they want about Martzke, but I think Mike Lupica of the New York *Daily News* put it best when he said, "It's amazing how all these guys are phoning Martzke, how all the TV executives and all the people in the television world jump and look at his column on Monday." I have to admit it, Rudy, I jump in on Mondays too. And I check immediately to see if I got the award for best analysis, strongest opinion, or whatever his boo-boo prizes are. We all look. We only pretend that it doesn't mean diddly.

Martzke wanted to know my feelings about the UNLV situation, but he also was trying to bust my chops about Valvano breaking into the television scene. Valvano had coached NC State for ten years before leaving the university to pursue a career as an analyst on ESPN and ABC. He is making his network debut Saturday at the Big Four Tournament in Indianapolis.

Valvano coached State to the 1983 NCAA championship

and took the Wolfpack to the Final Eight twice, but he left the school after suffering stinging criticism over a supposed lack of control over his student athletes and suffering through a year when the program was banned from postseason competition following an NCAA investigation.

Now, let's face reality. Why would anyone doubt that Valvano would make it in TV? The guy's got personality; he's always had it. He's got schtick, pizzazz, and his name ends in a vowel. "The bottom line," I tried to tell Martzke, "is this: If ABC has two teams and I'm not on Team Three, then I'm in great shape. It's when you're on Team Three, baby, that you start checking out the waiver list and the transaction pages. And the same with ESPN. If we've got five teams, you'd better not be on Team Six, baby."

I mean, I feel this way. I've had twelve years in the big time, an unbelievable run. If a rookie star comes in and makes you work harder . . . well, I'll just work that much harder, baby. I always welcome the challenge.

FRIDAY, NOVEMBER 30—

Who was sitting in the lobby reading the newspaper when I arrived at my hotel in Indianapolis? None other than Brent Musburger and Jim Valvano. After I stopped in my room, the three of us, along with Mark Mandel, the publicity director for ABC, went to lunch at Rick's Café down in the old Depot. We're sitting at lunch, sharing one laugh after another. The three of us—Musburger, Valvano, and Vitale—we all have something in common. We all got the "ziggy," the ax, and we all told stories about how the ziggy happened for each of us. We just laughed our heads off, and Mandel never got a word in edgewise.

From there, we went over to watch the workouts. We saw Louisville first and spent some time talking to Jerry Jones, Denny Crum's longtime assistant. Jones was telling us that Crum is very upset with Donald Swain, the university's president. Crum is angry because Swain changed the academic regulations for Louisville's athletes after a "60 Minutes" report that was critical of the Cardinals' graduation rates. "Dick," Jones said, "I've never seen Denny so affected by a problem."

Valvano, who faced the same kind of heat at NC State, told Jones he knows how Crum must be feeling. "I went through fifteen months with that baby hanging over me," he said. "Fifteen months of tearing you apart."

Next, we visited with Kentucky coach Rick Pitino,—Julius Caesar. He's the Caesar, baby, the Emperor, no doubt about it, the way he runs that Kentucky program. We met Ricky's wife, Jo Anne, and we teased her about all the gold and beautiful rings and necklaces she was wearing. I said things have really changed from when Ricky was an assistant at Syracuse. She was bright and happy, and Ricky looked like he was on cloud nine—which he should be. He's done an amazing job at Kentucky, rejuvenating that whole situation.

And then the General walked in, Bobby Knight, and immediately got all over Keith Jackson, my partner for tomorrow's Indiana–Louisville game. "Jackson," Knight said, "you've got to be a saint to be working with this guy. I really feel for you."

I got him right back. "I was really going to say at halftime that you were the No. 1 coach in the country," I said, "but I'm changing that right now and I'm going with John Thompson, man. I'm going with the big fellow. The heck with you."

I nailed him good at a charity roast earlier this month, too. I sent along some taped comments about the General and Billy Reed, who was there, said I had the Hoosier fans roaring. They gave me two minutes to roast the General, and I said: "I only have two minutes to roast you? I can't believe it. I need two minutes to toast you, because that's how long it will take me to say anything nice about you. But I need all day and all night to roast you."

Then I talked about Knight as a player. "You're nothing but a fraud, man," I said. "Your résumé says you were a player at Ohio State on the national championship team. All you ever did was get up on that sideline and stand on the bench and cheer and say, 'Do it, Havlicek. Do it, Lucas. Come on, baby.' Come on, man, you weren't a player. You couldn't play diddly. You couldn't guard anybody."

When we finally stopped laughing, Knight wanted to talk about the Vegas thing. He's a big believer in Tarkanian as a coach—he thinks Jerry teaches the best man-to-man pressure defense in America—but he said the NCAA ruling really surprised him. "Hey, I don't want to hear about feeling sorry for those kids," Knight said. "They had to know there was an investigation pending when they arrived at UNLV. They knew what their status was." I'll tell you, when the General lets it fly, he lets it fly.

One other Knight story: I was talking to his son, Patrick, a freshman on the Hoosiers, and I asked, "Is your dad allowed to give you a car, is he allowed to give you any cash, or is that a recruiting violation?" Patrick answered, in all seriousness: "My dad took my car away from me." It turns out that Patrick missed a class and got nailed. The General won't let anyone slide—not even his own son.

CHAPTER 2

I tossed and turned all night. I was so nervous, thinking about the doubleheader, the first big show of the season.

We had to be at the Hoosier Dome at ten for a photo session, and the arena was empty when we started to rehearse. People have no idea of all that goes on behind the scenes, all the little details. We huddled with Kim Belton, our producer; Geoff Mason, the executive producer; and a host of other people—directors, assistant directors, assistant producers, the graphics operator. It always seems like an eternity until tip-off—you get so exhausted and physically drained at times from all the pre-game stuff—but you've got to be prepared so there are no surprises when the game begins. Also, you have to learn how to fill time. If the game goes beyond 6:17, we'll have to fill until 6:30. I love filling in—that means AT, and to get extra airtime is unbelievable. I love the cameras.

John Saunders, who was making his network debut, opened the broadcast and introduced everybody to the Hoosier Dome. He was up in a skybox, and when he threw it down to Keith and me, Keith really busted my chops right from the start. "This guy's ready to e-x-p-l-o-d-e, and you know what that means," Jackson said. He was right. Keith and I are as different as night and day—as different as Vitale going head-to-head in a good-looking contest against Robert Redford—but he's a Hall of Famer, a man of tremendous ability, professionalism, and stature, and he knew what he was saying about me. I was so charged up.

We talked at the top of the show about the fact that Louisville has only three prime-time players—LaBradford Smith,

Cornelius Holden, and Everick Sullivan—and it made me feel good that the game bore that out. Indiana, which had already played four games, won by 20, 72–52, beating a Louisville team that was playing its first game. That always excites you when your analysis is correct, because there are days when you can't do it right. What the heck, I guess one out of a hundred is pretty good.

I talked about the management of a game—how a game really is broken down into four segments. You have your first four minutes, when you try to set some tempo. Next is the pre-halftime four minutes, which is an important segment psychologically. Then there's the post-halftime, when you need to get that good run to start the second half. And last, the final four minutes, winning time.

This one really was decided right after halftime; Louisville was down only ten at the half, but it could have been much worse if Indiana had played better on the offensive end.

As for Damon Bailey, he was almost invisible. Damon is a fundamentally sound kid and he's going to be a solid player eventually, but he doesn't have the good foot speed and the pace of the game really seems to be a step ahead of him. As I said at the top of the show, "Forget it if you think you're talking Magic, Michael and Isiah." You can see that he's eventually going to break out, but right now he's thinking too much and not just reacting on the floor and playing. He has to be more aggressive; he really does. He doesn't even look at the basket. In the first half, he was 0-for-1. It's hard to believe this kid scored more than 3,000 points in high school and was such a dominant force against real good competition.

Between games, we had to work. Saunders and I interviewed Tarkanian from Vancouver, where Vegas was getting ready to open their season against Alabama-Birmingham. Tark went through his spiel about the NCAA, how everyone is entitled to due process, and how he didn't get due process in 1977. Then I said, "Hey, Jerry, this is Dick Vitale. Rumors are rampant that you are are going to leave the program at the end of the year. What about that?" Tark's answer was that he's not a quitter and that he loves challenges.

After that, we did a halftime bit that was a riot. It was a takeoff on Siskel and Ebert, the movie reviewers. Saunders threw out some questions, and Jimmy V. and yours truly had to do point-counterpoint. We had a blast. We were screaming at each other. We were obnoxious. Musburger told us it was like watching Wrestlemania.

I had to leave the arena with about five minutes left in Kentucky's 98–90 win over Notre Dame, which has now lost four in a row and slipped to 2–4, but I made the plane in plenty of time. I sat on the flight with two NBA scouts, Dave Twardzik of the Charlotte Hornets and Eddie Badger of the Atlanta Hawks.

Badger was showing off his NBA championship ring he got when he was an assistant with the Boston Celtics, and then we got talking about Bill Walton, who played with Twardzik on Portland's 1977 championship team.

Walton came to the Celtics from the L.A. Clippers, where there was no leadership and all anyone cared about was stats. At Boston, it was different. K.C. Jones was coaching the team, and during one time-out Walton was talking away. Larry Bird immediately jumped in and said, "Hey, wait a minute, man, shut the bleep up. Listen to the coach, man." From that moment on, Walton never said a word. He just performed and played a big part in the Celtics' winning the championship that year. Walton has since gone on to become a great teacher, and Dale Brown invited him to LSU this fall just to work with his great center, Shaquille O'Neal.

SUNDAY, DECEMBER 2—

I had a message that Lute Olson called. Lute was upset with me for saying that he was crying over the fact that UNLV now is eligible for the tournament. He and Tark have been feuding ever since Lute succeeded Jerry at Long Beach State and he wound up on probation for violations that were committed during Tark's regime. I got back to Olson and explained that it was all done tongue-in-cheek, during that point-counterpoint with Valvano.

I guess not everyone thought it was a riot.

Howard Garfinkel was all over my case too. "You're a fraud, Vitale," he said. "The guy who made the best statement of the day was Keith Jackson, who said, 'Remember, Damon Bailey is only eighteen years old.'"

Garf is a big advocate of freshman ineligibility. Hey, Garf, if you read my first book, you know I agree. I think kids need a chance to adjust.

MONDAY, DECEMBER 3—

Flying to Syracuse is always an adventure, and today was no exception. There was a snowstorm, and we couldn't land. After circling above the airport for close to an hour, they took us to Albany. I had an appearance at 3:30 for a Windex sound-alike impersonation contest at the Syracuse student union, and I didn't know if I was going to make it.

I got to the student union about 4:30, an hour late. The place was jammed with several hundred students, and a lot of media was on hand. I spoke to the students, laid a few of my TO's and PTP's (prime time players) on them. It just floors me that this stuff has caught on the way it has on campuses.

They may love me, but I don't think Norman Chad of *The National* does. He pounded me again. "Hey, baby," he wrote, "if you want to avoid Dick Vitale and college basketball, throw your TV sets out the window." Then he told his readers what was good and what was bad about TV. Al Michaels, he loves you. Same with John Madden and Marv Albert. But he's down on Tim McCarver, Dan Dierdorf, yours truly, and my guy Chris Berman of ESPN. Rip, rip, rip. Get the knife out. Just spell my name right, Chadski.

I tried to call the coaches when I finally got to my hotel— I'm doing Day 2 of the ACC–Big East Challenge tomorrow, Seton Hall against Clemson and North Carolina State against Syracuse—but the teams didn't arrive on time and I couldn't get hold of Boeheim. So I watched the first two games between the ACC and the Big East on TV. These matchups, which were the brainchild of ACC commissioner Gene Corrigan and former Big East honcho Dave Gavitt, are really exciting. I think the whole idea is fantastic, because it captures the interest of the whole nation for a week and it generates reams of publicity for both conferences. The games are a chance for some teams to get a true evaluation of where they are.

Seton Hall, for example, hasn't played against a dominant team yet. Neither has Clemson. The same could be said for NC State.

Sometime after midnight, the phone rang. It was P.J. Car-

lesimo, the Seton Hall coach. I had left a message for him to
give me a buzz. I picked up the phone and he said, "Dick, you
want to talk about the Pirates?" I said, "P.J., I can't believe it.
You know what hour it is, man? It's after midnight."

He said it was the shortest conversation he's ever had with
me in his life.

TUESDAY, DECEMBER 4—

Whenever I come to Syracuse, I run into fans who are real
sports addicts. College hoops is what it's all about up here—
there aren't any pro teams—and I guess that's one of the reasons why Boeheim gets so much heat and pressure. There's
nothing else to take the pressure off him.

Seton Hall defeated Clemson, 78–62, in the first game, and
then Syracuse took the floor for the game against North Carolina State and the place began to rock and roll. The game was
a nip-and-tucker all the way. Syracuse finally won, by seven,
but the big story was LeRon Ellis getting into a shouting match
with Boeheim and storming into the locker room. I talked to
Jimmy about it after the game, and he basically brushed it off
as a moment of frustration. "He just had to go to the boys'
room," Boeheim said, "and I screamed at him. You get frustrated; it's the emotion of the game." I guess Ellis was frustrated too; he didn't get a lot of playing time in the second half,
because Conrad McRae was so nasty and really dominated
inside as the unbeaten Orange won their fifth straight game.

I'll tell you, Boeheim is really something on that sideline,
man. He really is one of the all-time crybabies, screaming and
moaning and groaning, always trying to get the extra call. He
really works that sideline. I always hear the same groans coming from Boeheim every preseason: "Dick, we don't have the
talent to match up with Georgetown and St. John's. We don't
have the talent."

But you know what? For the No. 1 crybaby, I've got to go
with the wimp, Wimp Sanderson of Alabama. Boeheim, you're
moving down the ladder. You're No. 2 now. And then we've
got to talk about my man, the wacky guy, Bill Frieder of
Arizona State.

As usual Billy Owens, Syracuse's junior forward, was su-
perb. He is so special. He makes it look so easy. He's got such

a fluid style about him. He's really improved his shot selection, can post inside, he can handle the ball exceptionally well in transition, run the floor, rebound. He's a total, total player. I ran into his mother, and she said, "Mr. Vitale, you better not say anything bad about my son Billy." I told her, "Billy's going to take you to the bank in style."

I couldn't resist teasing Georgetown coach John Thompson over the air about his cupcake schedule. Duke is playing Georgetown tomorrow, and I said: "Wait a minute, that must mean Duke-a-lola, baby, or Duke-moana, or Duke-mai from out of Hawaii. Is that really Duke against Georgetown?" Of course, I didn't want to get too carried away. John is 6-11 and 260. I'm not going to argue with him, man. I'm brighter than that. Besides, I played a bunch of cupcakes when I coached at the University of Detroit. Boeheim reminded me of that when I started teasing him about his schedule and told him about my "Jim Boeheim Cupcake Award." He just said, "I learned from you, Dick. Check out the Adrians and Oaklands, and all those teams you played."

WEDNESDAY, DECEMBER 5—

It was a snowy, depressing morning, and I had to get up real early to get to Chapel Hill for another doubleheader the next day—Villanova–Wake Forest and North Carolina–Connecticut.

I got a big kick out of an article in *USA Today* by Steve Woodward. The headline was "Vitale Will Change." Woodward had called me yesterday, and I told Steve I wanted to be a little more refined this season, that I planned to use a little less of my schtick and more X's and O's. He must have then gone to ESPN about what I had said, because the new vice president, John Wildhack, a young executive in his early thirties who is a big Syracuse hoops fanatic, called to reassure me that there was no reason to change. "I told the guy," Wildhack said, "that as far as I'm concerned this guy has knowledge, he's enthusiastic, and he's not afraid to be candid."

I got a ride to the airport with a guy I know here named Chick. He befriends a lot of the coaches who come up here. Chick is a beautiful guy. If you've got a 6:45 flight in the morning, he's waiting there at 5:45 to drive you to the airport—

just to be able to talk some Syracuse hoops. He loves Syracuse basketball. He knows all the inside stuff. He's constantly in contact with coaches.

At the airport, I ran into Bernie Fine, an assistant at Syracuse. He was jumping on a flight to L.A. to recruit, and I said, "Bernie, before you leave, let me pick your brain." I immediately got a scouting report on Connecticut and Villanova, two Big East teams that he's familiar with. He broke down the personnel for me, and I was scribbling. Some of the fans were teasing me. Somebody said, "That's where you get all your notes, right here in the airport?" I said, "You'd better believe it. You've got to be ready." Bernie didn't know much about Wake Forest, but Dane Huffman, who covers the ACC for the *Raleigh News & Observer,* overheard me and said, "Hey, I know a lot about Wake Forest. I cover NC State." So I picked Dane's brain too.

As soon as I arrived at the airport in Raleigh, my producer, Tim Rapley, grabbed me and said, "We're going up to Chapel Hill now. We've got to be at the Dean Dome at dusk. We're going to have you do a welcome, which we're going to use in the opening tomorrow night." I wanted to say, "Hey, I want to go to the hotel, relax, and get my preparation." But I had no say in the matter.

I was picking up my bags when I ran into Dee Rowe, one of my favorite people. Dee—one of the great X and O guys—used to coach Connecticut and had Valvano on his staff at one time. Now, he's the assistant AD up there. He was down for the game with his boss, Lew Perkins.

Dee really busted me. "Hey," he said, "you really killed Syracuse's recruiting last night. You talked about your daughter playing tennis and how sunny and beautiful it is in Florida, but it's ice cold here, and you said you couldn't wait to get out of the snowbelt. Can you imagine what the kids they are recruiting will think?"

"Come on, Dee, baby," I said. "Do you think those kids don't know about that? They know one thing: it's like a hundred degrees at the Dome when those 30,000-plus are rocking and rollin' like they did when the Orange beat NC State."

Once we did the opening and I finally got to my room, I called some of the coaches to get some more information. I called Villanova's Rollie Massimino, spoke to his daughter Lee

Ann, who's attending grad school here, and pretty soon he called me back and started screaming: "It's chuck-and-duck time, baby. This is Rollie Massimino, the genius of multiple defenses. I'm moving 'em up to full court." Rollie is a real riot. I've been teasing him, saying he's been on vacation since he won the national championship in 1985 and pitched that perfect game against Georgetown. We went over personnel for a while, and then he suddenly said, "Wait a minute. I'm doing all your homework, man. Send me the check." These coaches are always thinking about cash, baby.

I talked to Rollie about a number of things, and then he said, "Hey, help me out. I'm recruiting Jonathan Haynes. He just left Temple. You've got to help me out now. You've got to tell the world I just got off the phone with his mama. We'd like to have him down here at Villanova. He's a Philly kid. They always get on my case that I don't recruit any Philly kids, and I want to prove that if you're from Philly and you can play, we want you."

I said, "Rollie, I'll just tell the world that Jonathan is available. May the better guy get him, big guy."

THURSDAY, DECEMBER 6—

I got stuck in traffic after our 10 A.M. production meeting and got to the shootaround a few minutes late. Massimino wanted to talk about Jonathan Haynes again. "You know, I think he'll look good in our system," Rollie said. "Now, if you accidentally mentioned it tonight . . ."

Massimino wanted to discuss something else, too—Villanova's desire to get out of the Big 5, the round-robin deal in Philly that requires the five city colleges to play each other once a year.

"You don't understand it," Rollie told me. "It makes the schedule too difficult. Next year, we play eighteen Big East games. Throw in a Christmas tournament, a network game, and four Big 5 games and it's almost impossible to make the NCAA Tournament. Everybody's gunning for us in the city. We're the king of the block and everybody wants to eat us alive, chew us up. Every Big 5 game is a war. The kids are physically exhausted. I've got to go get me four games that are cupcakes, baby. I've got to get some wins."

Shootarounds are always a lot of fun. I get all my tidbits, get all my little notes. I ran into Jim Calhoun of Connecticut as we walked up the steps of the Dean Dome. He was looking at Carolina's roster and shaking his head. So many supers. From all over the nation. But that's a fact of life. A school like Carolina, with its tradition, facilities, and reputation, is going to get the top-level basketball recruit. But, as Jim said, "I've made a living at Northeastern in getting the Reggie Lewises, the LaFleurs, the players that really are just as good as some of the big names at Five Star."

Speaking of Five Star, I couldn't believe who showed up at this one: my man the Garf, Howard Garfinkel, the guy who runs the Five Star summer camps. I turned around when I heard his voice, and he said, "Yes, it's me." It was the first time in many years that I'd seen him at one of my games, and he immediately went into his song and dance. "Vitale," he said, "I'm giving you a name. Jerry Stackhouse. He's the best. He's a six-seven forward, the best sophomore in America. He's here in North Carolina. A tremendous talent. Vitale, I'm giving you a scoop. You've got to let the nation know that."

I spent part of the practice talking with Calvin Byrd of Villanova, asking him about one of his former high school teammates at St. Joseph's High in Alameda, California—Jason Kidd.

Jason Kidd. Remember the name. He and Rodrick Rhodes of St. Anthony's in Jersey City are the two best juniors in the country. Calvin was telling me how Jason worked out with Brian Shaw and Gary Payton last summer and held his own.

One of the first people I ran into at the Dean Dome was Dickie Paparo, one of the premier officials in basketball, certainly an All-Zebra Top 5. Last year I picked Jody Silvester as my No. 1 ref, and Paparo reminded me about it. "Vitale, you gave it to Silvester last year," he said. "Now it's time to give it to your paisano. It's Paparo, no doubt about it." I love his cockiness.

Villanova beat Wake in the first game. Lance Miller was brilliant, and Arron Bain was using all kinds of drop steps in the post. Rollie was in rare form; he had to make sure he reminded me that he's received ten calls already this week from kids who used to play for him. North Carolina won the second game by 15, and I loved it when my partner, Tim Brando, pointed out on the air that I said they would win by at least 13. Good job, Timmy B.

Connecticut was up seven at the half, but I said at halftime that Carolina would win going way. I'm not some kind of genius, but I'm going to tell you something: I have never seen Carolina, which is 4–1 but has already lost to South Carolina in the finals of the Raycom Classic, play so poorly in the first five minutes. Connecticut's pressure was eating them alive. King Rice, Carolina's senior lead guard, had a really tough night. The crowd was upset that he stayed out on the floor.

As we were leaving, I ran into Phil Ford, the former Carolina great who's now an assistant under Dean Smith, and we talked about the pressures facing Rice and the fact that just about everybody thought Rice would be a Phil Ford when he arrived four years ago. But there is only one Phil Ford, baby. I got a taste of him back in 1977, when he came to Detroit to play us. We had an outstanding team with John Long and Terry Tyler, and the game was close until Carolina went to the four corners, which Ford ran better than anybody I've ever seen. Dean held up the four fingers and it was time to throw in the towel.

CHAPTER 3

Who the heck's on my flight to Atlanta? None other than Mr. Superstar himself, Jerry West, one of my all-time idols and now the general manager of the Los Angeles Lakers. I'm sitting across the aisle from Jerry, trying to be cool as we're shooting the breeze about basketball. Jerry was saying how Cliff Rozier, Dean's freshman forward, really impressed him with his potential. I asked him who he liked on the national level, and he just raved about the silky, smooth one from Syracuse—that's right, Billy Owens. West sees him as a three-position player.

If that isn't enough, who do I bump into? Unbelievable! From West, we go to Mr. Laker himself, Kareem Abdul-Jabbar. Like me, he was going from Atlanta to Baton Rouge for tomorrow's Arizona–LSU game. He was headed down there at the request of LSU coach Dale Brown to work with Shaquille O'Neal, teach him a sky hook. I felt like getting my autograph book out. I didn't want to tell those guys, West and Abdul-Jabbar, but I was in awe.

Kareem was really in a great mood, talking about his daughter, who's now at UCLA, and his son. You could just see the enthusiasm as he told me about them. He said he travels all around the country for L.A. Gear, but that he's also got a production company that's putting out a movie. The flick is about a successful high school basketball coach who takes a college job and goes from being Mr. Integrity to someone who gets caught up in the whole big-time scene—the recruiting wars and the viciousness. Kareem also got a big kick out of an article I was reading in the *Sporting News*—about how you don't need a big post guy to win anymore, unlike the Abdul-Jabbar era.

We were met at the airport by LSU assistant Jim Childers, and after we got something to eat, I met our producer, Kim Belton, and the two of us hustled over to watch LSU play Chapman College. Chapman is coached by Bob Boyd, who used to coach Southern Cal in the 1960s. When Kareem was in college, he suffered only two losses. One was to Houston in that famous Astrodome game when he had a bad eye. The other was to USC in a slowdown game.

Southern Cal was the second-best team in the country that year, according to Kareem, but they couldn't go to the tournament because the NCAA took only conference winners in those days.

Bob spent some time at Mississippi State after he left USC, but he's back on the West Coast now. He called up Dale and said, "Do me a favor. We're coming into the Louisiana area. Give us a game."

Dale basically said, "C'mon down. You'll get a quick check. I'll get a quick W. And everybody's happy."

Shaquille just went through the motions. He knew he would get a much stiffer test seventeen hours later when LSU played Arizona on ABC. I said on the air that LSU–Chapman was like Roseanne Barr competing in a singing contest against Pavarotti.

Dale wanted me to stop by his office after the game. When I got there, he was watching a tape of the Arkansas–Arizona game, and he told me he thought Arizona was the best team he had seen in a decade. He was setting me up big-time.

And you know what? He kept it up all night. When I said I had to call my wife, Dale said, "No, let me do it." He just wanted to get me in trouble. He called and said, "Mrs. Vitale, we want to check a credit-card number. There's a guy who just walked in the Oriental Spa, where we're at, for a massage, and we want to verify this number."

My wife came back with a classic line. She said, "I hope he has a good time, baby."

Dale was hysterical.

SATURDAY, DECEMBER 8—

This game today is going to be really interesting, and not just because it's O'Neal against one of the best front lines in America. It's also because of the rivalry between the two coaches.

Lute and Dale played against each other in high school. Dale played for St. Leo's in Minot, North Dakota, and Lute played for Grand Forks Central in Grand Forks, North Dakota. I have to admit it, Dale, baby, Lute got the best of you. In fact, Dale was a sports reporter for the school paper back then, and he wrote that day that Lute was the best guy on the court. See, he thought the world of you, Lute.

And, really, from what they both say now, nothing has changed. Dale says Lute was the same guy then that he is today. He has that real poise. Dale says a lot of people thinks he's standoffish, but that's just his personality.

I stopped by Dale's office before the game, and it was an unbelievable scene. First, Dale whipped out his files—all kinds of criticism, articles about guys who have been successful in life but at one time were ripped from top to bottom. One of the things he showed me was a letter to *Sports Illustrated* from Adolph Rupp, the legendary Kentucky coach, who was responding to some criticism in the magazine. There were a million things like that in those files.

And then the parade of visitors began. In came Maurice Williamson, a sophomore who is off the team because of grades. On top of that, his dad, John Williamson, the former Nets guard, is fighting for his life with a kidney problem. Maurice and Dale talked about the Nets retiring John's number last night, and then I gave Maurice a little talk, tried to inspire him as much as I could. Maurice is obviously a concerned youngster, concerned about his dad and concerned about his future.

Next to drop in is Jamie Brandon. Remember him, Illinois coach Lou-Doo Henson? Brandon was rated one of the Top 10 players in high school, enrolled in a summer program at Illinois, left when the school ran into problems with the NCAA, and now is here at LSU. He's sitting out the year because of Proposition 48, but he'll play next season, and what a talent he is.

And then who comes in? Army Sergeant Phillip Harrison, father of the star of all stars, Shaquille O'Neal. He came marching in, and I started demonstrating how the hook shot can help Shaquille's game, using Harrison as a guide.

From there I went down to the locker room and talked to Shack. He thanked me for picking him No. 1 on TV, but said he didn't know if he really deserved it. I'll tell you what, baby, after watching him play he might be No. 1 in the NBA. As far as I can see, there are only three centers in the world who are better right now—Patrick, Akeem, and David Robinson.

The game was getting ready to start when Kareem walked on. The crowd at the Deaf Dome just exploded. Jessie Evans, an Arizona assistant, came over and said, "Vitale, we heard you saying that Shaquille is the best, and our big guys are ready. Brian Williams and Sean Rooks and all the guys are going to be ready." Well, man, they were ready. But so was the Shack. O'Neal was awesome—29 points, 16 rebounds, 6 blocked shots. I was going absolutely wackoville, watching him tear apart a big-time front line, giving the No. 2–ranked team in the country its first loss after seven straight wins.

Keith Jackson kept trying to get me to calm down. "Dick, he's only eighteen years old," he pleaded.

"You can't hide it," I said. "You can't hide this talent." I just couldn't believe Keith wouldn't get excited and give me a "Whoa, Nellie" like he does in football.

Arizona's perimeter game was nonexistent. They couldn't buy a jumper, and it led to their downfall. LSU played one of those emotional games and knocked off the No. 2 team in the country by ten. I told Dale earlier that I didn't think he could beat Arizona unless he got a superhuman performance from O'Neal. Well, that's exactly what happened.

Shaquille had some devastating dunks. I just wondered, looking at Kareem, what was running through his mind, because to stop Kareem, they took away the dunk during his era. Could you imagine Kareem with the dunk?

The only negative was fouls. Shaquille fouled out of nine games last year, and he was in foul trouble in this one as well. People pay to see Shaquille O'Neal play, and he shouldn't have to be sitting next to Dale Brown or an assistant coach. I personally would like to see the rules changed to keep players from fouling out. Leave it to the discretion of the coach. If a player picks up a fifth personal and the coach wants to keep him on the floor, let the coach get penalized. Give the other team two shots and the ball.

It was a riot driving to the New Orleans airport after the game with Kim Belton, our producer, and Alvin Patrick, our assistant producer. Kim, who set all kinds of scoring records at

Stanford before Todd Lichti arrived and was drafted by the
Phoenix Suns, was just going wild, slapping high-fives about
Shaquille, getting off on the fact I was screaming at the end of
the game, "He's a three-S man—scintillating, super, and sensational."

I rolled into the house about 1 A.M. It was just a wild, wild
day.

SUNDAY, DECEMBER 9—

Everywhere I went today, all people wanted to talk about was
Shaquille O'Neal. I went to church and I had guys asking me
about him. I went to dinner and they were asking about him.

As soon as I got home this afternoon, Dale Brown called. He
was still on a high from the day before. And he, of course,
wanted to talk about O'Neal too.

"Did I tell you he'd go off?" he said to me. Then he told me
Shaquille ended his day yesterday by working out for an hour
and a half with Kareem after the game.

MONDAY, DECEMBER 10—

I flew back to Chapel Hill today, and it was a beautiful, sunny,
gorgeous day, in the fifties. On my way over to practice to
watch Kentucky work out for tomorrow night's game against
Carolina, I picked up *The National* and my day was made when
I saw that Norman Chad, their TV critic, was ripping me for
going crazy over O'Neal. Mr. Chad, he's the Mister Scroogie.
Thank you, Scrooge. Every day I pick up the paper and read
Rip City U.S.A. by Mr. Chad.

Jerry Linquist of the Richmond *Herald-Leader* came over to
me recently and said, "Dick, you take criticism too hard, man.
You can't let it bother you. Be yourself. You made yourself."
I told him I could handle it but not when guys rip away with
no reason. I'm a human being. I have feelings too.

Rick Pitino has come a long way since his days at Boston
University. He was telling me that they once held Midnight
Madness up there with free champagne, and only fourteen
people showed up. Eleven of them were relatives. At Kentucky,
he says, he gets thousands for a shootaround.

I was teasing Pitino about the fact that he lost Cherokee

Parks to Duke and Tom Kleinschmidt to De Paul in the early signing period. He wasn't really complaining, but he did say that he feels he's fighting a bit of an uphill battle. "Dick," he said, "let's face reality. We haven't been on TV because of the NCAA sanctions. People have forgotten about us. I think after this year, when the penalties are over, you're going to start to see us really succeed in the recruiting wars."

I can really feel for Rick. The first day of the early signing period is when coaches become geniuses. That's when you become an absolute superstar. If you think it happens on October 15, when practice starts, you're wrong. Forget about it. It starts with personnel, it starts with players, baby. It starts when that phone rings, when a great player like a Cherokee Parks calls and says he's going to wear your uniform.

Parks is a 6-11 center from Huntington Beach, California, and Kleinschmidt is a hard-nosed shooting guard from Chicago. I'll tell you, those two really broke the hearts of the guys down at Kentucky. They had Parks down there for Midnight Madness—the place was sold out, just an unbelievable scene—and they really thought that would win him over.

But then, hey, it balances out. Sometimes the phone rings with good news. That's what happened at Indiana, where Bobby Knight, the mentor, beat out his former pupil, Krzyzewski, for Alan Henderson, a 6-8 shooter out of Indianapolis, one of the top five players in America. For weeks, nobody knew whether he would decide to play for the General or the King. Finally, he says, "Sorry, King, I'm going to play for the General. I'm going to Bloomington, Indiana."

The other thing is, the early signing period has become a farce. I don't believe any kid should be allowed to sign unless he has qualified under the NCAA's Proposition 48 standards. That means he has to have achieved at least a 700 on his Scholastic Aptitude Test and a 2.0 grade-point average. In a lot of cases, a kid will sign in November and then find out in April that he can't even be admitted.

And that leads me into a whole other area. I firmly believe that it's wrong for kids who don't belong there to go to college. I've been preaching and begging and pleading for the NCAA and the NBA to create a league for people not qualified for college. My only stipulation would be that each of the players involved learn a vocation in case that big paycheck doesn't come through. I don't think there's anything wrong with not going to college. What is wrong is to take a Chris Washburn or Lloyd Daniels who has not been prepared for college in any shape or form and put him in a calculus course. That is a sin. It's unfair. Then everybody wonders what happened when the kid doesn't graduate.

Oh, I almost forgot. I told Ricky about Dale Brown's suggestion. LSU and Kentucky are going to be playing each other once a year now because of the expansion in the SEC, but Dale wants to schedule another regular-season meeting.

"Tell Brown no way, baby," Pitino said. "I'll do it when Shaquille O'Neal gets out of there."

TUESDAY, DEC. 11—

Kentucky played well and Carolina struggled, but the Tar Heels won, 84-81, to increase their record to 5-1. Dean was upset at the press conference. "We're not a good team," he said. "We're going to be a good team, but we're not a good team right now."

Dean looked at me and asked, "Did your club turn the ball over at Detroit like we do?" He wasn't kidding. I mean, they are turning the ball over at an unbelievable rate, and that's not Carolina basketball.

The crowd was very quiet tonight. These people can't be fooled. Carolina really shows a lack of foot speed. They just don't have great athletic ability and they're not scoring a lot of baskets off transition. I think some adjustments have to be made before this is going to be a Top 5 team.

It's too bad, really, because Carolina is loaded up front. When you talk about the best frontcourts in the nation, you've got to go with UNLV first, with Larry Johnson, Stacey Augmon, and then George Ackles and Elmore Spencer in the middle. Next would probably be Arizona, with the "Tucson Skyline"—Brian Williams, Sean Rooks, and Ed Stokes. But Carolina is right there after that. George Lynch is an offensive rebounding machine. Peter Chilcutt is a steady, solid player. Rick Fox can play on the perimeter as well as on the baseline, and he can really shoot the rock. And then there are the two prime-time freshmen, Eric Montross and Cliff Rozier. They've just got so many bodies up front.

When I think of Carolina, I'm always thinking Top 5, Top 10, for sure. But this team would have a tough time playing against the Arkansases, the Arizonas, the Vegases. They still will be a good basketball team, I believe, once they get into their rhythm and timing, but I don't know if this will be a team that will knock people out until they can get positive, everyday contributions out of their two main freshmen, Rozier and Montross. Right now their confidence level has to be waning when they look at the numbers they're posting.

WEDNESDAY, DECEMBER 12—

I caught Providence and Boston College on TV. Eric Murdock really put on a show for Providence. He knocked down 34, but it wasn't enough.

Some things that happened tonight really got me thinking. Providence was playing without three players who were suspended after a brawl with Rhode Island. St. John's had to struggle to beat Brooklyn College because it was playing without two key players, Billy Singleton and Chuck Sproling, who were suspended for academic reasons. I mean, messages are being sent loud and clear. Academics will prevail in the 1990s in college athletics. Everywhere you go, people want to know graduation rates. Coaches have to be really selective in their recruiting process as a result. So many jobs are on the line today, if players aren't graduating. I mean, you can see how it's created all kinds of problems for guys out there, from Jimmy Valvano to Billy Tubbs. Denny Crum's under the gun right now at Louisville.

Many times it's unfortunate that the coach gets blamed. The players have got to start taking responsibility for themselves. But I guess it all starts with the recruiting process, trying to get to know the athlete. Pitino says he's intent on changing the way it used to be done at Kentucky and is trying to be very selective. Lute Olson does an unbelievable job at this: he makes sure his players analyze and evaluate the people he brings in, and he then asks his players whether or not they want the recruit to be a part of his program.

One of the problems in all of this is the recruiting restrictions. It's pretty tough to get to know a kid. You go to the kid's high school and the coach is always singing, "Oh, he's the best kid in the world, man, he's the best kid in the world." In the meantime, he's mugged three people, he's never been to class. But you want to believe the coach, because you know the kid can flat out play, and you think, "Well, maybe this guy is going to eventually turn it around academically. If he does, he can be the guy to take us to the winner's circle."

THURSDAY, DECEMBER 13—

You know how I can tell the season is kicking into gear? It's because I can't come home without getting calls from all over the country—writers, radio shows, people just wanting to talk hoops.

One of the calls I got today was from Steve Nidetz, the TV critic for the *Chicago Tribune*. He wanted to know my feelings about the game we're doing this weekend—UNLV against Michigan State at The Palace in Auburn Hills, Michigan—and what I think about these made-for-TV matchups. I told him I think they're great because they eliminate the cupcake and they match up two highly rated teams.

I also spoke to the Garf, who wanted to get on my case for praising Georgia on the air. "All you guys are frauds, Vitale," he said. "All you guys building up Georgia, saying Georgia's a real surprise." Let me tell you, baby, you don't have a discussion with the Garf. It's one way, *his* way, *his* opinion, and that is it. Final, closed case, he'll let you know, baby. He is the whole truth, nothing but the truth, when it comes to talking about hoopology. He's the doctor of hoopology, baby.

If you don't believe it, just call him up. I must have heard it from him at least five million times—how the Garf got me my start in college coaching. How he sold Dick Lloyd of Rutgers on me back in 1971 when I was a high school coach at East Rutherford in North Jersey. We had just won our second straight state championship, were working on a 35-game winning streak, and I wanted to break into college ball.

But I was getting more rejections than a guy driving the lane against Patrick Ewing. Then, at our banquet that year, I meet this guy, slicked-back hair, big glasses. And, he says to me, "Vitale, I'm going to get you a college job." And, oh, did he deliver big-time. But not even the Garf could have predicted what's happened to me since I got that first break.

Steve Woodward had another crazy idea in *USA Today*. He was writing about Tim McCarver being selected to host the Olympics, and he suggested that Chris Berman and I might make a good team if ESPN were doing the Games. What a dynamite duo! Can you imagine us hosting an Olympic show? I'd tell you what, we'd love it. We'd break every rule in television. But you know what, baby? We'd have the fans rocking and rolling, going wild. Can you imagine me screaming, "Awesome, baby" and Berman going, "Back, back, back, back . . ." at the alpine skiing. We might have some people throwing things at the set, too.

FRIDAY, DECEMBER 14—

I flew into Detroit today and was met by a big limo. I couldn't believe it, a big stretch limo. Fred King, our production assistant, was going to have somebody pick me up, but his car broke down and they had to send a limo at the last minute. So I got the big-time treatment, and it's great, especially since this is my home area, man. I like to impress these people. I have to big-time them a little bit.

I picked up the paper, the *Detroit News,* and I wanted to die. The headline said: "Vitale says State Has Little Chance to Beat Vegas." That's just a great way to be greeted here with all the Spartan fans and Spartan alumni. What I had said was, Steve Smith had to have a monster performance for State to win and that Vegas would have to play a very average game, based on the way the Spartans are playing. I mean, I've never been a politician, but I've always believed in being candid. Sometimes you've got to be a little political, I guess.

I was upset about something else, too. The day before, my buddy Billy Packer ripped me in *USA Today* for overhyping players. He mentioned that I once called Temple's Mark Macon "the next Oscar Robertson" and said I was doing the same thing now with Damon Bailey. Well, all I can say is, listen to the telecast, Billy P. Get a tape. I never said Macon was going to be the next Oscar Robertson. Macon was brilliant as a freshman for a Temple team that was ranked No. 1 in the country, and I simply said, "Macon has the size and some of

the passing skills and offensive maneuverability of the Big O."
As far as hyping Damon Bailey, give me a break. Damon
Bailey was hyped before I ever knew about him. He scored over
3,000 points in his high school career!

I went to watch Michigan State practice and I saw Billy
Cunningham, the part-owner of the Miami Heat, and Stu
Inman, his player personnel director. They were there to check
out Smith. Inman wanted to find out about Smith's upper-
body strength, so he went to the trainer. The guy told Inman
that Smith, who arrived at Michigan State weighing 175
pounds, was up to 200 now and had really worked on the
weight program. Inman also loves Larry Johnson of UNLV.
He thinks Johnson will be a phenomenal small forward, but
doesn't think he can be a power forward. I don't think he's big
enough, at 6-5 or 6-6, to play power forward either.

During the workout, Kim Belton asked me about who I
thought was the best player I've seen in my four years at ABC.
It has to be David Robinson. I'll never forget the unbelievable
show he put on against Kentucky when he was playing for
Navy. I jumped out of my seat—the first time I've ever given
a player a standing ovation.

I went back to the hotel and got a call from Tark. I mean,
he went on and on about a conspiracy by the NCAA, how he's
thinking about possibly instituting a lawsuit. He said he was
treated unfairly and that he finds it very difficult to accept their
penalty—which will ban his team from the tournament in 1992
and limit their TV exposure. He was going on and on like you
can't believe.

Then Tark started jumping all over my case. "Geez," he said,
"you make that Lute Olson into a God. I heard you the other
day in that game with LSU, Vitale. You helped to recruit for
him. You put players in their uniform. You said he was a great
guy to play for and that if you had a son you'd want him to
play for Lute Olson."

Hey, Tark, don't take it so seriously.

There were two other highlights from today. First, I was
doing a radio show in Kentucky, and the station really surprised the hell out of me when I heard they were giving out a
twenty-five-pound turkey for Christmas to the guy who does
the best impersonation of me. When I heard about the big
turkey, man, I tried to get something free. I gave them my best

Vitale rendition, and I think I'm going to be tough to beat, man. I gave one like, "Hey, Ricky Pitino, baby, get a TO, baby. Pitino, you're a PTP'er, you're solid gold." And, "Oh, is Reggie Hanson one of the real underrated players in America. Get him some PR and some ink, baby. The Kentucky Wildcats will be a team of the nineties. You heard it here, baby. The Wildcats will be cutting down the nets in 1995 and Pitino will be dancing and celebrating. It will be jubilation city." I think I ought to win with that rendition.

The other highlight of the day was that I found out I was nominated for an Ace Award, which is the equivalent of the Emmy for cable excellence. This is, like, my fourth time, but I've never been to the winner's circle. I'm the Mike Krzyzewski of television.

SATURDAY, DECEMBER 15—

I went to the arena, and the first guy I saw—again—was Dickie Paparo. He said, "Hey, Vitale, before you get on my case about the call you said I missed in the Wake Forest–Villanova game, when Rodney Rogers had a chance to get Wake within one, let me tell you something. Vitale, I agree, I flat out blew it!" Then Sonny Vaccaro came over. Sonny's all excited. He's promoting this game for charity. He's going to give a check for $125,000 to the Comic Relief Fund for the Homeless. "Let me pay you refs," he said, and he gave them their $400 for the game. They get only $500 for an NCAA championship game, and that blows my mind.

Another thing that blew my mind was meeting Michigan State athletic director George Perles before the game. George is going to make my All-Wide-Body team. I was teasing him about his weight, man. Boy, is he big. He looks like he's got to stay away from the table a little bit. He's putting on some big-time poundage.

I'll tell you another thing about Big George: He's taken on too much as both football coach and athletic director, and he's gotten into a big-time battle with the school president, John Di Biaggio, over whether he should do both. I don't see how he possibly can handle it at this level. I did it when I was at the University of Detroit, and it was tough enough there. There's no way a guy at the Division I level with football as a major revenue sport should be an AD and a coach. I think it's impossible to keep things running in a first-class way.

Pretty soon, the Tark walked in with his team. I grabbed Larry Johnson as he was walking by and said, "Johnson, baby, you look like Mike Tyson. You'd better go be a fighter. You're not six-eight, you're about six-five." He said, "Don't tell it to anybody nationally, Dick. It will cost me cash."

Well, I'm sure Larry won't have to worry—especially after performances like today's. He had 35 points and 14 rebounds as Vegas put together a spurt midway through the second half to blow out Michigan State, 95–75, and cruise to its third straight win this year.

I was teasing Larry Donald, the publisher of *Basketball Times,* afterward. He's assembled the best stable of basketball writers in the country on his staff—guys like Bob Ryan of the *Boston Globe,* Charlie Pierce of *The National,* Rick Bozich of Louisville, Mark Bradley of Atlanta, Mike Sheridan, who works for Larry and Skip Myslenski of the *Chicago Tribune*—heck, this sounds like an all-Jim Murray team. A solid gold writing staff. He ranked Michigan State No. 1 in preseason. "Larry," I said, "No. 1 in the country?"

Larry quickly let me know he also predicted Louisville to win the national championship in 1986 and he had Kansas in '88. Who knows? Maybe he owns a crystal ball.

CHAPTER 4

SUNDAY, DECEMBER 16—

You know, I said earlier that I don't object to made-for-TV matchups, but I do have a problem with the recent one involving Alabama-Birmingham. Gene Bartow, their coach and athletic director, played back-to-back games in Auburn and—of all places—Vancouver, just for the chance to make $75,000 and go up against UNLV in a game his team had no chance to win. UAB had to board a plane at 6 A.M. to get to Vancouver in time for the game. I said on our telecast Saturday that Gene was being unfair to his kids.

One other thing I don't like about these mega-matchups: I like to see the games played on college campuses, not in places like The Palace. That's the one thing I don't like about so many of the arenas in the Big East. Too many pro buildings. Places like the Cap Centre in Landover, the Hartford Civic Center, the Pittsburgh Civic Arena. Those arenas are just not college environments. You don't get the feel for college basketball the way you do at the Deaf Dome at LSU, Rupp Arena at Kentucky, or Duke's Cameron Indoor Stadium—or even at Vegas, where the pregame laser show is the best. You talk great environments in college basketball, Vegas has to be right near the top. You also have to mention Duke, Syracuse, Indiana, Kentucky, and Kansas. And you have to include Arizona. Lutemania is really getting to be something out there in Tucson. Lute has those people going bananas.

Tark was trying to tell me yesterday that Michigan State still had a home-court advantage, but it was only a mini-advantage. Michigan State was playing at The Palace for the first time. And besides, against UNLV, nobody has an advantage.

MONDAY, DECEMBER 17—

Well, here we are on the sixteenth. Or is it the fifteenth? No, wait a minute, it's the seventeenth. I got up real early this morning and I couldn't remember.

I traveled to Bloomington, Indiana, for Kentucky–Indiana tomorrow and I had a great flight. I bought my usual supply of newspapers—*USA Today, Tampa Tribune, St. Petersburg Times, Chicago Tribune, Miami Herald,* and *The National*—and read them all from cover to cover, especially the sports pages. The first thing I turned to was my usual Monday special, Rudy Martzke's column, and I read that Pat Summerall has a bleeding ulcer. Wow. I can feel for him, because I had a bleeding ulcer on three occasions—once when I was getting ready for a high school state championship game back in New Jersey—and let me tell you something, it is no fun. To this day, I'm on Carafate pills. They keep that stomach soothed. By the way, I read that Summerall said the first flowers he got in the hospital were really ugly and that he said to his wife, "Who sent me those flowers?" She looked at the card and saw they were from—would you believe it?—the TV flower man himself, Merlin Olsen.

Our crew was greeted at the airport by Jay Rothman, our producer, and Chip Dean, a former defensive back at Arizona State who is our director. We told Bobby Knight stories as we drove to Bloomington in the rain and cold. When we got there, we learned that Ralph Floyd, Indiana's outstanding athletic director and just a beautiful person, had died of colon cancer and was being buried today. We went over to the church. Knight was one of the pallbearers, along with IU football coach Bill Mallory.

We then drove over to Assembly Hall, and I decided to knock on the door of the General's private office. Sure enough, he was there. We talked about Ralph, and he was telling me how much he loved working with him and how he was so crushed to learn of his death because Ralph had stood by him through *many* controversies.

After we settled at our hotel, we went out to dinner. You'll never guess who was eating in the same place. Would you believe Bobby Knight and Scott Montross, Eric Montross's dad? Scott is a lawyer in Indianapolis. Indiana recruited Eric last year, and Knight had to be disappointed when the kid signed with North Carolina. When the two were spotted together, rumors started flying Eric might be coming home.

No way. Scott told me his son was happy in Chapel Hill, but that Scott spoke to Dean and asked what Eric could do to be more available offensively. Scott said Dean just simply told him the team doesn't have any rhythm to its offensive game right now and is doing a poor job of getting the ball inside. I reassured Scott that his son will be one heck of a player. He has tremendous work habits.

Ah, controversies. You can't be around Knight without them. Just last Saturday night, Knight was ejected from a game against Western Michigan. He said he'd had difficulty keeping his mind on the game as it was—he found out about Ralph's death just ten minutes before tip-off—and then came the incident. Knight demonstrated very vehemently for me what had happened. He said a guy walked with the ball four different times in one possession, then went to the goal and scored. Knight complained, got hit with two technicals, and was gone.

"I told the ref, '*You* should get credit for that basket. How the hell can you let that go?'" Knight said. "There have been times when I definitely deserved to get tossed, but I didn't deserve it here. If a guy blows a call, the official should be able to take a little blistering from a coach. That's part of it. Don't compound it by calling a technical after you made the error. I told him that and he blew the second T."

At that point, Norm Ellenberger, the Indiana assistant who's getting a second chance under Knight after running into problems with the NCAA at New Mexico, joined the conversation and presented Knight with a gag gift—a cassette tape filled with four-letter words. Press the button and you hear every choice word going.

There are, of course, two sides to Bobby Knight. Look at what he's done for Ellenberger, giving him a new lease on life.

Norm Ellenberger coached New Mexico for seven years, building the Lobos into a national power with a flashy, up-tempo style of play. But the NCAA felt he was taking shortcuts to success and dismantled the program a decade ago, placing the school on three years' probation and declaring seven players ineligible for alleged transcript fixing and a player-payoff scandal.

Ellenberger was suspended in November 1979. He was fired three weeks later. Ellenberger says now he deserved to be dismissed, but, by leaving without protest, he wound up shouldering all the blame and became a pariah in the sport. Ellenberger tried to get back into the game, applying for jobs at New Orleans, Chaminade, Texas–San Antonio, and other schools. But they were all dead-end streets. Finally, Don Haskins, an old coaching foe at Texas El Paso, offered Ellenberger a second chance as an unpaid assistant.

Ellenberger spent three years at UTEP, establishing himself as a valued member of the staff. When Haskins lost his voice because of an acute case of laryngitis last year and was unable to coach, Ellenberger took over on an interim basis and led the Miners to a 21–10 record and a trip to the NCAA Tournament.

Two months ago, he finally got the break he was hoping for when Knight, a personal friend and old fishing buddy, called and asked Ellenberger to join his staff. Knight had gone out of his way for coaches like Ellenberger in the past, giving Tates Locke, who had a problem with the NCAA while at Clemson, a chance to redeem himself. Locke is now the head coach at Indiana State. Ellenberger is hoping for a similar opportunity.

Knight often shows his tremendous love for the old-timers in this sport, and while I was there, he called up Hank Iba, the legendary former coach from Oklahoma State, and invited him down on New Year's to watch the football games and then see the Hoosiers play. The guy is truly a Jekyll and Hyde. He's always been super to me, and I've always enjoyed every visit I've had with him. Then again, I'm not an official who has to take his beratement on the court.

Watching Indiana practice later was like watching a clinic. The team was split into various stations. One was for the guards, who were working on beating Kentucky's traps. Another was for the wing players, who were going over dribble moves, change of direction, and shooting jumpers off the dribble. A third station was for the big men, who were working on their post moves. Ellenberger was posted up on the box with a big football dummy, and the big guys were smashing him as they tried to take the ball to the goal.

The whole thing was a riot. Ron Felling, one of the assistants, was trying to explain Kentucky's complex offensive options at one point when Knight interrupted. "Now, wait a minute now," he said. "Can you understand what this guy's saying? If you can, raise your hand." Nobody did, and then Knight said: "Well, I didn't raise mine, either, because even I can't understand it." He was just busting on Ron left and right, but Ron came back with a Bobby Knight imitation. "Kentucky's going to take the blankety-blank ball to the goal," he screamed. "Now do you understand?" Even Knight cracked up over that one.

I think this is where Knight is happiest—in the gymnasium, on the floor, doing X's and O's, breaking down a game, preparing a team for battle. He knows Kentucky's personnel are better than advertised, too. "Don't give me all this stuff about Pitino not having any players, Vitale," he said. "What are Reggie Hanson, Sean Woods, and Jamal Mashburn?"

TUESDAY, DECEMBER 18—

I made my debut on another weekly radio show this morning— this one's on a real popular FM station in Indianapolis—and one of the hosts, Mark Patrick, was doing an unbelievable Keith Jackson impersonation. I thought I was talking to Keith Jackson. "Wooh, Nellie . . ." It was incredible.

Rick Pitino joined us at our production meeting later in the morning. I had gone to see Kentucky practice yesterday, but Pitino wasn't there. He wanted to see Western Kentucky against Louisville—he plays both teams—so he had his assistant, Tubby Smith, run the workout. I kidded Tubby that I was going to say on the air that Pitino wasn't taking Indiana seriously, but the truth of the matter is, Kentucky already had its workout that morning before the trip to Bloomington. Yesterday afternoon was just a shootaround to get familiar with the baskets.

Pitino said he had decided to play LSU twice during the regular season, with the nonconference game alternating between Madison Square Garden and the Louisiana Superdome. Pitino thinks it will help his recruiting in New York, where he grew up and has a big name from coaching the Knicks.

I tell you, this guy thinks of everything. He covers every possible detail. You should have heard him breaking down the things his assistants do on the bench. He has an assistant, Herb

Sendick—who finished No. 1 in his class at Penn Hills High
and graduated with honors at Carnegie-Mellon—charting
every offensive and defensive possession so he can make the
right decisions late in the game. He also charts things like
deflections, to show whether his team is playing aggressive
basketball. The guy doesn't leave anything to chance.

The other thing about Pitino is he's got his own unique
vision of the game. Kentucky shot an average of 25 three-
pointers a game last season, and Ricky told us he's really upset
that they've been shooting only 18 to 20 lately. He'd like to go
25, even 30, a game. I mean, this guy doesn't just talk about
shooting threes; they come out and they work on it. I mean,
you have to see it to believe it. Ron Franklin, a big college
football guy who is doing the game with me, said it reminds
him of the run-and-shoot offense the Houston Cougars use.

Kentucky has played such exciting basketball the last two
years under Pitino, he's almost made the fans forget about the
probation. Chris Cameron, the Kentucky sports information
director, told me 1988–89 was the toughest year of his career.
The NCAA investigation. All the turmoil. That got me thinking back to the Indiana–Kentucky game and, man, I had called
for Eddie Sutton's resignation earlier that year and I had to go
back to Lexington. Man, I took some real abuse from some of
the fans who live and die with their Big Blue. They want to
believe in utopia and never want to hear anything negative.

But there were plenty of negatives that year. Not only did
Sutton and his entire staff resign, but the program was hit hard
by the NCAA. The Wildcats were banned from participating in
the tournament in 1990 and again this year. They were not
allowed to appear on live TV for a year and were allowed to
offer only three scholarships in the 1989–90 and the 1990–91
academic years. Ninety percent of the money Kentucky received from the 1988 tournament had to be forfeited because of
Eric Manuel's participation. Manuel's college-entrance exam
scores were questioned, and he was declared ineligible at any
NCAA institution. Manuel did not play last year after transferring to Hawasee Junior College in Tennessee. He has since
enrolled at Oklahoma City, an NAIA school.

But things have certainly changed. Within two years, with
Pitino in charge, I think Kentucky will be perennial Top 10.
The guy knows how to make adjustments. Look at the job he

did at Providence, taking them to the Final Four in 1987 when Billy Donovan was a senior.

I had lunch at J. Arthur's Pub in College Square. The place has a wall filled with Indiana memorabilia, photos all over the place. They even have a picture of me, wearing Steve Alford's jersey. Magnus Pelkowski, from Bogotá, Colombia, who played at IU two years ago, was sitting at a table with some ladies having a farewell luncheon. He's leaving tomorrow for home. I decided to have some fun. I told him I was going to say on the air tonight how miserable it was for him to play for the General. "Don't you dare say that," he said. "If you do, you'd better be sure I'm getting on a plane to Bogotá tomorrow morning and never coming back."

All kidding aside, though, Knight really is king here. With all its money, maybe Indiana should build him his own arena, a "Bobby Dome." Of course, they'd have to keep the chairs locked up so he couldn't throw any on the floor. Tickets to Indiana home games are almost impossible to come by. The students get to go to only four games a year, and the games are picked for them through a lottery. That really bothers me. Everything gets down to the people who can write out the checks. Everything is geared to money, money, money. The students, to me, should have first priority. They're the ones who live and die with the team.

They live and die with this interstate rivalry, too. Joe B. Hall, the former Kentucky coach who replaced the Baron, Adolph Rupp, once said his win over Indiana in the 1975 Mideast Regional finals was bigger than his national championship win over Duke three years later.

Amazing. But that's how much it means to the folks here. Indiana that year was undefeated, and had beaten Kentucky, 92–78, earlier that season. But Mike Flynn, a onetime Mr. Basketball in Indiana who played for Kentucky, had a great game that day and came back to haunt his state school.

It seems like there's always a transplanted Indiana kid on the Kentucky roster. This year, it's Sean Woods of Indianapolis. But, in the past, guys like Kyle Macy and James Blackmon have all crossed state lines to make a name for themselves wearing Kentucky blue.

Indiana won by three tonight, executing well enough down the stretch to hold off Kentucky, which had five guys foul out.

Jay Rothman was on cloud nine afterward because I got lucky. I predicted what Indiana would do on three consecutive possessions, and they scored on all three. Hey, sometimes the jumper falls and sometimes it's Brick City, U.S.A.

The end of the game was beautiful, watching Knight hug Pitino and tell him, "Your kids never quit. We had you by eleven. Your guys were in foul trouble and you scrapped and clawed and came back."

Kentucky, 5–2, has had two heartbreaking losses. They were like a pass away, a shot away from beating Carolina and Indiana on the road.

After the game, my partner, Ron Franklin, and I decided to stay in Indianapolis so we would be closer to the airport in the morning. As we were driving, we were listening to Iowa coach Tom Davis do his postgame show. He had just blown out Chicago State and he was laying it on about UCLA, his next opponent. You would have thought he was getting ready to face the UCLA teams of the John Wooden era. Davis is a master at stroking the opposition. Then we switched back to the Kentucky station, and the callers were questioning why Pitino didn't call a time-out at the end of the game. I couldn't believe it. All that criticism for a team playing over its head! Coaching is like a yo-yo—what have you done for me lately?

WEDNESDAY, DECEMBER 19—

Tonight was a great night to sit in front of the tube and watch some action, but you know what I did? I watched a tape that someone mailed me of the 1977 NCAA Mideast Regional semifinal between the University of Detroit and Michigan. That's right, yours truly in his last game as a college coach, going against Johnny Orr and the maize and blue. That team was like Muhammad Ali, the maize and blue. All we wanted was a chance to play them. We could never get them on our schedule. We had to do it the hard way—go 25–3 and win on the road against Al McGuire and Marquette, the No. 1–ranked team in the country. That's the game when I was yelling for a TO, baby, TO, and the kids wouldn't give me one. They figured I'd screw something up. Then Dennis Boyd hit a jumper at the buzzer and made me look like a genius. I did a Disco Duck dance with the cheerleaders after we won, and then I grabbed the microphone from the guys doing the postgame interview and I was off and running. I thanked everybody in the world, from the mayor, to my wife, to my parents, to every player, to every fan. I even thanked Al for his strategy down the stretch—allowing us, without any kind of pressure whatsoever, to take the last shot.

It was reminiscing time, sitting there. My daughter Sherri couldn't believe it when she saw my hair on the tape. I couldn't believe it myself. I had this strip of hair going across my bald dome, long sideburns, and these thick glasses. "How in the world," my wife said, "could I fall for somebody who looks like that?" You talk about a guy who got better looking; I *had* to get better looking. I was so ugly it was incredible. Man, I was one ugly guy. I was the ugly duckling. And, man, I came out dressed in a maize-and-blue outfit. I had the crowd at Rupp Arena down at Kentucky going berserk.

Earlier that day, I had one of the big thrills of my life when I got to introduce our team to two of the giants in the game—John Wooden and Adolph Rupp.

But you know what really excited me? Curt Gowdy and Wooden were doing the game on TV and they were talking about our program. It was just as exciting as anything. John Long had a big game for us, but Phil Hubbard was brilliant for Michigan. He really dominated on the glass. We ultimately lost, 86–81, but I was proud of my guys. We took so much out of Michigan that they were beaten in the next game by North Carolina-Charlotte with Cornbread Maxwell.

But back to today. I also caught a little of the UNLV–Princeton showdown—showtime versus slow time. Princeton came in undefeated and ranked in the Top 25. Can you believe that? Their coach, Petey Carril, man, he looks like he should be selling hot dogs in New York City under a super umbrella. His image is all Mugs McGuinness, not Ivy League button-down collar. But I'll tell you what, he'll run that backdoor on you and carve you to death, cut you to pieces. I know that when it comes to postseason time, nobody wants to go head-to-head with him. Just ask Big John Thompson. Or Nolan Richardson. They'll tell you. They've seen all they want to see of Princeton in the last two NCAA tournaments.

I get asked all the time how I rate Carril with the biggies, and

I have to put him right up there. He's one of the real outstanding tacticians and he always gets the maximum out of his kids, which is the way you really define coaching. Nobody in America gets more out of his talent than Pete Carril.

He seems happy where he is, too. I ran into him last summer at the Olympic Festival when he was coaching one of the teams there, and he said he was fed up with all the stars.

"Can you believe this?" he asked me. "One guy actually questioned me about executing the backdoor cut?"

Man, I got a kick out of him on the sideline tonight. He was out there with that Petey "do," with that hair all standing up. You've heard about the "Lou do"? Well, this is the Carril do. He looked as bad as his team played, too. UNLV just toyed with them and won going away, 69–35.

Everything isn't coming up roses for Tark, though. I read in the paper that the NCAA is charging UNLV with twenty-nine possible violations, many involving a highly publicized former recruit, Lloyd Daniels from New York City, who was supposed to be the next Magic Johnson back in 1986. It looks like the party is coming to an end for Vegas. They can't play in the tournament next year, can't play on TV. That's got to hurt recruiting, because this will drag on and other recruiters will use it against him. They say Tark's not implicated in any of the charges, but the bottom line is, he won't get the quality players he got in the past. There's also a big investigation going on over 6,000 tickets that are unaccounted for. The soap opera goes on and on, like a merry-go-round, and no one knows when it will stop spinning.

THURSDAY, DECEMBER 20—

Can you hear me, M.C. Hammer? You can't touch this. I feel so versatile. Two books and now a videotape. I had to leave the house at 7:45 to get to the Manatee Civic Center in Bradenton to make a tape—"Dick Vitale's Superstars in College Basketball." I'm going to pick my All-Rolls-Royce teams of the 1950s, '60s, '70s, and '80s, and my ultimate Solid Gold team. It will be marketed and sold on ESPN, a thirty-minute tape. I pull up in a Rolls in the first scene and introduce myself. Then

I say to James, a guy dressed up like a chauffeur, "Hit the throttle, baby. Take me to the hoop."

I led off with my team of the '50s. I know people are going to boo and hiss, and they have that right because there were so many great players, but I went with Bill Russell at center, Elgin Baylor and Tom Gola at forward, and Jerry West and Oscar Robertson at guard. Then we went to the '60s, and I lined up with Kareem at center, Elvin Hayes and Jerry Lucas at forward, and Bill Bradley and Pete Maravich in the backcourt. Maravich averaged—averaged!—better than 40 points a game. Can you imagine what he would have scored with the three-point line? Just think about it. Incredible.

We moved to the '70s, and I went with Bill Walton at center, Larry Bird and David Thompson at forward, and Magic Johnson and Phil Ford at guard. I took Ford over Austin Carr, which was a tough choice. Moving to the '80s, I chose Patrick Ewing as my center, Danny Manning and Michael Jordan as my forwards, and Chris Mullin and Isiah Thomas as my backcourt.

Then I went to my Solid Gold team. These were some very difficult choices to make. I mean, how could you pass up a Magic Man or an Isiah Thomas in the backcourt? But my two guards—forget about it, I love them, I'm prejudiced, but I just love these two guys—the Big O and Jerry West. Nobody ever did it any better. These guys could rebound, play defense, score. You talk about Mr. Versatility. I mean, PTP'ers, baby. We're talking flat-out supers. One day Oscar grabbed me at an ACC Tournament and whispered in my ear when he was sure nobody was listening, "Dick, you call all these guys PTP'ers, you call them superstars, solid gold, Rolls-Royce players. How would you describe me, man?" I said, "Oscar, there would be no adjectives to describe you."

There probably are no words to describe the guy I picked in the middle, either—Kareem Abdul-Jabbar. Chose him over Walton, Russell, Chamberlain, Ewing, David Robinson. To me, he was the consummate center when you look at offensive ability, defensive ability, passing the basketball, winning, doing all the things it takes for a post man to play.

My forwards? I don't know, a lot of guys say, "What about Elgin, what about Lucas?" But I went with Larry Bird, for carrying that little school, Indiana State, on his back to the final game in 1979. And I went for my Skywalker, the high riser, David Thompson. He was unbelievable on a collegiate level, he was Mr. Spectacular, showtime. Not a bad club, huh?

My all-time coach was a very easy choice: John Wooden. You can talk about Casey Stengel and all those wins with the Yankees, or Vince Lombardi of the Packers or any of the other guys who've had dynasties, but the greatest coach of all time, in any sport, has to be John Wooden, for winning ten national championships at UCLA and doing it with different personnel. We're not talking best four of seven, baby. One slip in the NCAA tournament and it's all over.

The whole thing was a lot of fun, and as part of the scene, the directors had me slam-dunk, even though the basket was only four feet high. I had some really great moves to the goal, man. I had some style and flair. Even Dominique "the Magnificent" Wilkins would have loved it. It was Jam City, U.S.A.

By the time I got home, my phone was ringing off the hook. The *Syracuse Post-Standard* has come out with a six-page in-depth exposé in which they allege Syracuse players are getting grades changed, are receiving money from boosters.

All kinds of quotes from ex-players and transfers. I'm amazed how guys come out of the woodwork after they allegedly take everything and their careers are over. Just once, I'd like to see one of these guys come forward before sticking out his hand and accepting the illegal cash and simply say, "Hey, a guy offered something illegal, and I don't want to be part of it. I don't want to be a prostitute."

FRIDAY, DECEMBER 21—

Life on the road, man. It's incredible. I left Sarasota real early—I'm going to Las Vegas for the Duel in the Desert, Ohio State–Georgetown and UNLV–Florida State—and there was a delay. Then I flew to Dallas and the plane was delayed again. I had to make the real long jaunt through the Dallas airport to get to my connection. By the time I got there, I was fortunate the plane hadn't taken off. And then we sat on the plane for about an hour because it was rainy and icy.

The good news was, I got a chance on the plane to talk some hoops. I ran into a guy who I watched play in the NIT finals at Madison Square Garden back in 1972, when I was a New

Yorker. He came in with the left-handed stroke and sent Notre Dame back home with a big L. That's right, Allan Bristow, now the vice president in charge of basketball operations with the Charlotte Hornets. He should have been the MVP of the tournament, but they gave it to Notre Dame's John Shumate. C'mon on, John, don't get mad at me. I know you played for me with the Pistons, but even you would have to agree to the victor goes the spoils.

Allan said he really loves Dikembe Mutombo, Georgetown's center. Charlotte needs a big player, so, from a value standpoint, Mutombo would be a guy who even ranks ahead of Larry Johnson for them.

Allan also said he just ran into one of my favorite guys. That's right, the guy from CBS who makes all the cash, Billy Packer, who was heading out of the Dallas airport on his way to Norman, Oklahoma, to do Oklahoma–Duke for CBS. It's about time you're working, Packer. That's your first gig. I've already done about twenty games this year.

I picked up the paper today and all I've read about are charges against UNLV, Syracuse, and now Texas A & M. What a sleazy mess.

A Dallas paper has telephone records stating that coach Kermit Davis has had conversations with Rob Johnson, a talent broker out of New York. Johnson was allegedly involved in arranging a transfer for Tony Scott, who left Syracuse last summer and resurfaced at College Station.

Johnson is the same guy who was identified in the book *Raw Recruits* as having allegedly steered players to Syracuse in the past. When is it going to end? These street agents taking advantage of the kids? But these aren't kids anymore. They got to look in the mirror and know right from wrong and that when they put their hand out and they accept clothing or cash, they're just as guilty. It's really one big mess, and it depresses me.

SATURDAY, DECEMBER 22—

I've been having an absolute ball here. It started last night, at a gathering in the Mirage Hotel. Brent Musburger and Keith Jackson were the emcees, and they introduced Jimmy Valvano and me along with the four coaches—Jerry Tarkanian, John

Thompson, Randy Ayers, and Pat Kennedy of Florida State. We did a little Q-and-A with the fans, and Valvano absolutely jumped all over me. He did a whole routine about my so-called love affair with North Carolina. "You're going to hear about it," he said to Kennedy, who will be joining the ACC next year. "You'll be up six with twenty seconds to go and all you're going to hear is, 'Michelangelo, he's a genius. Michelangelo, he can do this . . .' And if you play Indiana, you'll hear about the General, Robert Montgomery Knight." The place naturally went wild. Then I got up and said, "Let me tell you something, we're making an announcement here. A bulletin just came down, Valvano. I understand Jerry Tarkanian is hiring you immediately to be the academic adviser here at Las Vegas." Tark laughed hysterically.

Then I teased him about losing to Murray State last year in the tournament. "Valvano," I said, "that sounds like a dance studio."

I didn't spare anyone. I told Kennedy, "Kennedy, you got two days here. Enjoy one of them. Have a ball in the casinos. Go watch a great show. No use worrying, man. It's over. You're going to have one miserable day tomorrow afternoon when the pressure comes."

After Ohio State defeated Georgetown, 70–61, in the first game to win their eighth straight, Ohio State's sports information director, Steve Snapp, presented us with some cupcakes. Keith gave them to me at halftime of unbeaten UNLV's 32-point rout of Florida State and said, "Well, my partner's needling got me in trouble with the people down at Ohio State, talking about their cupcake schedule." But I'm not lying; they are playing cupcakes. And they beat a Georgetown team that was without Alonzo Mourning, who missed the game with a foot injury.

There was nothing to say about UNLV's performance other than "Awesome, baby!" I'm just so impressed with their defensive effort. Defense is the one constant in sports—winners all have it. I mean, there will be nights when you don't shoot well, when you can't knock down the J. But if your defense is going to lock up on people and force turnovers and create easy layups, you're always going to have a chance to get in the winner's circle.

Julius Erving, the great Doctor J, was at the game as a guest of Steve Wynn. During one time-out, Mark Jones, our sideline reporter, asked him how he would fit in on this Vegas team.

"Well," the Doctor said, "I'd probably be the Stacey Augmon type of player. Run the lane, get up in transition, and fly through the air a little bit." Watching Julius in Tark's system would be incredible. He was the most spectacular player in the history of the game prior to the arrival of Michael Jordan, and his acrobatic style would fit perfectly with the up-tempo pace the Rebels play. Can you imagine the dunk-a-thon he could put on, releasing into the open floor when Vegas got the ball out on the break?

Watching Augmon run the floor and defend is a trip. He may not have been a high school All-America when he played in Pasadena, but he looks like a lottery pick. Sonny Vaccaro made sure I knew about that. He also told me five years ago that Derrick Coleman, a late bloomer from Detroit's Northern High who signed with Syracuse, would be a better pro than J.R. Reid. J.R. was everybody's All-America in Kempsville, Virginia, before he signed with Carolina.

Coleman, I grant him, is having a great rookie season. But J.R. hasn't exactly been a bust down in Charlotte, even though the coaching staff there would like him to be a little more physical. Remember, this is only his second year in the league.

I saw Tark after the game, and I told him they better win it all this year because the future is dreary, dim and dark. I mean, if you can't recruit players, if you got to go to war with too many Roseanne Barrs instead of Michelle Pfeifers, you're going down the tubes. Tark agreed. "There's no question, Dick, our recruiting is dead," he said. "All this stuff has killed me."

But Pat Kennedy doesn't believe it's over. Check out who Tark had sitting behind his bench—6-5 J.R. Rider, one of the best junior college players in America from Antelope Valley, California, and Carroll Boudreaux, a 6-9 forward from Midland, Texas, Junior College whose brother plays for LSU. Pat said Tark's also got a shot to land Darrin Hancock, a freshman forward out of Garden City, Kansas, JC who was one of the top five prospects in the country last year.

SUNDAY, DECEMBER 23—

I walked in the house like a basket case after taking the red-eye. It was 8:30 in the morning. We all went to church, had lunch on the water, then we went shopping and I bought some gifts for the family. I met a lot of people in the mall who all wanted to talk basketball, and I was eating it up. But then a little old lady came up, and she broke my heart. "Hey, you're Vitale," she said. "You're that guy on TV. You're too loud for me. You blow my ears away. I don't like you, buddy. But I still want to wish you a merry Christmas."

I was thinking today about the teams that have been the biggest disappointments and the biggest surprises so far. Well, I'd have to go with Michigan State, Alabama, and Temple as the three biggest disappointments. Michigan State and Alabama were both Top 10 in my preseason magazine, and Temple was Top 20. In addition, Michigan State was the preseason No. 1 in Larry Donald's *Basketball Times.* Each of those schools has great individual talent. Steve Smith of Michigan State, Mark Macon of Temple, and Robert Horry of Alabama all look like future pros to me.

But all of these programs look like they have underachieved in December. Alabama is 3–2 and has already lost to Wichita State and Southern Mississippi. Temple is only 2–2, losing by 24 at South Carolina. And Michigan State has never been able to get it going, struggling to a 5–3 start with close wins over Furman and Cincinnati and losses to Bowling Green and Nebraska.

When you're talking about surprises, you definitely have to start with Nebraska. They have been doing an unbelievable job under Danny Nee. Georgia and South Carolina have been big surprises too. Georgia is just loaded with great athletes, led by Litterial Green. They are blowing people away. And South Carolina just had a two-point win at North Carolina, a very gutty performance. They also blew out Temple by 24. They've got a lot of homebred people on their team, a lot of South Carolinians, including Jo Jo English.

One other team that's got it going is George Raveling's gang at USC. It looks like the Rav finally has a team that can make some noise in the PAC-10, which, by the way, is one of the most improved conferences in the nation. I'll tell you, Harold Miner, their sophomore guard, is a flat-out big-time player. I caught some clips of him on TV the other day, and he's got to be one of the most underrated players in the nation. You never hear his name mentioned with the big stars, but he can play with anybody, anytime, anywhere. He had 35 against Notre Dame, and they just couldn't stop him. He did it inside, outside, the whole bit.

Later this afternoon, I was going through my mail and found a note from Gene Bartow. I knew right away what it was about. He wrote that he agreed with me and that one of the dumbest decisions he'd made was playing UNLV. He said he didn't do it for the cash, though it was because the kids wanted a chance against the national championship team.

My argument is, man, they never had a chance under those conditions.

CHAPTER 5

MONDAY, DECEMBER 24—

The other day on ESPN, they had me play Santa Claus and give out some gifts to three coaches—Knight, George Raveling of USC, and Boeheim. I did my thing and said, "Hey, I'm St. Dick, baby, and here's Santa to deliver to my guy Bobby Knight a zebra uniform. That's right, a zebra uniform and a whistle. Then I gave Raveling a new field house so he can battle Jimmy Harrick of UCLA on even terms. Finally, I gave Boeheim, who constantly gets maligned by the fans and the writers in Syracuse, a Dale Carnegie course in public relations.

TUESDAY, DECEMBER 25—

Christmas Day. I went to dinner at the Chop House and was greeted by two fanatics when I walked in. Both were from the state of Kentucky. One was a Louisville fan, the other was a Kentucky fan. All they wanted to do was talk hoops. I mean, it was Christmas. I wanted to talk about Santa Claus.

The guy from UK was really riding high, man. "They were burying us when we were on probation," he said. "But look at them squirming and suffering now. Vitale, mark it down— 1992. I guarantee it, Vitale. I mean, I flat out guarantee it. Take Kentucky to win the Final Four. It's lock city."

One of the guys had an eleven-year-old son, so I went out to my car and pulled out a Vitale Rock basketball. I said, "Here's a little gift. Take this home for Christmas to your son." Man, I made a fan for life. Eat your heart out, Packer. This guy will never come your way. He's mine all the way, in my pocket, you better believe it. Especially when I told him I liked Ricky Pitino.

I love playing Santa Claus and passing out the rock, man. The guys who put this deal together for me don't know what a monster they created, because I carry those balls in the back of my car. I'll meet some young kids playing hoops in the backyard and I'll just pull over the car and say, "Hey, how you guys doing?" Then I'll shoot a jumper or two with the guys and I'll pull out a basketball and say, "This is from me to you."

WEDNESDAY, DECEMBER 26—

Reading the paper today really broke my heart. I read that Scott May, an outstanding baseball player at Manatee High School and the son of Pittsburgh Pirates hitting instructor Milt May, was involved in a serious automobile accident. He is listed in serious condition with a head injury. The Mays are our neighbors and our friends. News like that really hits home a little bit more when you have teenagers of your own.

In the afternoon, I knocked off thirty-five commentaries for my syndicated radio show. They're one-minute commentaries and they're really a lot of fun to do. I did a number of generic topics, including my All-Rolls-Royce coaches, my All-Rolls-Royce team, my All-Rambo team, my All-Crybaby team, and the best team in the history of college basketball. It took me about an hour and a half to knock off the thirty-five shows. I have one more session to do another thirty and the whole year's completed. It's amazing what can be done through the magic of preproduction.

Hey, Rollie Massimino got some good news: Jonathan Haynes will be transferring from Temple to Villanova. He'll come in as a sophomore. What amazes me is that the kid played in one exhibition game and now he loses a complete year of eligibility. That, to me, is an absolute joke. They can't be serious. I mean, if a guy's injured and misses a few games, he'll get a medical redshirt. Here's a kid who plays in an exhibition game, not even a regular-season game, and it's going to cost him an entire year.

THURSDAY, DECEMBER 27—

Holiday tournaments are breaking out all over. At this time of the year, everybody tries to get two easy W's if they can, two bargain-basement goodies to kick in the New Year, particularly if they have the luxury of playing in their home arena.

Fans in New York will catch their first glimpse of 7–6 Shawn Bradley of BYU in the Holiday Festival, which also includes Maryland, South Carolina, and Rutgers. Arizona will attempt to protect its long home-court winning streak when it hosts Temple, Iowa State, and Pepperdine in the Fiesta Bowl Classic in Tucson. And Arizona State coach Bill Frieder may get a chance to face his old school, Michigan, if both teams advance to the finals of the Tribune Classic in Tempe.

I remember when I was at the University of Detroit and we ran our Titan Holiday Classic. One year it was Shock City U.S.A. The field included Michigan, Eastern Michigan, and Western Michigan. We drew Eastern Michigan in the first round, and the tournament was set up for us to play Michigan in the championship game.

I was so sure it was going to happen that I even went out and got a sponsor to donate wristwatches.

But Eastern Michigan didn't cooperate. We lost that night and lost again in the consolation game. We finished fourth. I had the most miserable holiday you could imagine. It was blues city.

I felt sorry for my wife and daughters, because I carried the losses so badly when I was a coach. I mean, I hurt and felt embarrassed. I wanted to sneak into the back of the church so I wouldn't be recognized. That was really immature on my part. That's one of the reasons why I'm not coaching anymore. I couldn't handle losing.

FRIDAY, DECEMBER 28—

Lou Holtz would be mighty proud of me and my family today. We've got a van, we've got a bunch of kids from Notre Dame with us, we've got all the Irish paraphernalia—the T-shirts and the sweatshirts and the hats—and we're on our way to Miami, baby, to cheer on the Irish in the Orange Bowl against Colorado and their coach, my buddy, Bill McCartney. McCartney gave me my first chance to speak in the Detroit area after I took the UD job—he was coaching at Divine Child in Dearborn—but I'm sorry, Big Bill, I'm coming down to root against you this weekend.

It took us four hours to go from Bradenton to the Hilton at Blue Lagoon, the home of the Fighting Irish. We walked in the lobby and we were greeted—that's right, greeted—by The Rocket, Rocket Ismail himself. My wife got a big kiss and hug from him. "Mrs. Vitale," he said. "Where's the picture I took of Mr. Vitale and the girls? I want to hang it in my room." Are you serious? Hey, Rocket, baby, you've got to know, I want *your* photo. Then, Scott Kowalkowski, their linebacker, came over and said, "Hey, a lot of kids on campus got a Dick Vitale T-shirt, and I don't have one."

Tonight we were joined at dinner by a kid by the name of Jason Beckworth, a walk-on freshman center from Michigan who made the traveling squad. He's 6-2, 230, and he said his indoctrination to college football was going up against Chris Zorich, Notre Dame's All-America middle guard, on a regular basis in practice.

"I've got the bruises on my body to prove it," he said.

Lou Holtz came over to the table and started talking about playing to your strength. Holtz is a big basketball fan, coached at Arkansas when Eddie Sutton took the Hogs to the Final Four in 1978. He said, "Dick, if it comes down to the last shot, you're not going to go to your fourth or fifth option." That's why I know he'll get the ball in the hands of the Rocketman at crunch time.

SATURDAY, DECEMBER 29—

Another fun day. The highlight for the players probably was the Everglades safari, where they got to watch some alligator wrestling. The guys all were trying to get Michael Stonebreaker, the All-America linebacker from Louisiana, to jump in the cage and take on a gator.

The guys were yelling, "C'mon, Stonebreaker, you jump in there, man. You're a Bayou guy, you know all about these alligators."

He naturally wanted no part of it, and I can't blame him one bit. In fact, the caretaker got bitten when he was demonstrating how he could open the alligators' jaws and put his hand in their mouths. His hand was bleeding like crazy.

I'd probably have given anything to go to school at Notre Dame. But my grades were so bad, there was no way I could get near the door. I was lucky enough Seton Hall gave me a break.

Tonight, at Lou Holtz's request, I addressed the Notre Dame team. I talked about what it meant to wear a Notre Dame uniform, how most kids they play against dream of wearing it. I also told them that every week they take the field, people are playing at another level and that they have to rise to the occasion.

I also talked about Chris Zorich. I have a special feeling for him. When my wife and I were talking to him, all he wanted to talk about was his mother, who he said was his inspiration. Zorich grew up on the south side of Chicago, a real rough area, and it was so beautiful to see this 6-1, 265-pound tough guy express his feelings. That's what life is all about, caring for others, giving back, sharing rather than take, take, take.

Little did we know, but three days later, when Chris went home after the game, he would walk into his home and find his mother dead on the floor.

After I finished, the team gave me a standing ovation. I can't tell you how much that meant, coming from a bunch of kids who are the definition of what a student-athlete should be.

In our hotel was a big New Year's bash. My wife and I dropped by and joined the crowd. Father Edward "Monk" Malloy, the president of Notre Dame, was right across from us. I remembered Father Malloy from a different life. He played on a great Archbishop Carroll High team in Washington, D.C., that included John Thompson, John Austin (who went on to play at BC), center Tom Hoover, and guard George Leftwich (who played at Villanova). Think they lost a game?

Father Malloy attended Notre Dame on a basketball scholarship, and I was telling him about my daughter Terri and how tough she said her classes were.

"When I was a freshman at Notre Dame, I had some engineering classes that threw me for a loop," he told me. "I had under a 2.0 GPA for my first year and I went on to become president of the university. So, if you apply yourself, anything is possible."

This was a really nice affair. My wife and I were dancing when Lou Holtz stopped over. "Dick, I'd like you to meet my wife," he said.

He was with a beautiful young lady. I mean, she was gorgeous. I said, "C'mon, Lou, baby. I know you're a superstar, but you're not in that league." It turns out the woman was the fiancée of his son, Skip.

Holtz was in rare form. Here it was, about one in the morning on the day of the game, and he was totally relaxed and having a ball. He wasn't the only one.

TUESDAY, JANUARY 1, 1991—

Bob Uecker should be so lucky. I had great seats, right on the fifty-yard line, courtesy of Steve Hatchell from the Orange Bowl. I paid for those babies, though. No freebies. Some of the Colorado fans were getting on my case because I was dressed in my Notre Dame finest, but we had a blast. I even won over the Colorado fans after a while. They were all upset when their quarterback, Darien Hagen, went out with an injury and had to be replaced by Charles Johnson, but I told them not to worry. "Hey, let me tell you about CJ," I said. "I know him, he's from out of Detroit. I met him last fall when I went to Boulder to speak on behalf of Joe Harrington's basketball team. This kid is going to be ready for this task." Harrington, a little word of advice. Johnson's from the same high school as Chris Webber, Michigan's high school phenom. Better get on the phone.

Sure enough, Johnson did the job. Led Colorado on their winning touchdown drive. It was one exciting game, even though the Irish lost, 10–9.

I thought Rocket might pull it out in the final minute when he returned a punt 91 yards for what looked to be the winning touchdown. But an official dropped a flag downfield for clipping, nullifying a magnificent play. If I had been doing that game, I would have been all over that zebra.

We were all disappointed when we went back to the hotel, but the Notre Dame kids handled it with class. So did Holtz.

I ran into him at about 1 A.M. and he said, "Hey, we got beat. I can't cry about it. We had our opportunities."

I walked away saying, "Wow." I know how I would have acted in the same situation.

WEDNESDAY, JANUARY 2—

We loaded the van and headed back to Bradenton. I've got to get back into the the swing of things. I have Notre Dame–North Carolina Saturday at the Meadowlands, and I'm going up there tomorrow to meet a couple of the guys I coached in high school.

Times like this help you remember where you came from. I've been lucky. I've been involved with some great players along the way: Les Cason at East Rutherford, Phil Sellers and Mike Dabney at Rutgers, and John Long and Terry Tyler at the University of Detroit. Those guys have been so influential in my career.

THURSDAY, JANUARY 3—

Every time I come back to North Jersey to do a game, it feels like a homecoming. I grew up here, got my start in coaching here. So I really enjoyed getting together tonight with three of my former players—Charley Rusconi, Dwight Hall, and Joey Solomini. They are three beautiful guys who were fierce competitors on my championship team when I coached at East Rutherford.

FRIDAY, JANUARY 4—

Today at the Meadowlands I had a chance to sit down for a while with Notre Dame coach Digger Phelps. Digger's off to a rough start and he's been taking some heat. He's also had it rough at home. He told me his father, who had surgery earlier in the year, was visiting the family over the holidays and had to be rushed to the hospital on Christmas Eve with pains in his stomach. Digger said he's gone to see his father in the hospital every day since then. His mind's on more than just basketball going into this game.

Then I saw Dean, and I immediately started teasing him about how I went to see Phil Ford for some information earlier and was told, "You've got to get everything from Coach Smith. I can't give you anything." That program is like the Secret Service, boy. The Man does all the talking.

Dean knows that I feel he's too protective, especially when it comes to his players. His argument is that it's unfair how much attention and publicity some of the kids receive, and that's true. But the bottom line is, part of being a great athlete is being able to live with all that, knowing how to handle it and deal with it. I know it can be tough, but the ones who can are the ones who are special.

Dean's got other things on his mind, though. All he wanted to talk about was how tough it has been finding playing time for all his blue-chippers. He tried to use Kentucky's situation to make his point.

"Pitino is doing a phenomenal job," Dean said, "because he's got great chemistry. Now they're going to get so good, they're going to start getting great, great players. And then the problems will start."

SATURDAY, JANUARY 5—

Notre Dame hung tough with Carolina for a half, but everybody knew that Carolina's personnel eventually would break it open, and pretty soon it was rock-and-roll time. Carolina won by 35. It's just tough for the Fighting Irish right now, who are a disappointing 3–9.

I suggested on the telecast that the Irish should join the Big East. It would elevate their recruiting to a new level. I know their athletic director, Dick Rosenthal, thinks they can make it as an independent, but it looks like their streak of NCAA Tournament appearances will be coming to an end this year.

The Irish definitely need to look into a conference, but only if it's the right one. What's happening with some conferences around the country is absolute lunacy. Marquette, Memphis State, De Paul, St. Louis, Cincinnati, and Alabama-Birmingham recently formed a new league called the Great Midwest. I'm not sure how UAB fits in with those schools geographically—just like I don't understand how Miami fits in with the Big East and Penn State fits into the Big 10.

What hypocrisy. It just blows my mind. The presidents are constantly screaming about reducing schedules. They go to their meetings, smoke their cigars, and make all these pronouncements about reform. But everybody's going after the dollar and forgetting about the kids. You tell me the logic of a tennis player from Penn State traveling to Bloomington for a match against Indiana. The kids will have to miss two days of school. It's that old mighty Uncle George Washington. Greed, greed, greed.

After the game, I ran into Lenny DeLuca, the little guy who runs CBS Sports. He says we look alike, that people are always mistaking him for me. I mean, come on, Lenny. If I look like you, I'm in big trouble. Lenny's one guy I'd like to play one-on-one, 'cause I could post the little sucker. Take him to the goal and score.

CHAPTER 6

SUNDAY, JANUARY 6—

Who's Rob Metcalf? Come on, all you basketball fans. Who's Bob Martin? Who's Willie Sims? Tell me who Patrick Tompkins is. I know they're not household names, man. When I got on the plane today to go to Madison, Wisconsin, even I didn't know a heck of a lot about them. But I guarantee you that when Minnesota and Wisconsin tip off tomorrow night, I'll know more about them than they know about themselves.

It was only fourteen degrees when we got to Madison, and we couldn't get into the gym right away for the shootaround because the doors were locked. I didn't have any gloves, and I was freezing. All I could think about was my wife back home in Florida. She was probably upset that it was only seventy-two there and not eighty-five or eighty-six like it has been.

When I finally got inside, Clem Haskins, Minnesota's coach, was telling stories about his days in the NBA. Haskins was the third pick in the draft in 1967, right behind Jimmy Walker of Providence and Earl Monroe of Winston-Salem. He said he got a $1,000 bonus from the Chicago Bulls and $12,000 a year. Can you believe that?

Haskins is really high on his players. He introduced me to Ernest Nzigamasabo, a freshman center from Baruni, Africa. What a brilliant young man. He's an A student in engineering—I mean, we're talking in the 3.67 area—and he speaks six languages fluently. Incredible. I asked him if he knew Dikembe Mutombo of Georgetown. He said he saw him play in Zaire but just knows him as "Hi." I said, "You guys ought to hook up together. He speaks *five* languages."

After a while, Clem and I started discussing the NCAA

investigation hanging over Minnesota's athletic department.
Clem said he feels there are only three or four violations being
alleged, that they are very minor involving basketball, and that
the school would not get any kind of sanctions. He did say,
though, that one of the alleged infractions involves Chris Webber, a 6-10 forward from Detroit Country Day School in Bir-
mingham, Michigan, who is the most sought-after high school
senior in the country.

Clem is really angry about the Webber business. He claims
the school didn't know it was committing a violation when the
president had Webber in a skybox with him to watch the Michigan State–Minnesota football game. He also thinks Michigan
State turned them in, because they're battling it out with Michigan to sign Webber. But you know what? Clem the Gem is
convinced that Webber's going to wind up at Minnesota. You
talk about a positive thinker and a guy who really believes:
Haskins isn't even allowed to call the kid or write to him until
the NCAA investigation is over.

"Hey, you never mention us, and we're going to get Chris
Webber," Haskins said. "He had his best visit when he visited
us. He loved it, absolutely loved it in the Minneapolis–St. Paul
area, and he wants to wear the maroon and gold." On top of
that, Haskins also said he expected to get guard Vashon Leonard from Detroit's Southwestern High.

I went to dinner with Steve Yoder, Wisconsin's coach. He's
6–4 and in a tough situation. Academically, it's so tough at his
school it's incredible. If he wins 15 or 16 games, he'll have done
a super job. He was telling me how tough it is, how people just
don't understand. He wants to be able to challenge the big
guys, but it's difficult when it comes to recruiting and trying to
build a tradition. Told me he was contacted about the SMU job
a couple years ago by the AD there, Doug Single, who used to
be at Northwestern and knew his work. But he decided to hang
in.

Tomorrow night's game is huge for them. Ray McCallum,
Yoder's assistant, came over to the table and said, "All our
recruits know we're going to be on the national tube tomorrow,
so you better say beautiful things about us." I said, "Yeah, I'll
talk about how this place is fit for the Eskimos, baby, out here
with this minus-three-degree weather. I'm freezing like an ici-
cle, here, I can't believe it." He said, "Hey, it's seventy degrees

in the gym every night, and I'll tell you what, the 'bleacher creatures' will have it up to ninety when they start rocking and rolling."

MONDAY, JANUARY 7—

I promised Yoder that I wouldn't talk about the cold weather tonight, but when I went outside this morning it was unbelievable. It was, like, minus six. Some guy outside said to me, "Hey, this is not cold at all. It's going to get colder." Are you kidding me? I can't believe people can live like this. I don't know about keeping that promise, Steve. If your recruits don't know by now that Wisconsin gets cold in January and February, then I don't think they can handle it here academically, baby.

Speaking of academics, we were holding our production meeting this morning and Mike Patrick and I got into a big battle with our director, Kenny Fouts, about graduating players.

Fouts just came back from Louisville. Denny Crum, you got a big fan, baby. Fouts says it's OK if the players don't graduate.

"So what?" he said to me. "The fact is, they're playing basketball. They're doing what they're there for."

Patrick jumped all over him.

"What are you talking about?" he said. "That's using players."

Kenny's argument is that the degree isn't the end-all in some cases, as long as the players are becoming better people.

I had to disagree. I feel you can't just use these kids for five years and, once their eligibility is up, send them to the sideline.

I made the mistake of bringing Bobby Knight into the conversation as a guy who cares about his kids.

Fouts was all over my case. He said, "Man, when are you going to stop talking about the General? We're in Big 10 country. It's the life of the Big General."

I stopped off to have something for lunch and ran into Bill Gardner, the scout for the Washington Bullets. We went over a bunch of different players. He told me he really likes the competitiveness of Minnesota guard Kevin Lynch, that Lynch could be a player he starts coming to see a little bit more. I asked him, "What do you think of Mark Macon?" He said John Chaney, Temple's coach, does a phenomenal job teaching the college game, but that when it comes to the pro level, a lot of his kids don't have a real feel for the transition game and they struggle a little bit. For that reason, he said he'd be a little worried about Macon.

I went back to my room and was trying to catch a little nap when I was awakened by a call from John Lewandowski, the basketball sports information director at Auburn. He was looking for some publicity. "Dick, we can't believe it at Auburn," he said. "Tommy Joe Eagles is doing a great job, we're six and one out of the gate, and nobody knows about it. You've got to give us some ink. You talked about your Diaper Dandies the other day and a lot of people were all upset that you never mentioned Wesley Person, Chuck's younger brother. He's averaging seventeen a game."

I said, "Wow, really?" I saw Person play against Alabama, and he didn't have a good game, but I could see he's got talent. I wish I could get down to Auburn and do a game. Unfortunately, I don't get into every arena, and I think that certainly tends, at times, to affect your opinions.

Jeff Gowen, our producer, picked me up at the hotel later and we went over to the arena to tape the first of "Dick Vitale's Fast Break" series, a two-minute commentary on a smorgasbord of college tidbits, which will air Tuesday nights at 7 on "SportsCenter" and Wednesday nights during the 11:30 show. I talked about underclassmen who might enter the draft. "Hey, baby," I said, "if you love college basketball, you better appreciate Billy Owens and Kenny Anderson now, because come the NBA draft, they're going to be gone. They're going to lay exorbitant dollars on Anderson. He's going to say bye-bye. Bobby Cremins is a players' coach, and he'll advise Kenny to take the money, tell him he's got to go." As for Owens, I said, "The university's investigation of the basketball program, which could lead to an NCAA investigation, is going to prompt him to move on."

Wisconsin played brilliantly. They outscrapped Minnesota, outhustled them and won by ten.

After the game, we went to a place called the Nitty Gritty, and the owner asked me to do a radio spot for him. So I laid it on them: "Hi, everybody. This is Dick Vitale from ABC and

ESPN Sports, here at the Nitty Gritty, where I make a stop every time I'm in town to do a Badger game. The place is awesome, baby. My guys here are PTP'ers. It's super." And he loved it. Naturally, it was a freebie!

Hey, they got a picture of Steve Bornstein, the president of ESPN, up on the wall. Steve was a grad of Wisconsin. I mentioned that on the air and Steve called me up to tell me he had been besieged ever since by alumni groups seeking donations. Said he'd remember that the next time we negotiated a contract. Only teasing, boss. Just tried to get you a little ink. You're the top of the ladder, one of the most powerful people in sports according to *Sporting News*.

TUESDAY, JANUARY 8—

I've been keeping tabs on the NCAA convention this week in Nashville, and I'm glad to see there appears to be a major move toward reform. The best move, so far, has been the decision to do away with athletic dorms. I totally agree with that. Regular dorms enable the athletes to mix with the student body, to be more than just one-dimensional.

I just wish they would have approved the Big East's proposal that would have given an extra year of eligibility to kids who enter college as Proposition 48 students and go on to prove they can do the job academically. These kids suffer enough. Right now, they not only lose a year of eligibility, but they can't even practice with their team their freshman season.

They come in wearing that shingle on their back, that label, and they deserve a chance to redeem themselves. And if they prove themselves in the classroom, like Rumeal Robinson of Michigan, they deserve the option of playing that fifth year, even if they choose to go to graduate school. Reward classroom performance.

It also bothers me to see coaching staffs being reduced. That decision is going to eliminate some of the young guys who are the future of coaching. Where are they going to get their start? For the few dollars you're talking about, it's absurd. If anything, I think staffs should be increased. Coaches are constantly blamed if kids don't graduate, if kids get involved with problems off the court. These guys need all the help they can get.

WEDNESDAY, JANUARY 9—

I just arrived in Durham, North Carolina, for the big ACC game tomorrow between Georgia Tech and Duke. It will be my first chance this season to see Kenny Anderson live. My partner Mike Patrick loves the kid. He calls Georgia Tech "Kenny Anderson University." He thinks Kenny Anderson's the best point guard of all time. Me, I have to give the edge to Magic Johnson because of his size and ability to post up inside. But Anderson might be the best small lead guard I've ever seen.

Kenny's been under a lot of pressure this season, carrying pretty much the entire load, but Duke coach Mike Krzyzewski was telling me today that he is one of Anderson's biggest fans. Mike coached him last summer at the Goodwill Games and the World Championships, watched Kenny make a pair of free throws with no time left on the clock to tie the bronze medal game with Puerto Rico and then take the game over in overtime.

Mike said that when it was all over, Kenny told the coaching staff, "I really want to thank you for all the things you did for me and all the things you taught me here this summer." Mike says he really got choked up.

"This is a special kid," Krzyzewski said. "Forget all the NBA scouting reports that say he's not physically strong enough. He's so much tougher than people believe. He's going to be a superstar in the NBA."

I ran into Tech assistant Kevin Cantwell a little later, and he had an honest evaluation of Matt Geiger, the Yellow Jackets' 7-0 center who transferred in from Auburn. Most assistants just praise, praise, praise. But Cantwell was honest to a T. "Hey, man, if we're going to be a good club, we've got to get Matt Geiger to get a little tougher," he said. "He can't play as soft as he is. He's got a great touch, great size, but we've got to get him to be a little bit more physical, a little meaner inside, to help us."

From there, I had to tape a locker-room scene in which I play the role of a coach—tie loosened, shirt rolled up, talking about containment and recovering and how they're going to be vital to Bob Hurley if he wants to control Kenny Anderson.

Then I went to the hotel and called Bobby Cremins. "Hey, Bobby," I said, "this is the NCAA, and we want to know about the $1 million payoff that was laid on Mr. Anderson by you and your people." I must have woke him up, because he kept saying, "Who's this? Who's this?" Then he recognized my voice.

I guess I have a voice that's not easy to disguise.

THURSDAY, JANUARY 10—

Cameron Indoor Stadium. The Cameron Crazies. There's nothing quite like this place. Or these students.

The doors opened at 7:30 for the nine-o'clock game, and the Cameron Crazies came storming in. They immediately started giving me the raspberries, because I was down on the floor shooting around with the Georgia Tech players. Geiger was feeding me, the big fella. He laid some assists on me, Big Geig, but I couldn't knock it down. I threw up a few air balls and the students let me hear about it. But it was the shirt, baby—the shirt was too tight—and the jacket. I just couldn't get the follow-through, couldn't get that normal release.

Everyone was talking about the NCAA convention before the game. Krzyzewski was particularly upset about the decision to cut scholarships from fifteen to thirteen over a four-year period. "Hey, we can't take things away from the kids," he said. Then he looked out on the floor at the three-man officiating crew that would be doing the game and said, "Why not have two guys referee? Eliminate the third guy and you would save all kinds of money. I have nothing against three-man crews, but you don't do it at the expense of the young people playing."

I can't really agree with you, Mike. I think the coaches can get by with thirteen instead of fifteen. Add three walk-ons and now you have a nice composition. Mike's argument is that you are going to have coaches running players off if they don't live up to expectations. I don't buy that argument at all. Part of the evaluation process is to make sure you get guys that fit your system.

The game itself was a blowout. Duke rolled, 98–57, to increase its record to 11–3. Tech, which got off to a slow start, is 9–4. Who'd have ever dreamed it? It was, like, a close ball game, then all of a sudden Duke put on a spurt and went up at halftime by 16.

This Duke team really plays some great pressure defense, and it looks like they've turned out another in a long line of supers—Grant "The Velvet Man" Hill. I mean, you talk about class. This guy can play three positions and handle the rock and penetrate. He's definitely one of the top freshmen so far, one of the Diaper Dandies, along with "Hot Rod" Rodney Rogers of Wake Forest, Adrian Autry of Syracuse, Shawn Bradley of Brigham Young, and Jamal Mashburn of Kentucky.

According to Krzyzewski, he just has to turn it up a notch. "Grant hasn't learned yet," Krzyzewski said. "I told him the other day, 'Grant, you're like this beautiful Porsche, but you're playing like a Chevy right now. You got to turn it into gear.' "

Hill's really got the great bloodlines, man. I was talking to his father, Calvin, at the NIT, and he was telling me how he knew his son didn't want to be a football player back when Grant was in the eighth grade. The two of them were out playing tennis in Reston, Virginia, one August day and it was ninety-five degrees out. The local high school football team was out practicing, and Calvin said to Grant, 'That's what you're going to be doing next year." His son looked at him and said, "You're dead wrong. There's no way I'm putting one of those helmets on, Dad."

Kenny Anderson put 25 on the board tonight, but I've got to tell you, he looked horrendous with a capital *H*. Hurley did about as good a job as you can with him. Plus, Duke did an amazing job cutting off the transition game in the first half and never allowing Anderson to get into the open court, where he excels. Anderson didn't have an assist in the first half. Can you believe that?

Krzyzewski asked me before the game whether Anderson was the best I had ever seen, and I said, "Yes, as a scoring point guard, a guy who can penetrate and score." But I really believe he feels the pressure now. He'd rather not have to score, that's the kind of kid he is. He'd rather find the open man. I mean, every time he goes on the floor, they're expecting him to score 30, 35, and that puts a big burden on him. He may be embarrassed by trying to force the play, but there's no way Tech can win without him.

Tonight, Hurley, baby, you were the star. You and Billy McCaffrey, who had a big night in the backcourt, too, knocking out 29. Hurley and McCaffrey look like two Boy Scouts, man, they look like they're ready to put up pup tents and go camping.

I'll tell you what, they're at the right place. Tents started going up outside Cameron right after the game. North Carolina's coming in next week, and the students already are lining up for tickets. They'll be camped out here in Krzyzewskiville all week.

FRIDAY, JANUARY 11—

What a life. It took me practically all day to go from North Carolina to South Carolina.

I was scheduled to arrive in Columbia to give a motivational speech to some Pepsi salespeople. I had a super time with the Pepsi gang, and then several of their execs took me to the South Carolina–Southern Miss game. We caught the last five minutes of the game. Southern Miss, which has now jumped into the Top 25 with a 7–1 record, won the Metro Conference game, 64–58, and I was really impressed by their 6-7 junior, Clarence Weatherspoon, in the little I saw. So was Mel Daniels, who was there to scout for the Indiana Pacers. Mel said he could be the next Charles Barkley.

Something happened at South Carolina's postgame press conference that really surprised me. Barry Manning, one of George Felton's players, got up and started to complain that the team was arguing with each other in the time-outs, that they were really on each other. He also questioned the guys who were shooting the ball at the end; he felt Joe Rhett and Jo Jo English should have taken the big shots. I could see that George was really upset. I know that as a coach you like to air those things out in private, not in public.

SATURDAY, JANUARY 12—

I had to go from Columbia to Charlotte today, and Bill Simon from Pepsi offered to drive me. Bill is a Connecticut hoops freak. He's really excited about the five blue-chippers Jim Calhoun signed in the early recruiting period. Told me his wife was a big Carolina fan, that they really had a war in their house when the Tar Heels played UConn in the Big East–ACC challenge.

But it was nothing like the crisis that's on the verge of taking place over in the Gulf. We got in the car and turned on the news, and the first story was all about Operation Desert Shield and the fact that the U.N. Secretary General was going over there for one last-ditch meeting with Saddam Hussein. Bill was in Beirut during the conflict in Lebanon. He went there on Christmas Day in 1983 on a destroyer. He was there when terrorists drove a truck with explosives right into the Marine compound and killed more than two hundred soldiers.

Bill had some really interesting observations about war. He said, "The toughest-looking guys, the guys you think are from the streets, who are really tough, big, six-two, six-three . . . they become like jelly, and the little, skinny guy from the rural country area gets as tough as nails at that time." He said he was living with such fear and worry when he was over there. He said you just pray and pray and pray.

The big news in basketball today was that Lawrence Funderburke, the 6-9 forward who got fed up with Knight and quit the team midway through his freshman year, is going back home. He's leaving Indiana and transferring to Ohio State. I'm a little bit surprised about that, because when I was in Indiana, the Hoosiers' Eric Anderson told me the word was he was going to Louisville. It will be interesting to see if Funderburke ever matures and becomes the star everybody has predicted.

Knight is really down on Funderburke. Bobby told me he would have taken him back, that he sat down with the kid early in the season and tried to give him some guidance. Hey, the kid is a great player. He was starting as a freshman. But Bobby said he never even said thank you after their meeting, and that really bothered Knight. Bobby also went to the players and asked what they thought about Funderburke possibly coming back. A lot of them said he had to show a hungrier attitude and make them feel that he really wanted to be a part of the team. Bobby said that's when he knew they had to go without him.

I got home about five, and the first thing I wanted to do was take a nice hot bath. I got in the tub and the phone started ringing like crazy. One of the calls was from Phil Richards, a writer in Indianapolis. He wanted me to give him my Final Four, because Indianapolis is the host city this year and his paper is getting ready to kick off its coverage. I said, "Final Four? This is January twelfth, baby!" But of course I did it. I gave him UNLV. You don't have to be a genius to say them. Then I went with Arkansas, North Carolina, and Arizona. I like Indiana, but I think they're a big guy away.

I also got a call that my assignment for Wednesday has been changed. Instead of Syracuse–Connecticut at the Carrier Dome, I'm going to North Carolina to do their game against North Carolina State. I was looking forward to going back to the Carrier Dome—Jimmy Boeheim, rock-and-roll time with the Connecticut Husky-mania—but you've got to go where the boss sends you. And besides, I just heard it's been snowing like crazy up in Syracuse. I love the Carrier Dome and Billy Owens, but not that much.

SUNDAY, JANUARY 13—

What a week I have coming up. Four monster games in seven days. Are you ready for this? Indiana–Purdue tomorrow, North Carolina–North Carolina State on Wednesday, Duke–North Carolina on Saturday, and Ohio State–Indiana next Monday. Basketball junkies would be drooling to have my seat.

On my flight to Indianapolis, one of the flight attendants came over to show me his watch. He's a big basketball fan who had a watch made in the shape of a basketball player. He wanted to know about Purdue. I know they blew out Michigan yesterday, 86–69, and they have a day to prepare for Indiana. Knight has had a week off. I can already hear Purdue coach Gene Keady screaming, "How does he get a week off to prepare for us? Not fair, schedule-makers, not fair." Naw, Gene would never cry, would he?

Keady will be coaching the Pan American team this summer. I've got some really strong feelings about that. A college coach is good enough to coach the Pan American Games, the World University Games, but not good enough to be eligible to coach the 1992 Olympic team. Oh, does that bother me, especially when you consider how highly Keady is thought of by his peers. Jud Heathcote of Michigan State says Keady gets more out of his kids than anybody else in America. Jud said the man is a miracle worker, that he takes good players and makes them into great teams because of his discipline, his intensity and emotion.

I was daydreaming during the flight, and for some reason I started making up a bunch of different hypothetical situations as my frequent-flier mileage just kept churning and churning and churning. That's life on the road, baby, up here in the big sky. The first thought I had was, I really would love to see a coach like Bobby Knight or Dean Smith switch roles for a year with a guy like Steve Yoder. I mean, Knight goes down to Wisconsin, to Badgerland, to take over that team, and Yoder goes to Hoosierland to take over at Indiana. Then let's check the W's and L's. I'm not saying Knight can't coach, and I'm not saying Yoder can't get the job done. What I'm simply saying is, it would be a great way of finding out how much a coach really means to a program. Hey, they have exchange students. What about exchange coaches?

Then I started wondering whether UNLV could beat a pro team, a team like the Sacramento Kings. I know you don't like hearing this, Mr. Richard Motta, but you know what? If you called up Jerry Tarkanian, I'm not convinced he'd want to give up Larry Johnson, Stacey Augmon, and Anderson Hunt for Lionel Simmons, Travis Mays, and all those young people you have on the Kings. I don't know, man, let's check it out.

Going through the papers, I read a funny quote from Marty Blake, the NBA's director of scouting, about Stanley Roberts. He went over to Greece, the seven-footer who left LSU after his sophomore year and is thinking about entering the NBA draft. Blake said he's ballooned to 300 pounds and is eating himself into the second round. "I think if Stanley went swimming, somebody would harpoon him," Blake said.

Blake rarely, if ever, misses on a kid. If you can play, he'll find you. He knew all about Scottie Pippen of the Chicago Bulls before anyone, when Pippen played for Central Arkansas. He introduced the world to three members of Portland's starting lineup—Terry Porter of Wisconsin–Stevens Point, Kevin Duckworth of Eastern Illinois, and Jerome Kersey of Longwood College in Virginia—at the Portsmouth Invitational. And he discovered Dennis Rodman at Southeast Oklahoma long before Rodman became the best defensive player in the NBA at Detroit.

I know how Bob Knight will sound when he finds out the tip-off for our game is 9:30. I can hear him already: "There's no way in the world we should be playing that late. My players got to get to class. By the time we roll into Bloomington, you're looking at two or three o'clock in the morning and this is not fair. This is not what college basketball's all about."

Indiana–Purdue is always a war. There's like 5 points separating these teams over the last 10 years and 20 games—5 points! Purdue is on top, 1,500–1,495. The rivalry should become more intense in the future. Purdue signed Glenn Robinson of Gary and Indiana signed Alan Henderson of Indianapolis, the two leading candidates for Mr. Basketball in the state.

The Indiana–Purdue game was the scene of Bob Knight's famous chair-throwing incident a few years back, and I just ran into Steve Reid, the former Purdue player who was on the line at the time. Reid, who now lives in Lafayette, says, "I played three years for Purdue, but that's all folks remember about my career."

"I guess that's better than not being remembered at all," I said.

When I got back to my room, I immediately turned on the Ace Awards. I got beat again for best sports analyst on cable, this time by former Cincinnati Reds star and Hall of Famer Joe Morgan. Whipped me. That's five in a row. Anyway, I got some laughs. Dr. Ruth and Richard Lewis were up there presenting some award, and she said, in her own language, "Do you know what the nominees all have in common?" He said "What?" and she said, "They all use condoms." Dr. Ruth—doing her little thing. She's unbelievable. Just take a look at her. She reminds me of the old Abe Lemons line: "You don't have to have a lot of experience to be an expert in anything." She's supposed to be an expert in sex, and you look at her and you know she has no experience.

MONDAY, JANUARY 14—

Man, what a morning I had. I walked into the shootaround and Keady immediately jumped on my case. "Pucker your lips.

Pucker your lips, Dickie, baby," he said. "Pucker your lips and say, 'Purdue, Purdue.' You're unbelievable. We win the Big 10 title, you're all over me, calling me every day. Now I don't hear from you. We don't hear the word Purdue mentioned once."

I was all ready to get back at him, but I was more concerned that my tape wasn't working. Keady, I thought you broke my tape. I went over to see my associate producer, Tom McNeely. These producers know what they're doing. "Tom," I said, "I'm going crazy. What's the problem?" He looked at the tape recorder for a second and then he said, "Dick, you're all done, you've got to go to the other side." Oh, what a dummy I am, man. If it weren't for basketball, where would I be in life?

Pretty soon Knight came strolling in, and the first words out of his mouth were: "Man, I'm tired of these nine-forty tip-off times. When is somebody going to take an interest in the kids and care about them?" He went on and on. "Maybe we should move to Ted Turner's station, go up against the Big East on Monday night and kick their butt," he said.

I've tried to remind the General—as I always do—that life is adjusting; life isn't always smooth. You got to teach players to be able to deal with adversity, baby. Come on, Robert, you always preach that.

Then we started talking about the NCAA convention. Knight is really upset about it. He said he didn't like the idea of reducing scholarships, and he didn't want to hear about walk-ons. "I don't need any walk-on players," he said. "Everybody in the university thinks they can play. These guys walk on, then they start moaning and groaning, thinking they should get a scholarship. It causes more morale problems than ever."

Knight didn't stop there. "They talk about cleaning up academics," he said, "but they voted down legislation that would have forced schools to graduate fifty percent of their seniors to maintain Division I status. Hell, that rule would have been such a positive move. It would have made guys go out and recruit student-athletes who have a chance to graduate."

I mean, the General was in rare form. Damon Bailey walked over, I said "Hi, Damon," and Knight exploded. "Now why would you say hello to Damon?" he said. "Why don't you go over there and say hello to my son, Patrick, and go say hello to Matt Nover. Why do you have to say hello to Damon?" I said, "Give me a break, will you please?"

I introduced McNeely to Knight and asked him if he followed boxing. Knight said, "Nope." I said, "Well, his father fought Floyd Patterson." "So what?" Knight said. Typical Bobby Knight, you know. He laid the intimidating eyes on McNeely. McNeely's about 6-1, about 220, a former football player, but he shrunk to about 5-1, 135. Incredible.

But Tom is so proud of his father, who's an assistant AD with the Massachusetts state prison system and still has a license plate, "KO," to remind him of his moment in the sun. You know who had that license plate before him. That's right, the Rock. Rocky Marciano.

Things didn't really settle down until Keady came over and asked for some advice about coaching the Pan Am team. The first thing Knight said was, "You've got to hire a guy to handle all the little details so you can just oversee the trials. Make sure you invite the players that you want and forget about the seniors. There's no way the agents are going to let the Larry Johnsons of the world play, so you have to know that." Keady wants to make a pitch for Shaquille O'Neal. Smart idea.

Those two are buddies, man, Knight and Keady. I'll tell you, you can just see the mutual respect for each other in their eyes, just looking at each other. There's no doubt about it. But you better believe that when that ball's tipped off, I don't think you'll see more intensity in a gym across America than you will witness here at Mackey tonight. I mean, this is INTENSE CITY. I mean, the bankers, the doctors, factory workers, and all the local people are completely into it. Purdue forward Jimmy Oliver described it best today when he said, "I'm walking through the campus Friday night and somebody says, 'Hey, are you ready for the game on Monday, man? We can't wait.' I said, 'Monday? We've got a game Saturday against Michigan.'" Poor Jimmy, he gets 35 against Michigan and it's like it doesn't matter. Everyone is thinking Hoosiers.

Knight was getting ready to leave when all of a sudden the word "tennis" popped up in the conversation. "I hear you play a lot of tennis," he said to me. "Well, let's hook up." He immediately went to his pocket and threw a wad of cash on the ground, a wad of singles. "Put it up," he said.

I couldn't believe it. I mean, the guy's a multimillionaire, he's got all kinds of cash, and he throws these ones. So I threw mine down, man. I had some twenties, I really did. I didn't have too many, I can guarantee you that. I'm not a betting man. I'll play him for a nice little dinner, though, I definitely will. Don't you be attacking my bad eye, though. "Come on, now," I said. "I know I can beat you, I just know it. Look at that gut hanging out there. I'll run you right and left. I've never seen you play and I know I can get a W over you, baby."

Knowing the guy, he'll be going to my bad eye, hitting to my backhand, putting me in all kinds of trouble. But I'll be running around that backhand like Andre Agassi, man, hitting my inside-outside forehand. He wants to play me next week when I come in for Ohio State–Indiana, and I'll get him on a court and lay a whipping on him. But you know what? That might not be the only whipping he'll get. He could take another one from his alma mater that night, and I think that one will hurt a little more. Only kidding, Robert.

After lunch and a few hours in my room, it was back to Mackey Arena for the game. The place was absolute bedlam—just like it was the day I did my first network telecast here back in 1986. I'll never forget it. I was a nervous wreck. I mean, if you can believe it, I was shaking. It was Purdue against Louisville and I was going to be working with my man Keith Jackson. I remember the Iowa Hawkeyes walked into the place the same time I did—they were going to be playing Purdue Monday night—and they all were teasing me, saying they were going to rate my work on the telecast. When I got back, Tom Davis, Rudy Washington, his assistant, and all the Iowa guys were yelling out grades. Someone said, "B-plus." Someone else said, "B." One wise guy thought I should get a "D." Then one Iowa player said, "I'd give him an A." I should have gotten his name down.

By the time I arrived at the game that night, the Purdue fans were wired. Mackey-mania. One guy up in the ozone flashed a sign that said "Sitting in the last row, Dick. Help us out."

I told Mike Patrick on the air, "If the guy had donated some money to the alumni fund, he'd be right up front."

Hey, he was lucky to be in the building. A lot of people wished they could have been here for this one. Indiana won, 65–62, and the intensity matched North Carolina–NC State, Duke–Carolina, and Kentucky–Louisville. The game was close the entire way, largely because both of Knight's forwards, Calbert Cheaney and Eric Anderson, got into serious foul trouble and played most of the second half with four personals. At one point, Purdue actually took the lead with eleven minutes to go, and Knight, who was resting both Cheaney and Anderson, put both back into the game. I thought he would yo-yo it, play one and save the other in order to get both on the floor in the last five minutes, but he gambled and won. Purdue kept trying to take the ball right at Anderson and Cheaney to try and force a fifth personal, but they never managed to get it done. In the end, the difference was execution. Youth vs. experience. Indiana, 15–1, played like a computerized team and Anderson was brilliant when it counted.

By the time we got out of the arena, it was 12:40 A.M. and we had to drive to Indianapolis. The police took us to our car, then some sheriff gave us a police escort all the way to Lebanon. I mean, he was traveling. Mike Patrick said, "I'm afraid I'm liable to get a ticket keeping up with him."

TUESDAY, JANUARY 15—

Ouch, did that 5:30 wakeup call hurt. I was home by eleven, though, and that made up for it.

I got a call today from Rachel Shuster of *USA Today*. She's doing a major feature on announcers and their response to charges that some of their terminology indicates racist views. Shuster says, for example, that a lot of people claim announcers constantly use the term "athlete" when they refer to blacks, yet they invariably refer to whites as being very heady or intelligent. I told her I can't speak for everyone, but I can't believe the guys I know would intentionally do that.

My definition of the term "athlete," with respect to basketball, is someone who possesses great lateral quickness, excellent speed, tremendous leaping ability, quickness to the basketball, and explosiveness to the passing lanes. When I do a game, I have no idea when a play is made as to the color of the skin of that player. No commentator I know goes into a game thinking about skin color.

I also got a call from a guy named Bob McKeon of Kodak. He told me that he's a basketball lover and he asked if I would do a favor for him and record a message for a colleague who's retiring. So I did a little bit for him. "Hi, everybody," I said. "This is Dick Vitale of ESPN and ABC, and today I send out a salute to my guy, that's right, Tom Levy. Levy, the downtown shooter for the Ohio Bobcats down in Athens, Ohio. This guy's a flat-out PTP'er, baby. He's awesome. He's the three-S man; he is super, sensational, and scintillating. Thirty years he's worked in the trenches at Kodak, and all his people want to say bye-bye because they admire the tremendous job he has done. Let me let you dream right now. It's Ohio U. against the Ohio State Buckeyes. It's a big chance for them to move up the ladder, baby, and play against the big boys. And hitting the jumper at the buzzer to win it: Tom Levy, a PTP'er if there's ever been one." The last guy I heard about from Ohio U. was Walter Luckett. Sir Walter Luckett. A cover boy on *SI*. Truth is, I've never seen Tom Levy play. I don't know whether he can shoot the jumper or not.

I get a lot of wild proposals like this. If the guy's bold enough to request me to do it, why not? Fun is what life's about.

Back to reality. WOR, one of the superstations out of New York, was interviewing a lot of people in Tel Aviv about the fear of a possible outbreak of hostility in the Middle East, and who pops up on the screen? Gene Banks, the former Duke All-America and NBA player who is now over there. He's anxious, and I don't blame him.

I spent the evening watching the Oklahoma–Missouri game, which ended with OU coach Billy Tubbs getting into a verbal battle with Missouri coach Norm Stewart. Tubbs and I have had some battles in the past. I got him mad at me several years ago when I said, "Tubbsie, you ought to take a clinic on how to play defense. I'm going to have Bobby Knight send you a Christmas gift—a videotape to teach you people how to play defense. You're scoring over a hundred a game, but you don't guard anybody and you're not going to win a national championship."

I've got to admit, Tubbs did come back strong. He said that maybe if I had hired him as an offensive expert when I was coaching in the NBA, I would still be in the league instead of getting the ziggy.

He even had T-shirts made up with my name on them, and he gave them out for outstanding defensive performances. Billy is a fun guy. He'll give up 90, as long as he can get 120 himself.

At least Oklahoma plays hard all the time. When I used to coach, I tried to instill that work ethic into all my teams. I used to operate on Lombardi time. You call a practice at 3:30. You expect your players there fifteen minutes early to work on their individual skills.

I can never understand why some big-time players want the star treatment, want to stroll into practice a little bit late, just to test you.

The worst big-time player I ever watched practice was Derrick Coleman of Syracuse. Do you hear me, Derrick? I know you had another big game for the Nets again last night—29 points, 18 rebounds. But anytime I watched you practice at Syracuse, it was always the same. You didn't like to practice.

I ought to pick my All-Non-Practice team. Yeah. Guys who didn't give 110 percent in practice. I'd start with Coleman, Charles Barkley of Auburn, Jay Edwards of Indiana, then go with Charles Shackleford of NC State and Sean Higgins of Michigan.

They tell me Marvin Barnes was a beauty too when he played in the pros. When I coached at the University of Detroit, Barnes was playing for the Pistons and he got arrested at the airport for carrying a firearm. Headlines all over the place, but do you think Barnes was embarrassed by the gig? Heck no, he comes strutting into the game in the second quarter, wearing a big leather jacket with MARVIN "BAD NEWS" BARNES on it and acts like nothing happened. The crowd went wild. I was looking at Bob Lanier, and he was just rolling his eyes.

It was like, "Am I in trouble?" Marvin said he used to carry—ready for this?—two guns, one in each pocket, when he played for the St. Louis Spirits of the old ABA, and he'd keep one cocked just in case the other one didn't work. Can you imagine making your living coaching those guys? Not me, pal. Can you imagine Marvin getting angry coming into the locker room? He's liable to cock that gun and blow the coach away.

CHAPTER 7

WEDNESDAY, JANUARY 16—

Operation Desert Storm went into effect tonight. I found out about it in my hotel room in Chapel Hill, North Carolina, just a couple hours before the North Carolina–NC State game. I was on the phone with my daughter Terri at Notre Dame. All of a sudden she said, "Dad, you'd better turn on the TV. They just announced that we're attacking, the United States is attacking Baghdad." I immediately went to the TV. It was an eerie feeling, a very empty feeling.

I went down to the lobby to meet Mike Patrick and head over to the arena. We both felt the game would be canceled, and we were having trouble getting our minds on basketball. For that matter, everyone in the crew would have preferred gathering around a TV set to hear the President's address rather than getting ready to do the game. But at that point, we couldn't. We had to do our jobs, do our preparation.

I went downstairs to the locker rooms, and it was somber. I was feeling for North Carolina's Peter Chilcutt, whose brother, Michael, is over in Saudi Arabia. You knew the last thing on Peter's mind was playing a hoops game against North Carolina State. And NC State guard Chris Corchiani was saying how all the guys on the team were trying to pick up the spirits of Anthony Robinson, who was really shaken up because his dad is in Saudi Arabia too. Corchiani pretty well summed things up when he said: "Boy, I'm not really in the mood to play tonight."

Back upstairs, I was talking to NC State coach Les Robinson when somebody came over and said the North Carolina officials wanted to meet with Les and Dean Smith about calling the game. Pretty soon, the official announcement was made. I thought it was a solid decision, particularly with all the military bases here and everything.

It was the first time I've ever been in an arena and felt that basketball was really meaningless.

THURSDAY, JANUARY 17—

The attitude was very somber today at the airport. Security was tight. Iraq was on everyone's mind. Nobody was questioning the decision to call off the game. Everybody's mind was on what's happening in the Middle East, and I found myself glued to the news, watching Peter Jennings, Tom Brokaw, Bernard Shaw, and Dan Rather. They're the stars of the real media world.

I saw on TV where Connecticut coach Jim Calhoun said he wished his game with Syracuse had been called off. Galid Katz, one of Calhoun's players, was in the Israeli army and his family lives over there. "We have to try to get him in touch with his family," Calhoun said, "and make sure everyone is safe."

I also saw an interview with Mike Krzyzewski. He certainly has a special feeling for the Iraq situation, because he graduated from West Point in 1969, spent five years in the service, was an artillery captain, and knows a lot of guys over there. He is in genuine support of the troops' being there, and he thinks that even though it's very insignificant playing basketball with what's going on in the world, we must show our troops that we have a positive attitude. Mike's philosophy is that the country can't come to a stop, that we must keep things going.

I got home and watched the reports of the Scud missile attacks on Israel for a long time before I finally had to go to bed. I've got to get up real early and fly to Boca Raton to tape the Foot Locker Slam Fest. After today, I'm hoping it will be a welcome relief.

THURSDAY, JANUARY 17—

I felt a little bit ridiculous going to this thing today. It was very difficult with everything going on to get into a mood to be saying "awesome, baby," and "slam jam, baby," but we all have to do our jobs. It's the only way to look at it.

I flew today on Sunshine Airlines. That's right, you are my sunshine, my only sunshine . . . Sunshine Airlines. It's like an eight-passenger job, baby. The pilot climbs in through the window. I'm telling you something, it was shake, rattle, and roll time. Bill Haley at his best. Maalox time. My stomach was shaking. It was only an hour flight to the Fort Lauderdale airport, but it seemed a lot longer.

The event should be exciting, with baseball players Ken Griffey, Jr., Barry Bonds, Dave Justice, Deion Sanders, Ben McDonald, and Delino DeShields; football players Chris Doleman, Barry Sanders, and Michael Dean Perry; and track stars Larry Conley and Mike Powell, all demonstrating their slam-dunk ability.

Reports are coming in about the attacks on Israel last night, and everyone is wondering whether the Israelis are going to get involved in the crisis. That's something we hope doesn't happen so they can keep the allied coalition together. I've never spent as much time, to be honest with you, reading the front pages.

I walked into the meeting at 10:30, and I was immediately greeted by this little guy, and I have to admit it, I didn't recognize him. Barry Sanders of the Detroit Lions. Powerful legs, powerfully built shoulders, and an affectionate smile. He's the best running back in the NFL.

"Barry, baby," I said, "they didn't get you the ball enough. You've got to run it twenty to twenty-five times every game. You'd put a hundred and fifty to two hundred yards on the board every game."

I watched the Lions play Tampa Bay in person last fall, and I have to say, I don't want all those Tampa people to get angry, but I had to cheer for my guy Sanders. But he never got the ball. C'mon, Wayne Fontes, get him the pigskin. He strolled over and said, "Hey, Dick, wait until you see what I do with the rock."

What a field. The track guys have dominated the competition for the last three years. Powell, a world-class long jumper, won last year, and Conley, a world-class triple jumper, won the two previous years. But in most people's minds, the guy to beat was DeShields, a former hoopster who originally signed with Villanova, then chose baseball after the Expos offered him a big signing bonus.

Guys like Conley, who played at Arkansas and has names for all kinds of dunks, can use the $50,000 first-prize money. To guys like Sanders and Bonds, this is probably pocket change.

Sanders, a defensive back with the Atlanta Falcons, is playing two sports, like Bo Jackson, and is hopeful of latching on with the Atlanta Braves. I'd like to have his paycheck.

Bonds came over to me and said, "Hey, you still selling your house in Bradenton? I might want to buy it."

"I think you can afford it," I told him.

Barry told me he had to submit his numbers for arbitration today. Hey, Larry Doughty, GM, you better sign him for a lot of years. Bonds is coming off an MVP year with the Pittsburgh Pirates. Heck, he beat out my Brandenton buddy, Bobby Bonilla.

He told me, "If I don't get 3.2 [million], if I don't get what Canseco and Mitchell are making, I ain't gonna play. I'm gonna become a free agent."

It's unbelievable when you think of the cash out there. But, when you perform, you want to get paid in relation to your peers.

Bonds challenged me to a game of h-o-r-s-e, and while I was out on the court fooling around with him, Kim Belton, Jimmy Valvano, and John Saunders decided to play a practical joke on me. They took away my pride and joy, my tape recorder. Hid that sucker.

After I finished my game, Jimmy came up to me and said, "Hey, I've got a great story for you. They're hiring Mike Slive at Syracuse to look into all the so-called violations there. He's the same guy we had at NC State. This guy, he finds out more than what was initially laid out." I thought it was a great little tidbit and I wanted to get it on tape, but I couldn't find my tape recorder. I looked all over and was beginning to panic. All those guys were making like they were helping me look, but then all of a sudden Valvano said, "Hey, what about your shoot-out with Bonds? How did that go? Let's get that on tape." I turned around and Valvano had the tape on and they all were laughing hysterically, like a bunch of kids.

The crowd at the competition that night loved Deion Sanders. Neon Deion. But DeShields was the class of the field, smooth and silky. Beat Eric McMillan of the Jets in the finals. He was the choice of a judges' panel that included Bobby

Jones, Calvin Murphy, Artis Gilmore, Connie Hawkins, and Wilt Chamberlain.

Afterward, Wilt came over to me and said, "Let me tell you something. I'm going to scrutinize that tape, and if you say anything negative about me . . ." I hope he doesn't see my "Superstars of College Basketball" tape. If he finds out I chose Kareem as my all-time center, he's going to go up a wall.

FRIDAY, JANUARY 18—

I read today on my flight to Durham that Iraq attacked Israel again last night. This is just incredible. I have to be honest, I just can't believe this insanity going on with Saddam Hussein. Absolutely wacko. The all-time wacko.

I rode to the airport in a cab driven by a history buff. I mean, this guy was a fanatic. He had every answer for every problem in the Middle East, every possible solution for President Bush. It was really early in the morning, and this guy didn't stop. I mean, he made me seem shy and introverted. I couldn't get a word in. Do you believe that? Then again, I wasn't in the mood to get a word in. I was absolutely exhausted.

Anyway, turning to the sports pages, I read where Duke's Bobby Hurley has picked up on the fact that I put him on my All–Bill Laimbeer Crybaby team. He really shouldn't be offended. He's a competitor, a fighter, and I use the term "All-Crybaby" in a very positive way. I mean, Rick Barry was one of the biggest whiners ever. Do you think you would want Rick Barry in your lineup? What about Magic? He moans and groans every time he gets a foul called on him. And Bill Laimbeer?

I told Bobby at practice, "You're too good and too talented to be crying and moaning on every foul." He said, "Oh, I know I show a lot of facial expressions when I play." Where Bobby's concerned, it's just his desire bubbling through.

I also saw that the ACC has rescheduled the North Carolina–NC State game for February 7. That means the teams will be playing each other back-to-back, Wednesday night in Raleigh and Thursday in Chapel Hill. Who do you think got the better of that deal when you look at the rosters? North Carolina has a deep bench. State can go only five deep.

I had a quiet night tonight. I think I really needed one. When

I got into town, Jay Rothman, our creative producer, took one look at me and said: "Hey, you look whipped. Go get some sleep. You look like you've been hit by a truck."

Man, I'll tell you what. I always look like I've been hit by a truck.

SATURDAY, JANUARY 19—

The official population of Krzyzewskiville was 1,600 last night. That's right, they keep a tally of how many students are camped outside the arena in their tents waiting for tickets. These tent cities are a regular sight before big games, particularly when Carolina is coming to town. The only real rule is, someone must be in the tents at all times or they lose their spot.

Duke played a road game at The Citadel Wednesday night, and I think one of the reasons Krzyzewski did that was to keep his players away from the students. They've been wired for this game for almost two weeks. That's all the students want to talk about—Carolina, Carolina, Carolina.

Krzyzewski's got such a great working relationship with the students here. Rothman shot some great footage of him inviting about six hundred students from the tent city into the gym the other night and going over a scouting report on Carolina. Krzyzewski does things like that all the time—buying pizza for students, sharing time with them. He's taken Duke's great tradition and carried it to another level.

When the doors opened tonight, the students came flooding in and immediately began to get on the Carolina players warming up out on the floor. Then they started getting on me, because I said in my midseason report on ESPN that Arizona had the best fans. Hey, no doubt, they've been a big factor at that PAC-10 power, which hasn't lost at home for over a year.

Well, as I said on the air later, Cameron is the best environment in college basketball, all things considered. I'm talking about the whole scenario—size of the arena, closeness to the floor, priority given to the students. It really is one wild scene, with the students right on top of the action.

The game was a defensive struggle, with both clubs really getting after each other. Thomas Hill and Greg Koubek, two names you don't expect to hear a whole lot about, were sensational in the second half for Duke, and after falling behind by 17 early, Duke came back to win, 74–60, and take over first place in the ACC with a 4–1 record.

After the game, I wanted to spend some time preparing for Ohio State–Indiana Monday night. Randy Ayers is really an amazing story. He was an assistant under Gary Williams, and when Williams left to take the job at Maryland, there was a lot of speculation that the school would go for a big name like Nolan Richardson or a more established name like Jim Crews, a former Knight assistant now at Evansville. But Ohio State gave Ayers a chance, and he has made the most of it.

The same scenario occurred at Virginia, where AD Jim Copeland gave assistant Jeff Jones a chance last year, and Jones has done well in his first year. Sometimes there are quality applicants right under your nose. All too often, AD's feel compelled to go out and appease the alums, the fans, and bring in a guy from out of town who has a big reputation.

I remember when I was an assistant at Rutgers and Dick Lloyd resigned and I went after that job. I felt I had done a good job recruiting players like Phil Sellers and Mike Dabney, who eventually took Rutgers to the Final Four in 1976, and I begged and pleaded with the athletic director, Fred Gruninger, to give me a chance. I was such a dummy. I went in and said, "Give me the job at the same amount of money I'm making now as an assistant, and if I don't do it in one year, fire me." I felt in my heart, having coached high school level in New Jersey and having done a good job under Lloyd as a recruiter, I was the perfect guy for the state university. I really felt that, given the chance, I could have done a heck of a job.

When I went in to talk to Gruninger about it, he had a stack of applications on his desk from head coaches around the country, major college assistants, and small-college coaches who all wanted the job.

He said to me, "Why do you think you are more qualified than these people?"

It was his belief that he wanted to get a proven head coach. He was chasing all the big names. Guys like Frank McGuire, George Raveling, and Pete Carril were the type of names that were popping up in the news every day. Gruninger was counting on Sonny Werblin, the owner of the Jets, to help bring Frank McGuire—Dapper Frank—in.

Well, things worked out better for me in the long run, but I do think that AD's have a tendency not to give people a chance in those situations. Do you hear me, Freddy, baby?

SUNDAY, JANUARY 20—

As soon as I arrived at the hotel in Bloomington, Indiana, I received a phone call from Bobby Knight. "You bleep bleep son of a gun," he said. "Where's your racket? Come on, bring it down. Come on, you told the nation last week in the Purdue game that you could whip my butt, that you're going to pummel me in tennis. Well, I'm at the Tennis Center right now and I'm ready for you."

I told him I didn't bring a racket, but that didn't stop him. "I don't want to hear that nonsense," he said. "I've got any size you want, any kind of racquet here at the Tennis Center. And don't tell me you don't have any shoes, because I've got any size you want. Get your butt down here."

If I had said, "Yes," he probably would have made me wear Adidas sneakers. I'm a Nike guy, baby.

Fortunately, I got out of it by telling him I was tired. This guy was all fired up. Do you think I'm going to play him now? He'll blitz me.

Knight, by the way, is really high on Ohio State's young coach, Randy Ayers. Told me he felt this was the best-coached Ohio State team he'd seen in years. Randy Ayers, thirty-four years old and coaching one of only two unbeaten teams in the country. Coming in to play the Master.

MONDAY, JANUARY 21—

This day was unbelievable from the very beginning. I went down to the lobby. I was just besieged by fans looking for tickets to the game. The prize was the guy who wanted to know where he could get four. Hey, call up the General and ask him. No way I'm going to get you four tickets. My stomach was already in knots, and it was still twelve hours from tip-off.

I did my weekly radio show with J.P. McCarthy in Detroit, who ranks right up there as an interviewer with Larry King and Roy Firestone. After we talked a little about the Indiana–Ohio State game, J.P. tried to ask me about the Celtics, who are in town to play the Pistons. I said, "I don't want to hear about that game. It means nothing. It's not like the game tonight."

The Celtics. The Boston Celtics. Just thinking about them really got me going. "You tell their coach, Chris Ford, baby, he is really on my bad-guy list," I said. "He's never called to thank me for making it possible for him to be the star he is today. He'd be working somewhere in the auto industry if I didn't trade him for Earl Tatum when I was coaching the Pistons. Thanks, Al McGuire. You owe me a favor. You said Earl Tatum was the 'black Jerry West.' You told me, 'You've got to take him.' Yeah, Earl Tatum. America's guest. He'd been traded to so many teams. He could stroke the J. But he couldn't do much else. Ford goes to Boston, gets a championship ring, and now he's a head coach with the Boston Celtics. I get fired. Unbelievable." I think Red Auerbach should send me a ring for being the architect of the Celtics.

My next jolt came when I got word from my guy Freddie Gaudelli, our producer, that John Wildhack said I should watch my weight. C'mon, John. You didn't hire Robert Redford. You hired me for my mouth. Besides, I'm in Bloomington. I want to go to Leslie's for a special Italian dish. What are you trying to do to me? Come on, give me a break, big John. Let me eat. I think he's worried about my expense account.

We went over to the gym this afternoon to shoot my "Fast Break" series, and I had to climb above the rim on a stepladder because we were talking about all of the giants, like 7-6 Shawn Bradley of Brigham Young. The crew was teasing me about being a wimp. I guess I was a little scared. I have a phobia about heights.

I stopped in to see Knight a little later and he was going through his mail. I asked if he knew anyone who was in Operation Desert Storm, and he said, "Hey, I've got a lot of guys who are there, officers who I coached." Then he said he had a letter he wanted to share with me. It was from a Lieutenant Colonel Wally Wojdowski, of Gunnison, Colorado. He played for Knight in 1970-71 and graduated from West Point in 1972. It was such an emotional letter. It was all about the things he learned from Bobby at West Point, how he's in real battle now and how he just wanted to thank Bobby for everything he taught him about discipline and about life.

I told Knight I wanted to share the letter on the air, but he immediately said no. He didn't want to look like it was self-serving. "Heck," he said, "if you want to just mention his name, fine."

This was the emotional side of Bobby Knight, the side most people never see. And I got another taste of it a few minutes later when a guy called and asked if Knight and I could make a tape to send to a friend in Saudi Arabia. Bobby was just so agreeable. This guy, really, I'll tell you something, he does a lot more for people than you'd ever believe.

It was two hours before game time, and we were just sitting there having fun. We started talking about baseball—Bobby's a baseball nut—and he was surprised to find out I was too. "You know what?" I said. "Maybe I should do some baseball." He said, "Hell, maybe you'll do a hell of a lot better in that sport, because you certainly screwed this one up."

Bobby loves guys like Ted Williams. We were talking about great hitters, and I think I shocked him when I said, "Williams. Let me tell you about Williams, Billy Goodman, Dom DiMaggio, Vern Stephens, Bobby Doerr, Mel Parnell . . . What else do you want to know about the Red Sox teams in the fifties?"

Knight shook his head.

"I have to admit it," he said, "I'm impressed. Now name me the starting second baseman for the Phillies' Whiz Kids in 1950."

"That's easy," I said, "Mike Goliat."

After a while, I could see he was getting a little tense. "Boy," I said, you really look like you're feeling it now all of a sudden." "Yeah," he said, "my stomach is churning. I feel this way almost every game. The expectations. Every time we play, people come to beat us. It's like Notre Dame football. People play at another level, and you're always worried if you can sustain it and keep it rolling."

Well, guess what? Ohio State played at another level for most of the game. This was supposed to be a showdown of two Top 5 teams—Ohio State came in at 15–0, Indiana 16–1—but the Buckeyes took most of the suspense out of it early. They jumped out to a 48–29 lead and wound up winning, 93–85. Jamal Brown, Ohio State's guard, really put on a show. He had 26 points to offset a big finish by Calbert Cheaney, who struggled so badly early that Knight didn't start him in the second half. I know they had to be celebrating down at Blocks' Bagels in Columbus, where owner Steve Block is a big Buckeye fan. You keep eating those bagels, Steve, you're gonna join George Perles on my All-Wide-Body team.

I'll tell you, we were celebrating too. We all felt we had a great telecast, and it really feels good when it happens in such a big game, with such a large audience.

TUESDAY, JANUARY 22—

All that people wanted to talk about at the airport was the big game. And as soon as I settled into my seat on the plane, I heard this loud voice saying, "You had the JV game last night, Dickie. The real game, the big-time game, was the Lakers and Pacers." It was none other than Jack Madden, one of the premier officials in the NBA. "Jackie, baby," I said, "I'm going to slap a T on you. It's too early." This guy was fired up. I think he still had the adrenaline flowing from last night when his crew made headlines by whistling eight technical fouls. I've always said the worst thing that can happen to an official is to read about himself after a game.

I've been living on planes. I've been on a plane almost every day for the last two weeks. Today, I headed back to Bradenton for a day of R and R before heading out again for the Duke–NC State game. I really felt like I had a strong game. It's like I told the crew; you feel it in your heart. It's just like a player who knows when he plays well or a writer who knows when the prose is flowing. My feelings were reconfirmed when I picked up a paper and read that Bobby Knight said, "Hey, we told our players at halftime that we had to play it in segments and get it down to ten points at the ten-minute mark." Those were his exact words. And mine, too. It makes you feel good when you're right on target.

WEDNESDAY, JANUARY 23—

I was checking in at my hotel after flying into Raleigh, and the girl at the counter asked me for my autograph. "Can you make it out to Kelli?" she asked. "I told my dad I was really anxious to meet you." I said, "Oh, really?" And she said, "Yeah, my dad is Les—Les Robinson. Boy, we're so excited about tonight's game against Duke. I hope we can bounce back after being blitzed by Wake Forest."

Hey, I'm excited too. Tonight is Vic Bubas Night. Vic Bubas played at North Carolina State, scored the first basket at Reynolds Coliseum when he played for Everett Case, and later coached at Duke. He took the Blue Devils to three Final Fours. At one time, he had a staff that consisted of Hubie Brown and Chuck Daly. We have a photo of it, and we're going to use it on the show. Man, Hubie and Chuck, you guys were so young and dynamite-looking. Vic was just one of those special guys who was ahead of his time. In fact, I always thought he left coaching too early. He really had it rolling with guys like Art Heyman, Jeff Mullins, and Bob Verga. He could have been a Dean Smith; he could have had a Dean Smith kind of record.

Before the game, I went into the State locker room and had some fun with Chris Corchiani.

I had him going crazy. I said, "Chris, I just got done talking to Bob Hurley. He told me he has no fear of playing against you. He told me, 'Are you kidding me? I'm not worried about Corchiani. I just got done playing against Kenny Anderson and some of the great guards in the ACC. Corchiani, he's on the bottom of the list.' " Corchiani said, "Coach, he really said that? Did he really say that? I can't wait 'til this game starts."

His teammates jumped in on the joke too, chiming in with, "Yeah, yeah. He said that."

At that point, I had to break down and tell him the truth. I didn't want him telling the media he was all fired up over something Bob Hurley didn't say.

Then I ran into Gabe Corchiani, Chris's dad. Gabe coached Chris at Hialeah Lakes High in Miami, where he scored 3,400 points and had more than a thousand assists. Chris was the only guy in the history of Florida to be selected Mr. Basketball two years in a row, and yet some people questioned whether he could play big-time basketball. Has Corchiani shocked them? Has he done the job? His next stop could be the NBA. Corchiani knows how to play. By the time he finishes his career at State, he will pass Sherman Douglas as the NCAA's all-time leader in assists.

Today, *USA Today's* basketball writer John Bannon referred to Corchiani and Rodney Monroe as the best backcourt combination in America. Sorry Johnny B. They are the best offensive backcourt in the nation, but in my mind, I rank them behind UNLV's set of guards, Anderson Hunt and Greg Anthony, who also play on the defensive end.

Tonight they really put on a show. Duke was a little passive, didn't play with the fierce intensity I saw against North Carolina, but it didn't really matter. Monroe scored 35, Corchiani dished out 14 assists, and State rolled, 95–89, to jump back into Top 25 consideration with a 10–4 record.

THURSDAY, JANUARY 24—

I got a call when I got home today from my agent at IMG, Peter Goldberg. He said I was in the running with one other guy to do a car commercial. You know who the other guy is? Tommy Lasorda, the manager of the Los Angeles Dodgers. I have no chance, man. That's an M & M'er. That's a no-chancer. Lasorda, I'm trying to nip you. I'm trying to come down to the wire, but he's too dominant for me. I mean, Lasorda is *really* big-time. I can't believe it. There was a time, and I want you to know this, Lasorda, years ago, while I was teaching the sixth grade back in the 1970s, I would run around and ask Lasorda for his autograph! "Tommy, give me an autograph." I still do that when I go to Dodger Stadium. I say, "Tommy, give me some baseballs, man, give me some balls."

Tommy and I have gotten to be good friends since I got into broadcasting. I was visiting with him recently and he wanted me to be a batboy at one of the games.

"C'mon," he said. "Massimino and Michael Fratello did it."

I refused. Maybe I made a mistake. It might have been good PR.

Let me tell you about Lasorda. I was there one time and he was telling the media about what sport he felt had the most pressure. You think lining up that little white ball for a big putt or getting ready for a big serve of that yellow ball is tough. Get those tennis guys and golf guys out there and have them stand in against Nolan Ryan, throwing ninety-five mph, with the ball rising and dropping and all these guys yelling and screaming and throwing beer. That's pressure. I never understood why the crowd felt it was necessary to keep quiet at those other sports.

"C'mon, Vitale," he said to me, "you ought to broadcast golf or tennis. Liven it up."

I also got a call from the *Indianapolis Monthly*. They want to do a cover story on me for their Final Four issue in March. Naturally, I was delighted to accept. Do you believe they want my mug on their magazine? Hey, Tom Cruise, move over, I'm becoming a cover boy. I might be absolutely the sexiest guy ever placed on that cover.

CHAPTER 8

FRIDAY, JANUARY 25—

I had to go to New York today to tape some voice-overs for the Foot Locker Slam Fest that ABC is carrying. It was absolutely chaotic from the moment I arrived.

First, I was at the airport looking for my driver when finally this little guy popped up with a sign that read, "D. VETELIY." I couldn't believe it, so I decided to do some interrogating. He didn't speak English, so it was really tough. I mean, I had to spend ten minutes trying to get this guy to understand me. Finally we agreed that I was the guy, but when I told him I was going to the Parker Meridian Hotel in Manhattan, he had to call and get directions. I knew I was in New York. Mayor Dinkins, you've got to help me.

I picked up the New York papers later and there was a big story about Jerod Mustaf, the rookie forward with the New York Knicks. He's upset with coach John MacLeod over his lack of playing time. I couldn't believe his quotes. "It's an insult to me," he said. "A lot of things are not fair, and this is not fair to me. To be honest, I can learn by staying at home and watching on TV." Can you believe this guy, twenty-one years old and supposed to still be in college, moaning and groaning about PT? I mean, like he's ready to dominate and perform on the NBA level. He should have stayed at Maryland where he belonged. Only the "supers" are ready to come out—the Magics, Isiahs, Michael Jordans. Believe me, Mustaf isn't in that class.

I'll tell you, it just drives you nuts how these guys all want to be coaches. They have all the answers. It's time for Mustaf to grow up and learn to be patient. When things got tough down in Maryland, he ran out, took the cash and left. He left his school hanging, left Gary Williams hanging. Gary Williams, who did everything he could to make him a player and would have made him an even better player if he had stayed.

Oh, I know, Jerod, you probably were "misquoted"; I hear that often too. "I didn't really say that." "Who, me?" "I would never say that."

Sorry Jerod. Maybe I've come down too hard. He is young. He does have a future. I guess my message is simply BE PATIENT.

SATURDAY, JANUARY TWENTY-SIX—

Can you believe this town? I had a banana muffin and a cup of coffee for breakfast at my hotel this morning. The bill was over $10. It's just absolutely incredible! New York, New York. Baby, I'll tell you. This is some kind of place. What's a tip, $10? The other day I was in Carolina, and for $5 I got a turkey dinner. A whole turkey dinner with everything, with the dressing and the stuffing. I got stuffed right there, baby, I got stuffed big-time style. You figure it out.

When I arrived at the studio to do our taping, Valvano whipped out the new book he wrote with Curry Kirkpatrick. It's called *Valvano: They Gave Me a Lifetime Contract and Then They Declared Me Legally Dead.* He is really excited about it. Jimmy has told me there is no way he would want to get back into coaching and the rat race of recruiting now that he likes what he is doing—speaking and TV. That's why I found the note on the back of the book so interesting. "People ask me if I miss coaching," he wrote. "In the last 23 years I've seen it all. From the bush leagues to the jet leagues. From White Castle to the White House. From good kids to bad kids and all the in-betweens. From doting mothers to doubting fathers. To the fans who were either at your feet or at your throat. I don't miss the one-point loss in double OT or the bad calls from the refs. But the emotional locker room, the ecstasy of the big win and the big game, you bet I miss it."

I know how Jimmy feels. I miss that camaraderie, watching guys fighting, sweating for the honor of their school, the honor of the jersey they wear. It's just a high when you get that W. You really feel like you're in utopia, walking out of that locker room to meet the press. But then there's the L, when you have to go to practice the next day, listening to guys complain about their lack of PT, getting calls from angry alums, listening to all of the criticism from those Monday-morning quarterbacks.

I know all the cameras focus on the winning coach after a big game. But I still sneak a peak at the other guy.

We did the taping and then I raced to the airport to catch my flight. I was anxious to get home, because I'm going to the Super Bowl tomorrow for the first time ever. The flight was a little more relaxing than that trip through the Lincoln Tunnel, man.

On the plane, I sat next to a pilot who was flying home to Fort Myers. You talk about having it tough. I moan and groan about my job, but are you kidding me? You talk about pressure. They can't afford to have a turnover. One little turnover up there and it's lights out.

SUNDAY, JANUARY 27—

Super Sunday. Showtime. I was anxious to go down to Tampa and party, be part of the whole scene, see what it's all about. But you know what? I think I went down there with a little chip on my shoulder, thinking it might be like the Final Four but that the NCAA Tournament is better. I didn't see how this could compare to the NCAA.

But, hey, I wanted to give this a fair shake. I wanted to give these pigskin guys a chance. Prove to me that this is better. I don't know, football, it's OK, but it takes so long to play. I'm glad I don't have to analyze a football game. I mean, it's forever. Those guys are in that booth for more than three hours. And the preparation—you've got to go in on a Thursday for a Sunday game. It would just drive me nuts.

When we got there, the parking was a nightmare and the hustlers were everywhere. One guy knocked on the car door and offered me $1,000 a ticket. I couldn't believe it. He wanted to buy all four of them. My wife was ready to roll the window down and take the $4,000, but I thought the guy might have been a vice cop and that we would get arrested. Can you imagine the headline—"Vitale Peddles Super Bowl Tickets"?

We went to an ABC party, and the place was filled with celebrities. You're not going to believe who I ran into: M.C. Hammer.

I'll tell you the big star I am. I really rated, I got great seats. I was on the ten-yard line. Guys kept coming up to me and saying, "Dickie, this isn't like in basketball where you sit at midcourt."

You think I had it rough? I looked to my left and I saw one of my former players, M.L. Carr, down at the goal line.

But you know what? I loved it. I was with all the real people. I was cheering for the Bills and Jim Kelly. I'm a Kelly guy. I like him. I certainly like the Giants' coach, Bill Parcells, who's from North Jersey. But he won the championship in 1986, and I thought I would like to see Marv Levy get a chance to win it all.

It hurts me to say this, but it was just one unbelievably great event. It was a very emotional night. Whitney Houston sang the national anthem. The New Kids on the Block performed at halftime and they escorted a bunch of kids whose moms and dads were serving in Operation Desert Storm onto the field. The game was filled with drama, too. What an awesome finish. You really had to feel for Scott Norwood, the Bills' kicker, who missed a goal on the last play. I saw the pain in his face as he walked off the field right in front of us.

Yes, I have to admit it. The Super Bowl was rock-and-roll time. But I'll still take the Final Four. No way in the world does the Super Bowl compare with that. It is an NC, baby. No contest. And believe me, my thinking will not change on that. The Final Four has all that color and pageantry packed into three days. I love that college atmosphere, and I still get goose bumps before the start of the national semifinals when all four teams still have a chance to win.

MONDAY, JANUARY 28—

We got home late last night and I didn't get much sleep because I had to get up early to go to Champaign, Illinois, for the Illinois–Iowa game tonight. My stomach was churning all day like you couldn't believe. I was Mr. Weatherman, checking the reports out of the Midwest.

Getting to Champaign is never easy, but you really have to worry when you're traveling on the day of the game. Normally, my bosses John Wildhack and Mo Davenport want me there a day early, but I got special permission to fly today because of the Super Bowl.

Let me tell you, there is no love lost between these two teams. Illinois coach Lou Henson is upset because his school went on NCAA probation this season, and he blames two people—Digger Phelps and Iowa assistant Bruce Pearl. Henson makes no bones about it; he feels they turned him in to the NCAA.

Pearl made a tape of a conversation between himself and a recruit, Deon Thomas, a 6-9 prep All-America forward from Chicago Simeon. On the tape, Thomas allegedly said Illinois assistant Jimmy Collins offered him $8,000 and a new Chevy Blazer to attend school there. Thomas eventually signed with Illinois, but Henson is still steaming. He claims Pearl called the kid on twelve different occasions and got him to say some things that weren't valid.

My gut feeling is that Illinois will rebound from the probation and get back to the first division of the Big 10 faster than a lot of people believe. They're banned from the NCAA Tournament for two years, but they're still allowed to be on TV, still allowed to give out scholarships. The state of Illinois produces loads of quality players, they have a great environment to play in, and they're in a first-class league. Plus, they have Henson. He really gets a lot of unfair criticism. They play some super defense at Illinois, and they do it year in and year out.

The problem is, Illinois people don't want to hear any of that right now. You can just feel the bitterness. I mean, this is some vendetta. The St. Louis papers were filled with it. Collins was quoted as saying, "If Pearl's a man, he should definitely show up." Thomas said the two games with Iowa will mean more to him than any other games this season. Henson made it very clear he does not intend to shake hands with the Iowa staff, told me this particular game means a lot to Deon.

Lou is on the warpath these days. He's mad at the Iowa staff. He's mad at the NCAA. He's mad at Digger because he feels Digger played a big role in the LaPhonso Ellis situation, where the NCAA investigated claims that Ellis was offered money from the Illini. I was taping my "Fast Break" series and Digger, I got to tell you, I got some boos when I mentioned your name.

When I got to the hotel, I gave Tom Davis a call to talk about the scene. He said, "Dick, all I can do is prepare my team. I can't be concerned about all the outside stuff. Naturally, I wish it was a better situation, but it's not and there's nothing more I can do."

Davis told me Pearl would be at the game. He said Pearl was a member of the staff and had the right to walk in there and be treated like a human being. As long as there's no physical contact, Davis said, the fans can scream and boo all they want. That's their prerogative.

When I arrived at the arena, the Pearl situation, of course, was all everyone wanted to talk about. Then Pearl walked in, came right over to me, and sat and talked with me under one basket. I was teasing him. I said, "Bruce, don't stand next to me now, man. I don't want any bottles or bullets flying out of the stands." We started laughing.

Deep down, I think, Pearl regrets taping the phone conversation. I mean, if a school feels somebody has cheated, it has the right to contact the NCAA, let them know about it, let them look into it. But I thought it was just unethical to take a teenager and throw a tape on without him knowing about it. Bruce knows my feelings about it and I said as much over the air. Bruce had a very good reputation before this incident, but he may have committed professional suicide. I just hope he hasn't damaged his chances of becoming a head coach.

Fortunately, there were no incidents during the game, although Henson didn't go near the Iowa bench during the introductions. Illinois jumped off to a 15-point lead and held on to win by three, 53–50, to increase its record to 13–7 during this bittersweet season. Collins refused to shake hands when Pearl walked over after the game.

TUESDAY, JANUARY 29—

Are you ready for this one? My 7:15 wakeup call never came, and when I finally woke up it was 7:25—only twenty minutes before my cab pickup. I was hustling. When I went to put my contact in my eye, I couldn't find it. So I panicked. I called downstairs for a bellman.

He came up and we were both on our knees in the hotel room, scraping and clawing and looking for my contact. John Madden, my favorite analyst, the best analyst in all of sports, would really be proud the way we were scratching and clawing to find that lens. We were looking all over and we couldn't come up with it. Then—you're not going to believe this—I felt a little discomfort in my eye and the bellman spotted the contact. It was folded in there—right in the deep corner of my eye.

I was able to get the contact out, sprint down to the lobby, jump into the cab, and get to the airport. But through it all, I felt so bad. I never laid a tip on the bellman. Hey, do you think maybe he thought I was Billy Packer?

WEDNESDAY, JANUARY 30—

The first time Duke played Georgia Tech this season, the Blue Devils stomped them, 98–57, in Durham and Hurley forced Kenny Anderson into one of the most horrendous games of his career. Anderson said his team played like a bunch of pansies and vowed it wouldn't happen again. He said he couldn't wait for the rematch tonight. I couldn't wait, either.

Today at our pregame production meeting in Atlanta, one of the guys told me that Auburn center Robert McKie did an impersonation of me during the opening of the Kentucky–Auburn game last night. They said it was real funny. I missed it. McKie, I'm going to give you my microphone and I'm going to stay at home and let you do the games, baby. But I'm going to get the check.

Anderson was really fired up when I saw him before the game. He told me he had gained more confidence in his teammates and wasn't looking to shoot as much. Then he asked me if I would say hello to his mom. I told him I wasn't allowed to do that, but I was only kidding. A guy with talent like his deserves anything he wants.

Anderson told me his two favorite players in the NBA were Kevin Johnson and Isiah Thomas, and he played like a combination of the two against Duke. Georgia Tech lost by two, but Anderson put on a helluva show—32 points, a school-record eight steals, eight rebounds, and six assists. He put on two moves that had me jumping right out of my seat. I kept screaming, "I can't believe it. I can't believe it." I felt sorry for Hurley, because this kid was on fire.

Still, Duke held on, 77–75, to go 17–4. They made all the big plays down the stretch and dumped it inside to Thomas Hill for the winning basket as time ran out. Tech dropped to 12–6. I was talking to Tark earlier in the day—I'll be in Vegas Sunday to do their game against Rutgers—and he was saying that he really likes Duke. He likes their intensity, their defense, and he thinks that next year, when they get Cherokee Parks, they're going to be really sensational.

Back at the hotel, everybody was talking about the game, naturally. But I couldn't believe it when I heard a few guys complaining about Anderson, saying he choked when he missed a free throw at the end. I couldn't take it.

"You can't be serious." I said.

Everybody knows who Anderson is. But Jon Barry, one of his teammates, is still trying to escape from his father's shadow. His mother Pam approached me tonight, told me Jon was really trying to establish his own identity, and she said, "He'd appreciate it if you guys in TV wouldn't always refer to him as Rick Barry's son."

I tried to explain to Pam, who's now divorced from Rick, that's something he can't change. The name is Barry and he has to live with it. His dad was a Hall of Famer. I can understand where she's coming from. It must be difficult for children of famous parents.

THURSDAY, JANUARY 31—

Whenever I come home, I'm always greeted with a stack of mail. I just love reading it all. My wife was on me about it today, saying, "When are you going to end this nonsense? Here you are, at your age, lying in bed reading all these papers and reading all this mail. Give me a break. You've got to take care of all the bills, you know. You've got to take care of some of the family things." But, hey, this is when I do all my catching up—late at night, when I get home. This is when I get a chance to see what the fans are thinking.

Here's just a little of the mail I went through today:

Susan McKay, of Columbus, Ohio, wrote to say I'm a traitor; that I like Indiana over the Buckeyes, and that I used to be such a good Buckeye fan. I mean, she's really all upset. I just like basketball, I have no personal preferences. The Buckeyes certainly played well against Indiana. Come on, Susan, you can't be serious.

Debra Novak wrote to tell me that the best-kept secret in

college basketball is John Taft of Marshall University, who is averaging better than 25 points a game. She wanted me to get the guy some PR. Look at these ladies that love basketball!

Robert Wagner, who sent a copy to Mike Patrick, wrote to say that Mike and I were homers, that we were absolutely all for Indiana against Ohio State and didn't give the Buckeyes enough credit. Hey, I listened to that tape, Robert. You are way, way out of line. We told it like it is. We gave the Buckeyes all kinds of praise. Robert's from Homer City. It figures.

I got a lovely letter from the parents of Jimmy King that said it was an honor to hear me talk about their son signing with the University of Michigan. Yes sir, Jimmy King is going to be an outstanding player for the Michigan Wolverines. He is one of America's highly rated players, a tremendous athlete from East Plano, Texas. That's right, they're looking for Jimmy, along with Juwan Howard, to step right in next season and help the Wolverines get back into the upper class of the Big 10. If they ever get Chris Webber, Mr. and Mrs. King, your son will really be a standout, because people will have to occupy Mr. Webber and your son will be slashing to the goal.

Eric Schwager, from Flushing, New York, wrote to say that he wants to be an announcer. Eric, I wish you lots of luck. It's a great way to make a living, my friend, but please don't be a PTP'er. Don't come in and take my job. I've already got too much competition.

John Sanford, of Fairview, Michigan, wrote to say that he met me when I was with the Pistons and that he still has one of my bumper stickers, the one that says, "R-E-V-I-T-A-L-I-Z-E-D, baby." Yeah, I was revitalized. Are you kidding me? They shipped me right out of town.

Finally, J.C. Harper, an assistant on Notre Dame's football team, wrote to thank me for speaking to the team at the Orange Bowl. No, J.C., I didn't do a good enough job. I got a big L. Mike Patrick has been on my case about that. He said my speech caused the Irish to get beat. Come on, baby, I need another chance. Let me speak when I've got an automatic, man. Give me a cupcake. Can I speak when you're going to play Navy? Uh-uh. Don't get mad at me, midshipmen. I just need a W. I'll leave the Miamis and the Colorados to Holtz.

FRIDAY, FEBRUARY 1—

You'll never guess where I was today. The answer is Indianapolis, to do a personal appearance for the Indianapolis Ice, a minor league hockey team, at one of their games.

I was hoping all day that they wouldn't want me to do any play-by-play, because I couldn't tell you what the blue line is, the red line, the green line. I don't understand a thing about hockey, John Ziegler. Don't get upset with me, Big Z. The Big Z, man, is the commissioner of the NHL. I couldn't tell you anything, other than I know who Mario Lemieux and Wayne Gretzky are.

I was asking Frank Beckman on WJR Radio in Detroit for some advice in the morning. He said, "I'll give you very simple advice: Bring some boxing gloves, baby." These guys always put on those fights, man. I don't know how they allow it. Can you imagine basketball if they allowed that? Stop the action and go after each other? I mean, you're talking chaos. How do they permit that in a sport? That blows my mind.

Roy Hurley, from the Indianapolis Ice front office, made me feel like a million dollars, as he had a stretch limo waiting for me when I arrived. He took me over to my hotel, and then it was off to the offices of *Indianapolis Monthly,* where they took a picture of me for the cover of their special Final Four edition. From there, we went over to Q95, the radio station, where I went on with Mad Dog and Chick, their two afternoon hosts. Q95 has one unbelievable promotion they run every Friday. It's called "Will It Float?" Get this: They actually go into a bathroom and drop a big cookie, about six inches in circumference, into the john. Then they have people call up and decide whether it will float or not. I had to describe the action.

Then they rushed me to the arena for a live shot with Ed Sorenson, a local sports anchor. Sorenson was wearing a skullcap to make him look like yours truly. Apparently, I wasn't going to be the only bald man in town. They were doing a thing where guys were getting their heads shaved for $95 and some Speedway gas. Guys were lined up. One guy we called Grizzly. He had a mop of hair and a big beard. These two women barbers started shaving his deck. I grabbed a pair of clippers, went over to him, and said, "I want to take your beard off."

"No, no," he said. "Do anything, but don't shave my beard off."

Then they had a Dick Vitale sound-alike contest. Some little guy won, about thirteen, fourteen years old. He really had me down. When I found out first prize was a trip to Toronto and a color TV, I tried to enter. I gave the crowd my best General material, but the crowd still booed.

That night, before the game, they had me introduce the players. I had to announce the starting lineups—you know, the right defense, the left defense, the center and the goalie, and I used PTP'ers, Rolls-Roycers, and Diaper Dandies to describe them.

Then, when the game got going, I sat in the penalty box and called the action from a mike that carried through the entire arena. I had the place going wild with some of my comments. Guys were fighting against the boards and I said in a little girl's voice, "Fellows, you shouldn't do that. Your mother didn't teach you to hit. Come on, guys, don't fight. That's not fair. They don't do that in basketball." Another time I said, "I want to see some J's baby. Get rid of that little puck. Let's see some J's, some scoring, some action." Man, it was wild. There was one whole section of people wearing skullcaps, all bald Vitale look-alikes. I mean, it was an absolute riot.

It was 1–zip after the first period. I mean, my head was going left, right, blue line, red lines, offsides, icing. To be honest with you, I had no clue, but Ray Compton, the president, seemed happy. Ray used to work for the Indiana Pacers, and he's done an amazing job with promotions. I mean, this team is averaging more than 6,000 in attendance, and this is minor league hockey.

Of course, when you bring in guest stars like Kathy Ireland, it doesn't hurt. She's the model who's been on the cover of *Sports Illustrated*. She's about 5-10, 5-11, and they claimed she dressed in a micro mini, and had the place going absolutely wild. They really wanted her in a swimsuit, but that was a no-go, baby. She wouldn't go for it. Who would you like to see do their thing? Kathy Ireland in her bikini or Dick Vitale screaming, "It's awesome, baby"?

SATURDAY, FEBRUARY 2—

As soon as I arrived in Vegas, I went to watch UNLV work out and immediately had to take all kinds of heat for picking Vegas to lose at Arkansas February 10. Stacey Augmon, Greg Anthony, and Anderson Hunt greeted me by chanting: "Arkansas, Arkansas, Arkansas . . ." Tarkanian was laughing. Then he started teasing. "Anthony," he said, "work on your shooting. Let Vitale help you. Instead of forty-eight percent, you'll be down to twenty-five."

I was trying to be serious. "I can really work on your shooting," I told Anthony. "Did you watch Kenny Anderson the other day?" He hadn't, but it was clear that it wouldn't have mattered. "Who won the game?" Anthony said. "I want to know, who won the game? . . . The bottom line is winning. Look at us, we win. I'm not worried about points, I'm not worried about producing all those numbers. All I'm worried about is getting W's, me and my buddy." And he gave a high-five to Anderson Hunt.

Tarkanian has done an amazing job indoctrinating these guys to the philosophy of winning and being unselfish. Anthony is the catalyst for all of that. He's going to be a politician—he worked in Washington as an aide during the summer—and you can see why. This guy will be the governor of Nevada someday—Governor Anthony. I can see it now. Tarkanian, move over. And what an entrepreneur. He's already part-owner of an apparel business, doesn't take any scholarship money. I mean, this guy Anthony has got it together. He has success written all over him.

Vegas has been hogging the headlines, on the floor and off. They have a chance to become the first team since UCLA in 1972–73 to win back-to-back national titles, now that they've cut that deal with the NCAA that will allow the Rebels to participate in this year's tournament, but ban them from competing in postseason play next year as well as limiting their TV appearances. Robert Maxson, the school president, was at practice today and he told me UNLV made the trade-off for players like Larry Johnson and Stacey Augmon, who passed up the NBA draft to return for their senior year.

"Well," I suggested, "they could always go somewhere else."

"Other schools wouldn't have scholarships available in July," he tried to tell me.

"Mr. President," I said, "for Johnson and Augmon, schools will *find* scholarships."

After practice, Tark and I were walking out to the parking lot, and I couldn't believe all the fancy cars the players were driving. "Yeah, I know," Tarkanian said. "Greg Anthony's bought a car and everybody in town is all upset about it. I don't even know what kind of car . . . I don't know the makes. They tell me it's expensive." I said, "Yeah, a little bit. New 300 Mercedes. He told me about it earlier."

These guys work these deals out, get loans through their parents, who co-sign. I'm sure it's on the up-and-up. It's bending rules, not breaking rules. There's no way the players are going to cheat on something like this, because they know the NCAA is breathing down their backs. In fact, Anthony told me that whenever the guys buy a car, they immediately call the NCAA and notify them how they're going to finance it.

About the only thing I don't like about this Vegas team are those black high-top sneakers they wear. I told that to Tark. "It reminds me of the old YMCA, Tark," I said. "Back when you used to play with your underwear hanging out of your shorts." He said he didn't like them, either, but that the players voted to wear them.

Tark wanted me to go to dinner with him at Piero's. "Well, as long as you're springing," I said. Tark hasn't sprung for a meal in his life. I don't think he's been billed for a meal since he's been out here. I said I would meet him as soon as I finished watching Rutgers work out and we had our production meeting.

I didn't have to spend much time with Rutgers coach Bob Wenzel to realize that even he didn't think tomorrow's game was such a good idea. "But we have no choice, no choice," he said. "We're trying to build our program, trying to get national publicity. We know we're about the third shot here for ABC. I've been going to ABC every summer, trying to sell Jack O'Hara, their program director, on the idea of putting us on TV. How could I reject them and say no?"

Originally, ABC had penciled in Oklahoma to meet Vegas, but Tubbs backed out. Then they went to Missouri, but the Tigers had a scheduling conflict. At least they're catching Rutgers at a good time. The Scarlet Knights just blistered Temple by 20 Friday. No one knows how they'll play after flying cross country, though.

Things were really loose at our production meeting. Someone had a Johnny Most T-shirt on, and that sent Kim Belton off. Belton loves to do impersonations of the legendary Boston announcer, and he couldn't refuse telling us about the game Most called a couple years ago when the Celtics played a Yugoslavian team in the McDonald's Classic in Madrid.

Johnny couldn't pronounce any of those big Yugoslavian names, so he decided to improvise. "Well, the Yugoslavs have the ball, the blond guy's got the ball. He passes over to the guy with the mustache, who passes to the guy with the hair hanging out of his armpits. Wait a minute. The blond guy is mad. He didn't get the ball back."

When someone asked Most about it afterward, he just shrugged his shoulders. "Screw it," he said, "nobody back home will know who they are anyway."

You should have heard Belton doing his Johnny Most. You should have heard me busting on Tark later in the lobby. Watch this, I told Joe Calabrese of the *Newark Star Ledger*. I had him going crazy. "Jerry," I said, "don't get nervous, but ABC took film of the cars out in the parking lot—the BMW that Stacey Augmon has, the BMW that Anderson Hunt's driving, the Corvette convertible that Larry Johnson's driving. We're going to run that on ABC." Tark flipped. "Dick," he said, "they can't run that. Those kids, those are just friends' cars, they don't really own those cars. Even though everything has been done legally, we'll get in all kinds of trouble. That's all I need."

Tark just went on and on. He told me how he tried to talk Anthony out of buying the Mercedes, how it sends bad signals to the NCAA, how he doesn't need that kind of aggravation. I mean, the guy was going to have a heart attack. Finally I said, "Jerry, I'm only busting your chops. I'm only teasing you, baby. Don't get so nervous." "Why do you do that to me?" Tark said.

CHAPTER 9

SUNDAY, FEBRUARY 3—

Dinner last night with Tark was one unbelievable scene. We were sitting there at Piero's, eating the best Italian food, and Jerry was just being besieged with people coming over, Tark fans. This guy's so big that Piero's owner, Freddie Glusman, who's one of his main men, had pictures made up, and Tark was autographing pictures for the fans.

In between autographs, I got Tark all nervous again when I started talking about who his successor might be if he ever stepped down. One guy at the table said, "I think Bobby Cremins. He's tight with the president, Bob Maxson. Bob really likes him." They both have ties to Appalachian State, where Bobby was head coach prior to his arrival at Georgia Tech. "Naw," I said, "he's got no shot to get Cremins. There's no way. This guy had a chance to go to Kentucky and he wasn't interested. There's no way he's leaving."

Then somebody brought up Big John Thompson of Georgetown, who loves Vegas. This time Tark spoke up. "There's no way he's going to leave Georgetown to come out here," Tark said. "If anything, he's going to be a GM in the NBA."

Finally, Billy Tubbs of Oklahoma came up for discussion. "Tubbs would come here in a minute," Freddie Glusman said. "Tubbs loves this place." You know what? They're right. I think Tubbsie would come out here. But who would want to follow the Tark? You win 20 a year here and you could get the ziggy. You'd better win 25 and sell 17,000 tickets.

After a while, Freddie started telling me all about the tickets. This is how big UNLV basketball is out here: They have a point system. You donate big bucks, you're entitled to four postseason tickets. Freddie said he had to donate $25,000 to the scholarship fund to keep the tickets he bought this season. All the high rollers go to the games, sit on Gucci row. Freddie and his wife, Bonnie, sit down there, next to the Wynns. That's right, Elaine and Steve Wynn, the owners of the Mirage and the Golden Nugget Casinos.

After dinner, we got in the car and went over to several clubs. We wound up at Sharks. That's right, Sharks. Tark has a club named after him. You talk about disco lights, music blaring. You can't touch this, M.C. Hammer. There were bodies crawling next to each other. I mean, it was body-to-body. It was as wild as can be—minis running all over the place here. Even the scene outside was crazy—lines that went on forever. Tark went into the special line and they all went wild. All of a sudden, these foxy ladies came running up to the Tark. They wanted pictures. He is treated like royalty in this town. He's Mr. Vegas. Wayne Newton may be big here, but he's No. 2 to Tark.

Then I got lucky. All these people were yelling out, "He's awesome, baby. Get a TO, baby. He's a PTP'er, baby." When we got inside, I was drinking my orange juice and guys were running over and saying things like: "What about the St. Louis Billikens?" "Hey, Anthony Peeler of Missouri, AP, told me to say hello if I ever see you." "Hey, Vitale, you're crazy. There's no way the Razorbacks are going to beat our Rebels." Pictures, snapshots, you couldn't move, couldn't budge. My orange juice spilled and somebody screamed out, "Get a TO, Vitale. Get a TO!"

Orange juice. That's my favorite drink. Maybe I should call up the folks at Tropicana in Bradenton. Tell them I'd be a great spokesperson. Just call me O.J. Vitale.

In the morning, reality hit. It happens every time you come to Vegas. I picked up the paper and saw this big headline on the front page: "Tark the Shark, Biggest Fish in High-Paying Pond." The story claimed that UNLV pays Tarkanian more than any other university pays its hoops coach. It went on to speculate that Tark is making more than $600,000 a year, $203,976 from the university. Hey, come on, Tark is probably making more.

When I spoke to Tark about it later, he was defensive. "They're crazy," he said. "I don't make $600,000. I don't have camps like these other coaches. I make about $400,000." Oh, really? Only $400,000?

Tark then tried another way to soften the news. "Hey, wait a minute," he said. "What about Lute Olson and Bobby Knight? I don't get one-third of what those guys get." Hey, Tark, I'm pretty good at math. If you make about $600,000, that's $1.8 million for Lute and Bobby. Wow, I've got to do a lot of work to catch those guys.

Tark really didn't have to apologize. What people don't understand is that certain coaches have become entrepreneurs. It's the same as the leaders in the corporate world, leaders from Ford Motor Co., General Motors, and Chrysler. They get all these bonuses for excelling, all these bonuses for sales. Coaches now are being treated the same way in terms of tickets sales, revenue from tournament play, revenue from merchandising school items. Guys like Dean Smith, Bobby Knight, Lute Olson are the Lee Iacoccas of the college basketball world.

The paper ran pictures of the ten highest-paid coaches at state schools. Yeah, they had Tark, Knight, and Olson, but the second-highest-paid coach after Tark—and he was far ahead of everyone else—was Bill Frieder of Arizona State. Frieder's salary was listed at $152,000. Next was Olson at $130,000, then Dean Smith at $120,185, Jim Calhoun at $120,000, Knight at $114,500, Denny Crum at $110,022, Jud Heathcoate at $99,500, Randy Ayers at $81,120, and Nolan Richardson at $78,045.

The paper also had a chart that showed each guy's perks and incentives. I'll just give you a sample here. Here's what it had about Olson, whose total income was estimated at more than $600,000:

TICKETS PROVIDED FOR: four.
INCENTIVES: 1/12 of his annual salary for each of the following accomplishments: winning the Pac-10 conference; reaching the third game of NCAA playoffs; reaching the Final Four; and if and when his athletes attain a graduation rate of 85 percent over five years.
PERKS: a car and free use of an accountant and lawyer.
SIDE DEALS: TV and radio shows.
ENDORSEMENTS: $150,000 shoe deal with Nike.

Can you imagine the professors reading this? I can't believe it. It was one of Jimmy Valvano's big downfalls when he was at NC State. When they started posting all the numbers, the profs went nuts, they went bananas.

You know what, though? I'm a former coach, and these guys are under constant pressure to produce, produce, produce. Unlike the NBA, where the players are king, the coaches are the big show in college basketball. The stability factor. They're also faced with scrutiny, scrutiny, scrutiny. If players don't graduate, they're buried. If players get involved in drugs, they're buried. Don't win and you get the ziggy, ziggy, ziggy.

It will be interesting to see how long Tark sticks around. They've just changed AD's out here and Maxson has brought in a lot of his own people. A lot of Tark's guys are not big fans of the interim AD, Ron Finfrock. They're upset about the way ticket distribution is being handled. Tickets are such a big thing out there. The story says Tark receives 216 tickets as part of his contract, but he claims that he has 160 and that a lot of them go to recruits and people from the university. As far as selling tickets, he said, "I sell only a few, and basically it's right on my income tax. It's all legal and taken care of—as long as I document and don't scalp, and I've never done that."

Jerry says the president has been super to him, even sends him letters of appreciation. But there's another side out here that claims Maxson would rather not have Tark around. These people say Maxson would like to bring in somebody who's a lot more low-key and doesn't have Tark's exposure and notoriety.

I'll tell you, this whole UNLV scene is one unbelievable soap opera. It goes on, man, it beats "General Hospital." I've got to talk to Dennis Swanson, the No. 1 guy at ABC, about a new soap opera on ABC. We can call it "Tark's World." I want to play a lead role in that. I mean, I want to play Tark.

The game was a wild scene too. Bill Cosby, the Cos, was there, and he is absolutely one of the funniest guys you could ever want to meet. He was wearing a Harvey Mudd College shirt and he was in rare form. Tark came over, and Cos said, "Hey, don't get a haircut like the Tark, Dick. Look at that."

Cosby made me feel really good. He said, "Hey, whatever you do, don't let criticism from the media bother you, and don't change. You relate with the people." He surprised me; he's a heck of a basketball fan. He loves you, Kenny Anderson.

He says that move you laid on Hurley the other night was something he'll always remember.

We did our opening from the Rutgers locker room, and I talked with Earl Duncan, another Syracuse transfer who's now the starting guard for Wenzel. Duncan, Keith Hughes, Matt Roe, Richard Manning, Tony Scott. You could make an All-Transfer team with the guys who left Jimmy Boeheim's program. Guys like that are always moving on for one reason. PT. Playing time.

Duncan was a high school All-America from L.A. when he enrolled. He's ballooned up to 240 pounds following arthroscopic surgery last summer. The players started calling him "Donuts." Donuts Duncan. He's back down to 215 now. We talked about how he would have to protect the basketball and not turn it over for Rutgers to have any shot at all. When the game was on, unfortunately, they turned it over and turned it over. It was apple turnover time. It was blitz city. The score was 57–39 at halftime, but that didn't indicate how much UNLV was dominating. The final was 115–73.

Even though it was a blowout, I still think it will be a learning experience for Rutgers once they put it in perspective. The Atlantic 10 has some good basketball teams. Look at all the other good basketball teams that have been blown out by Vegas—the Princetons, the Florida States. UNLV, which has now won 18 in a row this season, is on another level. At times, they make you look like a junior high school team.

MONDAY, FEBRUARY 4—

Welcome to Champaign, Illinois. I'm here to do Illinois–Northwestern tonight. I flew out of Vegas right after the game and got in at 1 A.M. There was a message at the hotel when I arrived. It was from Northwestern coach Bill Foster. "Hey, what's this guy doing double-dipping?" it said. "He's working Sunday and Monday, boy. Making some big money. Tell him to get out to practice to see us tomorrow at eleven in the morning."

When I walked into Northwestern's practice, Foster was in a great mood for a guy whose team has lost 41 consecutive road games in the Big 10. Here's a guy who's turned around programs at Rutgers, Utah, and Duke, and I mean, you've never seen anyone so optimistic. I feel it's unfortunate he has to go through what he does at Northwestern, because he has a very creative mind and a great understanding of the game. His teams play hard, have a good attitude, do things the right way, his players all graduate. They'll probably be the CEO's of tomorrow. But my gut feeling is that unless Northwestern wants to make a serious commitment to athletics, these kids should be playing in the Ivy League where they have a chance to win. I just feel the school has got to give them a fair shake in admissions. Indiana has done it. Michigan has done it.

If not, they're always going to be living off selective memories. I flew down here with a Northwestern grad, and he told me, "Several years ago we beat Indiana." I remember that. The Zoo Crew went wild that night. But it was only one night.

"That's the problem," I told him. "You guys always live off that dream of pulling off the one W, and that's not what it's about. You got to be able to compete on a regular basis."

Foster hopes the future will be brighter. Bill laid his recruiting class on me. He's really excited about the kids he got—Matt Purdy, Dewey Williams, Dion Lee, and T.J. Radford. I'll give you one thing, they sound like great names, Bill. They really do. Dewey and T.J. and Dion. They sound like big-time players. I didn't want to break his heart and mention that Michigan's getting Juwan Howard, one of the top five players in America, from his own backyard in Chicago, and Jimmy King, the best guard in Texas; that Purdue's getting Glenn Robinson; that Indiana's getting Alan Henderson. That's the problem. For every recruit Northwestern brings in, the other schools in the conference are getting twice the talent. That makes it difficult to survive.

The point spread on tonight's game is 18. Kenny Fouts and Tim Rapley, our director and producer, both wanted to run it on the air. But Tim Brando and I were vehemently against it.

"No, no," I said, "we can't do that. Remember the NFL even frowned on ESPN running the point spread. I know we did it because it's a fact of life. But I'm against it on the college level."

"Aaah, what are you afraid of?" Fouts said. "Are you afraid of the General?"

Well, we finally agreed to check with the brass at ESPN. And the brass said, "No way."

For once I was right.

As it turned out, I only saved Northwestern some temporary embarrassment. But, as you might expect Illinois won in a blowout, 73–59, and Northwestern fell to 5–14.

TUESDAY, FEBRUARY 5—

I knew as soon as I got up that it was going to be an awful day for traveling. The fog was scary. My 6 A.M. flight was canceled. The 7:10 was canceled. The next one was delayed. My partner Bob Carpenter wanted me to drive three hours with him to St. Louis, then connect out of there. But I said no. That was a big mistake. I didn't get out of Champaign until around noon, and I didn't walk in the door at home until seven that night. That's a fourteen-hour day. I could have gone to Hawaii and back.

While I was waiting, I spoke with Mike Soltys of ESPN's PR department. He was still upset about the General screaming about the 9:30 starts.

"Hey," he said, "what about the General and his practice sessions? What about his triple sessions? He talks about academics and kids missing class time. What about the fact that, after some losses, he keeps them in the gym a long time?"

That's right, General, what about that? Come on, now, you know Mike has a point. There's no question the games are late. But haven't you gone overboard yourself? Just one time I want the General to say, "Look maybe I pushed the issue too far. Maybe my kids can adjust." I mean, they're only being asked to do this once, twice an entire year. But the General won't let up. He's just like his favorite guy, Feinstein. Maybe I should invite the two of them to lunch. I'll even pick up the tab.

WEDNESDAY, FEBRUARY 6—

My phone has been ringing off the hook all morning. People are calling from all over the country. Most of them want to talk about the big showdown coming up Sunday between UNLV and Arkansas. That's all I heard all day—how come I'm picking Arkansas? Tarkanian, you're driving me crazy with this team. Hey, Packer, they should be calling you, not me. I'm not doing that game. I'm doing UCLA–Arizona, an important conference game. UNLV–Arkansas is just a made-for-TV game. Only kidding.

I took my wife to dinner tonight, and she plunked some old tapes from WJR in Detroit into the cassette deck in the car. I couldn't believe it. The tapes were vintage 1973, the year I got hired as the coach at the University of Detroit. The late Vince Doyle, who was an institution in Detroit, and Norm Plummer were hosting a show called "Sports Line" and I was their guest. It was just incredible listening to all the comments. I was recruiting like crazy, trying to get Tom LaGarde to go to UD instead of North Carolina. LaGarde was a star in that town. I was a nobody, trying to build a following. I sounded just like I do now on TV, the voice, the fast talk, the same thing, baby. And that was eighteen years ago. Vince, bless his heart, was the guy who introduced me at my press conference, and he called me Vinnie Vitoli. They didn't even know my name when I arrived.

We listened to the callers asking different questions. Who am I? What about my background? Can this guy coach? What about my recruiting ideas? I'm telling about my goals, how someday I'd like to maybe even become a pro coach and how I'm going to pack that place at Calihan Hall. I talked about getting the white alums from the suburbs to come back down into the city. My wife taped the show at home and I could hear my daughter crying in the background. Now, eighteen years later, she's gone, she's at Notre Dame. It's just totally unreal, because at that time I was making about $16,000, $17,000 a year, chasing a dream.

We were rolling in the car when I told one of the callers about my idea for a paint-a-thon. Are you ready for this? One of the administrators wouldn't give us enough money—it was, like, $20,000—to paint the seats, the chair backs, at the arena. I wanted to paint them red, white, and blue. So I said, "Please, just let me go out and get somebody to buy the paint, and I'll get all the students in a paint-a-thon and we'll all paint the seats and work around the clock and have fun and get it done." The administrator said, "You've got to be crazy, putting a paintbrush in those kids' hands." I said, "Wait a minute, we can put a gun in their hands and they can go into the service. They certainly can paint." Vince Doyle was laughing hysterically, and sure enough we had a paint-a-thon. Can you imagine Dean Smith or Bob Knight getting involved in a paint-a-thon?

We did all kinds of stuff like that. Once we had Hoop Hysteria—a twenty-four-hour marathon. For twenty-four hours we kept the gym hopping with games every two hours. That's right, we got the local police to play the fire department at one game. I had cafés bring their people to play after the bars closed. We had one game that matched Willie Horton's café against Joe Strawder's café, because I figured these former Detroit sports stars would help draw a crowd. Every two hours we had a game. We culminated with our intrasquad scrimmage at 8 P.M. Saturday night. Anything to create excitement.

THURSDAY, FEBRUARY 7—

Rudy Martzke did a big feature on me for *USA Today*. It was a very positive article, but, boy, if I made the money he says I do, I'd be able to retire immediately. I mean, I'm a mini, mini, mini John Madden, both in terms of physical stature and in terms of finances. Of course, Rudy also had to throw in a little shot that some media guys were criticizing me. Who's criticizing me? The Norman Chads of the world? Some writers? All I ask is that these critics spend a day on campus with me and then make a judgment.

On my way to the airport—I'm flying to Greensboro, North Carolina, to do a speaking engagement tonight—I stopped at a phone to call Michigan coach Steve Fisher. I wanted to talk to him before I do Ohio State and Michigan on Monday. Fisher's team is really in struggle city, because he came up empty in recruiting last year. He really thought he was going to get Eric Montross because Eric's parents both went to Michigan, but the kid basically wanted his own identity. It's so bleak at Michigan right now that Fisher's even got a walk-on starting, a 6-5 guy named Freddie Hunter. When's the last time that happened, a walk-on starting at a major school like Michigan? But Fisher's bringing in a good class—Howard, King, and Ray Jackson, another good guard from Texas—and he reported that he's still in the hunt for Webber. It's not locked up yet, though. Fisher said he's a little worried that Webber is visiting Duke this weekend for the LSU game, then staying on campus

Monday. Naturally, when Webber sees that environment, it could really excite him.

I was introduced at the Greater Greensboro Merchants banquet by—are you ready for this?—a funeral director. His name was John Forbes. I didn't want to shake his hand, man, I was scared. I said, "Forbes, that's all I need is a guy like you saying all these beautiful things about me. It's like my eulogy. Man, I don't need you." Then I went into my routine. I said I had read an article that listed all the coaches Dean Smith had beaten en route to 700 victories. The list even included me. "Hey," I said, "Dean shouldn't be bragging about that, baby. A lot of guys have wins over me. That's no great accomplishment. I mean, you don't have to be a genius to do that."

On the way back to the hotel, we passed by Guilford College, the alma mater of guys like M. L. Carr, Bob Kauffman, and World B. Free. Kauffman is the guy who hired me with the Pistons. Carr played for me. And Free? I was recruiting Phil Sellers for Rutgers and I went to Brooklyn to see him. He had some guy standing with him. "Coach," he said, "I'd like my friend to join us on my recruiting visit." I'm saying like, "Who's this guy?" I felt like a fool when I found out.

By the way, North Carolina came back from losing last night in Raleigh to beat NC State by 22. Isn't that the way I said it would happen? Carolina just wore 'em down with its depth. Plus, the game had the revenge factor.

FRIDAY, FEBRUARY 8—

The new issue of *Sports Illustrated* had a great story on Michelle Marchiniak from Allentown, Pennsylvania. She's probably the best women's high school basketball player in the country right now, and she has signed with Notre Dame. I'm sorry, Curry Kirkpatrick. There's no doubt he's a great basketball writer, but I never got to the college basketball section. I couldn't get through the bathing suit segment.

SATURDAY, FEBRUARY 9—

Four hours into my flight to the coast, this flight attendant started talking to the guy next to me, complimenting him on all his accomplishments in the field of physical fitness. It turned out that the guy was Jack LaLanne. This guy's seventy-six and he looks about forty-five. No wonder I didn't recognize him.

LaLanne had been in Tampa to promote a new line of vitamins. Boy, the shape he's in. I can't believe it, this guy is like rock. Are you ready for this? At age seventy, he swam a bicentennial mile in Long Beach Harbor towing thirteen boats with seventy-six passengers. One time, he set a world record—right on "You Asked For It"—of 1,033 push-ups in 23 minutes. He said he has a very simple philosophy: Anything in life is possible.

Meeting Jack LaLanne was a great experience, and I had another one when I got to my hotel. The place was right on the beach and the view from my room was beautiful. Oh, wow, I wished my family could have been out there with me in this baby. The whole thing was gorgeous, I mean, absolutely gorgeous.

Even though I was staying in Santa Monica and the weather was beautiful, I couldn't leave the room right away because I wanted to watch the end of the Notre Dame–Syracuse game. Syracuse won it at the buzzer on a put-back by Billy Owens. They were originally supposed to play without six kids they suspended for alleged rules violations, but the NCAA gave the kids the OK to play. Digger still had his guys hanging tough, though. He even brought out new lime-green uniforms for the occasion.

Those uniforms were the same color as the first new car I ever bought, back in 1969. A new green limelight Bonneville convertible. I was driving it the day I met my wife. I guess I was a little luckier than Digger.

From there, I watched Arizona practice and then I went over to the Sports Arena to watch Southern Cal play Arizona State in an afternoon game. George Raveling has started bringing a lot of excitement to the school, but he definitely needs an on-campus facility to help with recruiting. When I walked in, he was up on that sideline, dressed in his finest threads, trying to get the crowd going. Trying to give a course in Cheerleading 101. There were only 4,000 people there, and they were quiet because the Sun Devils had come in and really played well. I was so excited to have a chance to see Harold Miner, USC's sophomore star, but Arizona State denied him the basketball. He didn't take a shot for the first nine minutes. He ended up getting 14 points, but it wasn't enough. Arizona State jumped out to a 16-point lead, then held on, 88–83, to improve its record to 14–7 and PAC-10 record to 5–6.

If you're Southern Cal, this is the kind of game you have to win. You just beat UCLA, you just beat Arizona, you're at home, you've got to close it out. You have 13 wins, you want to get to the next level, get a postseason bid. You can't afford to lose this. It was a big loss for George's team.

Frieder was just as wacky as ever. He had that towel around his neck all during the game, and then afterward, he sent his camera guy over to ask if I would be part of the school's highlights film. I told him to throw the mike on. Hey, a little airtime doesn't hurt anyone, right, Frieds? Maybe I'll get a free meal out of you down the road. You're one of the cheapest coaches in the history of coaching. Come on, Frieder, at least give me a T-shirt.

Frieder, the Big 10 misses you. How could you ever leave? When you left, the Big 10 dropped a couple notches. I think Frieder's recruiting madness really forced everybody else to keep up because you knew if you're an Illinois, an Iowa, you better go out and get some horses.

Gary Grant, one of Frieder's best recruits ever, and Pooh Richardson were both at the game. Gary's a guard for the Los Angeles Clippers these days, pulling down about $900,000 a year. "Hey, Dick," he said, "I owe you a lot of that cash—you made me a star in a year."

Pooh was a Philadelphia playground legend who played for UCLA during the Walt Hazzard era and is now a starting guard with the Minnesota Timberwolves. These guys are making megabucks now. Pooh had a diamond-studded pendant around his neck with the name "Pooh" on it. "I was the only guy on the West Coast you ever gave any publicity to," he pointed out. "You didn't think any of us could play except for me."

"That's because you were an East Coast guy who went west," I said. I was really down on West Coast basketball for a while, and I got into it more than once with Lute Olson and Hazzard. But times have changed, with an influx of aggressive coaches like Frieder.

Frieder was in no mood to joke around at his postgame interview. One of the local writers told him Jim Harrick of

UCLA questioned the fact he would shift to a slowdown after playing fast-break basketball all year.

"Let Harrick run his own team," he snapped. "Why is he trying to tell me what to do with my team? Ask Harrick how he's managed to lose seven games with all that talent." My guy Frieder. Everywhere he goes, there's sparks.

From there, I drove over to Westwood to watch Jim Harrick's UCLA team practice. Boy, the traffic in Southern California is brutal. UCLA was just finishing up, and their point guard, Derrick Martin, came over to say hello. I said, "Congratulations, Derrick. You just broke the school record with fifteen assists in one game." He had a look of shock all over his face. "I know more about you," I said, "just like I know about your forty-four points in your last game in high school, just like I know about the fact that you wanted to get out of your letter of intent. What else do you want to know about yourself?" I cracked him up.

Martin then started telling me how his teammate, Don MacLean, has calmed down. I'll have to see that to believe it. MacLean has really been tough on his teammates in the past, screaming and yelling, moaning if he didn't get the ball, complaining, always talking a lot of trash on the floor. He's definitely a member of my All-Crybaby team.

"No," Martin said, "coach Harrick's done a great job with him. I had a talk with him, too, because he and I had gotten into a couple screaming matches. I mean, he embarrassed me. I don't need that aggravation."

MacLean then walked over. I was standing around with Ed O'Bannon, America's number-one high school player from last season who is recovering from major knee surgery, and when I saw MacLean I said in a joking fashion, "Eddie, if you were healthy, MacLean would've been the best sixth man in college basketball." MacLean said, "Are you kidding, man? I would have walked, I'd have been gone. Sixth man! There's no way I'm sixth man."

MacLean then told me he was thinking seriously about skipping his senior year and turning pro. "Wait a minute," I said. "Don't you think about it. You just stay in school, you need another year in school."

I mentioned it to Jimmy Harrick later, and he said, "Naw,

he's just putting you on." I don't know, though. I think he might be serious. He had that look in his eyes.

A little while later, we were having our production meeting and Jack Arute, our sideline reporter, cracked us up with a story about the security at the Super Bowl. It was at the height of the war, you know, and the deal was there would be two security guards stationed in the broadcast booth in case anyone tried to break in and grab a microphone to make a political statement or take someone hostage. Arute said these FBI agents were giving instructions to the crew and that he nearly died when one guy said, "If somebody grabs your microphone and takes you hostage, be very calm, try to get confidence, and the biggest thing is, step away and try to leave some space so one of our sharpshooters can get them."

I said, "You've got to be kidding me, man. He grabs my microphone, you think I'm going to fight him for it? I'm going to give it to him. He can have the microphone. It's his, baby. That's one way to shut me up and get me no AT."

SUNDAY, FEBRUARY 10—

I was getting ready to leave for our game when I ran into some Vegas fans. They were upset that the Rebs were down four at halftime. But by the time I walked into Pauley Pavilion, everything had changed. Our production crew was going crazy. "Hey, did you hear about the blowout?" one guy asked me. "Blowout?" I said. "Yeah," he said, "Vegas came out, scored the first ten points of the second half, went on a sixteen to two run, and blitzed them, 112 to 105." I couldn't believe it.

Lute Olson said Vegas put on just an awesome performance in the second half. In the UCLA locker room, Tracy Murray was giving a detailed description of the incident that got Larry Johnson and Todd Day ejected at the end of a physical game that was laced with taunting. Day and Johnson were battling for a rebound with just 2:27 to go and had to be restrained from tearing into each other—as well as official Jody Silvester, who tried to intervene. Silvester gave both the hook before total chaos broke out. Hey, Day, you got to be smarter than to hook up with Johnson. That's like Tyson versus Vitale. You're lucky you did that in front of the cameras instead of in some back alley.

Yeah, I heard all about it when the students started flocking in. They were razzing me good for picking Arkansas. Keith Jackson got all over me too. He told me he's going to bring his Arkansas Hog hat and put that thing on my head the next time we work together.

But I won 'em over. Drilled ten in a row from the line before the game, even though my shirt felt tight. Then I challenged big Mike Lanier, UCLA's 7-6 redshirt center, to a little game of one-on-one. Blew by the big guy, scored with an underhanded reverse scoop that shocked even me. The student body erupted. Keith Jackson jumped in jubilant style. It was a shot made for the movies, but there were no cameras. I ran into the stands, laying high fives on all the Bruin faithful. Tinsel Town became Fun City at its best.

Our game was terrific. I mean, you talk about intensity, you talk about excitement. Back and forth, back and forth. Arizona finally won in overtime, 105–94, but they needed a shot at the buzzer by Chris Mills to stay alive in regulation. The Wildcats are now 19–4 and look like they're in good position to win another PAC-10 title with five of their final seven games at home.

So much for MacLean's new image. He really impressed me with his offensive skills, but he made a big mistake late in regulation when he threw a ball at Brian Williams, who was lying on his back. MacLean got hit with a technical, Arizona made one of the two free throws and got the ball out of bounds, and the momentum shifted.

I had to get all over MacLean for being so immature. I felt his antics in the Arizona game turned the game around. Childish actions such as this carry over to all the players on the floor, and it affects the mental attitude of everyone. It's a downer, baby. MacLean is too talented, too gifted, to be wasting his time groaning and moaning and carrying on like he's back in first grade, where it's Dick and Jane time.

MONDAY, FEBRUARY 11—

Sometimes I even amaze myself. L.A. to Chicago last night. Chicago to Columbus, Ohio, this morning. And in plenty of time to make it over to the student center for the Windex Dick Vitale Sound-Alike Contest. They had numerous contestants, and there were some really great impersonations. The winner was a guy by the name of Steve Biro. They call him Woody, as he does a great Woody Hayes impersonation and he's Mr. Popularity on the Columbus campus. He had me down pat.

All the local TV stations were there, and it was just one big happening. I mean, who am I kidding? This attention is so flattering. I can't believe I'm being paid to have fun. We used it for our "Fast Break" series. We had Biro do his impersonation of me as I busted onto the stage. "Get out of the way," I said. "Let the real Dick Vitale come on."

When I arrived, the students presented me with a bunch of cupcakes for my constant criticism of Ohio State's early-season schedule. I told them, "Get rid of those cupcakes. I'll set the schedule for you. Play Cincinnati. Open up with Cincinnati. Then let's go to Lexington, Kentucky, and play the Kentucky Wildcats and Ricky Pitino. Then we'll go down to Duke and play in front of the Cameron Crazies. We'll get this club ready, big-time style, for the Big 10. We're talking playing all the heavyweights." They roared. They were really excited. They loved it.

On second thought, maybe we ought to cancel that trip to Durham, after what Duke did to LSU yesterday. Shaquille O'Neal might be the No. 1 talent in the country right now, but Christian Laettner did a number on him, holding him to just 15 points.

Laettner looks more and more like one of the top ten players in the country. But Bobby Hurley's not sure about Shaquille. "I wasn't that impressed," Hurley said. Don't get carried away, Bobby.

What a time for Chris Webber to visit Duke's campus.

An hour or so before the game, I stopped into the Michigan locker room and I could just see the tension on the players' faces. Fisher wasn't in such a great mood, either. He was worried that he might have lost Webber. "Hey, did you hear the report, Dick?" Fisher said. "They're saying Webber committed verbally to Duke, although we checked with his mother and she totally denies it." You're getting too nervous, Fisher. I really don't think he'll go out of state. I also think Michigan has moved ahead of Michigan State in the sweepstakes.

I think Michigan State made a major blunder when they turned in Minnesota for having the kid in the skybox, I really do. I think that's an example of a school getting a little carried away. I mean, if a team's blatantly breaking rules and they're blatantly laying out money and doing things of that nature, that's one thing. But if a kid goes into the president's box to watch a football game, I mean, give me a break. And I think Jud Heathcote has to pay because of an overzealous supporter.

Ohio State won tonight, 81–65, to improve its record to 20–1, but I thought they played poorly. If I were Randy Ayers, I'd be concerned that my guards are not playing like they did earlier.

I got a chance to talk to Lawrence Funderburke after the game. "Coach," he said, "don't put me on your coulda been, shoulda been, woulda been team." I said, "Lawrence, you mean you listen to my teams? I don't want to put you on that team. I want to put you on the All-Rolls-Royce team. You've got talent. You've wasted a whole year, and now it's time to change."

"Well, you know, I'm young, you make mistakes," he said.

"Yeah," I said, "but that excuse is running out. You're not as young as you think anymore. It's time to get on down and do it. You're coming to the end of the road. You have to make a decision what to do with your life. You've got size, intelligence, ability. Now you got to prove you can fit in as a total person, prove you can be an integral part of a team and stop blaming coaches and players."

When it happens in high school and college, it's time for a gut check. Time to look in the mirror. Everybody can't be wrong. I told him, "If you can't play for Randy Ayers, you can't play for anybody."

TUESDAY, FEBRUARY 12—

I received a call from a Syracuse writer after I got home today, and I didn't like what I heard. The school has been conducting an internal investigation of the basketball program, and apparently they've discovered all kinds of things. Jimmy Boeheim's going to go through a tough time. I don't know whether he can survive this or not. The Boeheim bashers are out in force. I wouldn't be surprised if the administration asks him to resign if there are NCAA violations involved. Jimmy has a low-key personality and is not charismatic like the Lou Carneseccas or

Ricky Pitinos. That makes him susceptible to a lot of criticism if he doesn't advance deep into the tournament. Television has become a monster. If you don't have one-liners, you'd better win big.

I also got a call from Rudy Martzke. He wanted to know if the fact that UNLV is the prohibitive favorite coming into the tournament will affect television ratings. He said John Madden has a theory that when you have a big team and everybody is chasing that big team, it makes for exciting television. But Rudy said this year's Super Bowl convinced Madden that he'd rather see two evenly matched teams.

Well, I think you're definitely looking at a monster team here in Vegas, but the best team doesn't always win the national championship. Take a look at Villanova–Georgetown in 1985. Somebody would have to pitch the perfect game to beat Vegas, but it can happen. Remember, in college basketball, it's a one-game shot. It's Russian roulette. You lose once and it's all over. It's not four out of seven à la NBA championships, the World Series, or the NHL playoffs. That's what makes it so special. In a one-game shot, Vegas can be beaten.

WEDNESDAY, FEBRUARY 13—

It's Valentine's Day tomorrow, so the first thing I did when I got up today was order a dozen roses for my girls and my wife. Then, of all things, I got a call from Jim Spadafore of the *Detroit News,* who was calling different celebrities to find out how they met their spouses.

"How did I meet her?" I began. "I showed my recruiting prowess, man. She shot me down on two occasions. I went to ask her to dance, with all my buddies sitting there around the table. I was embarrassed; it was worse than losing a twenty-point game and coming back in the locker room and facing the media. I had to come back to that table, and they jumped in my face like you couldn't believe. All the guys were laughing hysterically.

"She's told me since then what a nerd she thought I was. She said I kept trying to impress her by talking about my favorite team—the Knicks. But it was all Greek to her. She had never gone to a game in her life. I was throwing all these names like

Willis Reed and Clyde Frazier around, and she had no idea what I was talking about.

"But I wasn't giving up. She had the hot pants on, the white boots, the red hair, looked like dynamite. I walked over the third time and said, 'Got no chance, honey, you're going to have to dance with me.' Or maybe I said, 'I'm going to call a technical on you if you don't dance with me.'

"Finally, she did. She danced with me, and we've been married for twenty years."

Ohio State coach Randy Ayers led the Buckeyes to national prominence. He was also the recipient of my pre-season Dick Vitale Cupcake Award for easy early schedule.

Damon Bailey, last year's frosh phenom of Bobby Knight's Indiana Hoosiers.

Arizona's MVP of Big Apple NIT, Chris Mills.

Here I am with my buddy Jim Valvano. Who said all Italians are in the construction business?

GREG CAVA

I'm with Tark the Shark, Jerry Tarkanian. My feeling is that Tark belongs in the Hall of Fame, not the Hall of Shame.

I can shoot the rock, baby!

The one and only Robert Montgomery Knight...the General.

Billy Owens, the multitalented
three-position player of the
Syracuse Orangemen.

Rick Pitino, Kentucky's vibrant
leader, has rejuvenated Kentucky
basketball—the Cats are back!

Here I am with All-American Jimmy Jackson, Mr. Clutch of college basketball.

Lute Olson, Arizona's coach, has developed Lutemania in Wildcat country.

Hey, look who's shaking my hand! Shaquille O'Neal, the 3-S man— Super, Scintillating, Sensational.

Chicago's Michael Jordan, the nation's most electrifying performer, a genuine Rolls-Roycer.

CHICAGO BULLS

Three basketball junkies...Dick Paparo, America's No. 1 zebra, Sonny Vaccaro, Nike's entrepreneur, and yours truly.

Brian Watson of McDonald's, John Wooden, and Dicky V. at the McDonald's All-American game. Wooden is my choice as best coach of all time—he won ten national championships at UCLA.

Georgia Tech's brilliant Kenny Anderson. He's awesome, baby!

I can't believe it! My partner, Mike Patrick, is letting me get some A.T.— Air Time, baby!

Showtime at the Final Four. From left to right, here are Bob Ley, Mike Krzyzewski, Jim Valvano, and me.

This is basketball heaven, talking roundball at courtside with UNLV's Jerry Tarkanian and Mr. Showbiz himself, Bill Cosby.

Mike Krzyzewski, 1991 NABC Coach of the Year and Duke's all-time winningest coach, is a PTP'er who is a master at blending personalities into a team.

Georgetown's John Thompson. At 6' 11" and 260 pounds, he is without doubt the heavyweight champ of college coaching.

Keith Jackson, one of America's premier announcers, with yours truly. Whoa, Nelly, it's a jumpshot, baby!

Two basketball wackos sharing a laugh. Arizona State's Bill Frieder is a recruiting wizard.

North Carolina's Dean Smith, the Michelangelo of coaching, is a real artist at work and a genuine Hall of Famer.

Here I am with my favorite people, the fans, doing what I like best—watching and talking hoops.

CHAPTER 10

I can't believe Jimmy Boeheim. First, he called ESPN to complain about a quote I had in *USA Today* concerning the Syracuse situation. Then he went on the air on "SportsCenter" and asked ESPN to give me the ziggy.

I'm really upset that Boeheim wouldn't call me like a man. These guys never call you if you say five thousand great things about them, but you say one thing that they question and they're all over you. And besides, my quote wasn't that strong. It really gets to be a one-way street. I get criticized by many people for being an ambassador for the coaching fraternity. I can take the heat. I don't want to be Chadski. Not me. It's not my personality to be Rip City, U.S.A. All I want is for the coaches to be fair. In this case, Boeheim was not.

I told Martzke that Boeheim has been one of the most maligned coaches in college basketball, that he's doing an amazing job this year with a team that has limited bench strength. But I also said that with all the NCAA reform taking place today and the track record of many of his current and former players off the court, the ammunition now is there for the Boeheim bashers to come after him. I said it would not surprise me if the administration asks for his resignation if they find NCAA violations took place. That's just a gut feeling I have. I didn't say he should step down.

So what does Boeheim do? He calls my boss Mo Davenport to complain, then he goes on the air and says I should be fired. I'm very, very disappointed, James Boeheim. You call me up. Groan, moan, complain. Then, if you're not satisfied, take it to the next level. But it's difficult to respect a guy when he goes this route. Jimmy had to be fed an inaccurate quote that got him all riled up. I guess the heat is beginning to build, and I start to sense some panic going on within the program. The NCAA investigators are on campus, asking questions. And, with that internal investigation, there's bound to be some dirt being turned up. Otherwise, there is no way he would react like that.

Hey, Jimmy Boeheim, I want to really thank you. Maybe I should send you a dozen roses for Valentine's Day. I mean, I had to answer calls all day, Boeheim. My phone was ringing off the hook. It was radio stations, it was reporters, it was ESPN execs, everybody. Thanks a lot, Jimmy B. My wife is waiting to go to dinner and I'm on the phone, calling the Martzkes of the world. I'll remember you always on February 14. Maybe, from now on, I should call it St. Boeheim's Day.

FRIDAY, FEBRUARY 15—

Bobby Paschal called today. He's the coach at South Florida and he was all excited about Radenko Dobras, his three-point shooter from Yugoslavia, and his team's big win last night against Alabama-Birmingham, Gene Bartow's team. Bobby was telling me how they had things beginning to roll in their program. I'll always remember I did their first game in their new arena when they hosted Duke. In the stands that night was George Steinbrenner, the big Yankee guy. Bobby was trying to sell me on driving over for a game. Hey, I love it in the Tampa area. I would have driven over tonight to see Ray Charles in concert—Ray Charles, baby; he's one of my favorites. Mr. Pepsi. You got the right thing baby, uh-huh—but I've got to leave town early tomorrow for the Ohio State–Indiana rematch on Sunday.

SATURDAY, FEBRUARY 16—

Jimmy Boeheim and I have been trying to contact each other. He finally got back to me yesterday, and I think we got things straightened out. He really thought I was calling for him to be fired, but I told him that wasn't the case. We've been friends for so many years, and I've been one of his biggest supporters. I mentioned time and time again on ESPN that he allows guys to play and doesn't overcoach like so many people do in today's game. In fact his flexibility, I believe, plays a great role in why his players succeed at the next level. Think about it. Rony Seikaly of Miami was voted Most Improved Player in the league two years ago. Sherman Douglas made the All-Rookie team. Derrick Coleman was the Rookie of the Year. Billy Owens may be the No. 1 pick this year. Hey, wait a minute. With all that talent, how come there are no championship banners flying in the Carrier Dome? What am I doing praising you, Boeheim?

The conversation ended with him saying, "I'll just scream at you a little bit when I see you, and we'll have a little fun." Chill out, Jimmy baby.

The Garf called last night, too. He said he was in the process of selling fifty-one percent of his Five-Star camps to an assistant coach. I knew there had to be something funny about that. He wouldn't tell me who it is, but I know who he is, Garf. It's your buddy, the guy you love down at Wake Forest, Dave Odom's assistant, Jerry Wainwright.

The reason Garf's doing this is so he can continue to bring in college coaches to teach at the camp. Garf is in a real battle. Under the new rules, coaches now can only work at camps run by representatives from NCAA schools, people such as Wainwright. And even that is subject to change. The NCAA feels, and so do a lot of coaches, that coaches employed by camps have a tremendous recruiting advantage. That's why a proposal is in the works to have the NCAA sponsor all camps. Spearheading this drive is George Raveling of the University of Southern Cal. It is getting really ugly. Name-calling and personal vendettas are being launched along the way. In fact, Raveling has broken his relationship with Sonny Vaccaro of Nike. For people in the basketball-know, Raveling was Vaccaro's best man at his wedding. Now they are not even on speaking terms because of this scenario. Those camps would employ only high school coaches and would be the only place where college coaches could observe players over the summer. This proposal would wipe out all private camps—Nike and Five-Star . . . all of them.

I know Garf won't want to hear this, but if I was still coaching, I wouldn't like guys like Wainwright and Pete Gillen living with prospects for a week. I think that gives them a tremendous advantage. Why not just use high school coaches like Bobby Hurley of St. Anthony's in New Jersey.

One last note: I got a kick out of *Sports Illustrated*'s dream team for the Olympics. Chuck Daly, the new Olympic coach, was on the cover along with Magic Johnson, Michael Jordan, Patrick Ewing, Charles Barkley, and Karl Malone. Take those pros and throw in some new kids like Shaquille O'Neal, Kenny Anderson, and Larry Johnson, and you're on your way toward reclaiming the gold medal. We're looking at Blowout City, U.S.A.

My man Al McGuire can't be serious when he tells Rudy Martzke an all-star team wouldn't beat a European team. I can't coach a lick, but I could go on the road with that team and wipe out the competition. That's a better lock than Yale. Before you call, Garf, I know it's one of your lines.

I can just see those Soviet guys talking to themselves when the Magic Man comes down, kicks and dishes it to Jordan, and Jordan dumps it inside to Ewing. I mean, they'll be talking to themselves. "Comrade, what's going on here? I can't believe it. Comrade, please, let's get a TO, baby, like that guy Comrade Vitale says."

It'll be just as bad as what happened a couple years ago when the Soviets came over here to play the Milwaukee Bucks in the McDonald's Open. The night before the game, the country was making the shift to standard time and the Soviet coach, Alexander Gomelsity, had his players get up at two in the morning to move the clocks ahead. I knew then they were in big, big trouble.

SUNDAY, FEBRUARY 17—

It's always a big event when Bobby Knight comes back to his alma mater, but today it was even bigger than usual. Ohio State, 21-1 and No. 2 in the country, was hosting Indiana, 22-2 and No. 4, in a game that was likely to decide the Big 10 championship. St. John's Arena was crawling with national media. And I'll tell you one thing, it was one of the most exciting college basketball games I've ever been a part of in my twelve years of broadcasting.

Ohio State won, 97-95, in double overtime, and the game

had all the drama you could ask for. Damon Bailey, the highly publicized freshman player, starred in front of the national TV audience with 32 points, and Calbert Cheaney added 26 for the Hoosiers. Jimmy Jackson (Mr. Clutch) led Ohio State with 30 points and 11 rebounds, and moved from forward to point guard after Mark Baker got hurt early in the game. Jackson also made the big play at the end to win it. He took the ball in a clear-out situation, ran the clock down to two seconds, drew a double-team, then dumped it off inside to Treg Lee, who hit the game-winning five-footer.

The environment was just incredible—St. John's has become a real rock-and-roll place. One of the reasons for that was Gary Williams, who really got things going before he left for Maryland by getting the students seats at courtside. I was teasing Keith Jackson about it during the game. "Come on, Keith, baby," I said. "You have to admit this is better than football. Football can't be this good."

Keith not only disagreed, he got me back. During one of the time-outs, he placed on my bald dome an Arkansas Razorback hat, the one he had promised for picking the Razorbacks to beat UNLV. I'm sure he got the hat from his good buddy Frank Broyles, the former football coach and current AD at Arkansas who used to work with him at ABC.

MONDAY, FEBRUARY 18—

The Chris Webber recruiting sweepstakes is really heating up. That's all everyone was talking about when I arrived in Ann Arbor for the Michigan–Purdue game tonight.

After speaking with his father, Macy, I really think Webber will stay local and choose between Michigan and Michigan State. And I think a lot will depend on which school has the best recruiting class. "Chris wants to play in an environment where you have other outstanding players and he has a chance to win," his father said. "He doesn't want to be in an environment where he's got to carry the load and be the man, be the star."

That being the case, you'd have to say that Michigan is leading. But before Webber makes his final decision, his father said the family wants to see who Steve Fisher hires to replace Mike Boyd, who left the Michigan staff in November to become the head coach at Cleveland State. If it's Perry Watson, currently the head coach at Detroit's Southwestern High and a close friend of the family, I think it's over for everyone else.

Watson is a big name in the Motor City. He's won the Michigan state championship the last two years and has all kinds of players. He coached Antoine Joubert and has two great ones this year—Jalen Rose and Vashon Leonard.

I spoke with Jud Heathcote today too. He said his assistants have been on pins and needles about Webber, but he didn't agree that he was falling behind. He also denied turning in Minnesota to the NCAA. "The NCAA came to us because some TV station found out about it," he explained. "I'm not going to turn them in on something like that. I would have just simply picked up the phone and called up Clem at the end of the year. I don't think Minnesota's going to get him anyway. That's what I told my administration."

Webber was sitting at midcourt tonight, the big superstar. I talked to him at halftime and everyone was wondering what he said. Then he got all the Michigan people really nervous when he left before Purdue finally won in double overtime.

"He just told me he's going to Michigan State, so don't worry about it," I said, straight-faced. "He'll be back here. He loves Crisler Arena, but the next time you see him, he'll be wearing a Michigan State uniform."

I really was kidding, you know. All Webber really told me was that he's getting frustrated with all the heavy recruiting. My gut feeling is, it's Michigan. I mean, they're going it without you, Friends. Fisher proving he can do it without you. Only teasing. The first big battle in the state for a super of this caliber was won by Michigan State with Magic. The law of averages could be against you, Jud.

TUESDAY, FEBRUARY 19—

After the game last night, I had a chance to talk with Fisher about Perry Watson. Perry makes an awful lot of money right now—it comes to about $85,000 when you throw in all his extras: he heads a summer program in Detroit, works the Nike camp, does speaking engagements. But Perry's going to have to give in a little bit, because Michigan will open doors for him.

Perry has to realize, at age forty, that if he wants to get into college coaching, he's got to make a move and not worry about the finances. Besides, I think Michigan could put together a package that will excite him. I think he can look at about a $60,000 salary, plus another $10,000 for a summer camp. Throw in a car, and before long he's right there banging on the door. I don't think money will become a problem. That name "Michigan" is a big entrée into the coaching world.

Heck, I remember leaving my high school job and taking a pay cut to go to Rutgers for $11,000 a year back in 1971 because I knew that was what I wanted to do. The dream of going straight from high school to a head coaching job in college is all but dead. I know, Gerry Faust did it at Notre Dame and Bob Wade did it at Maryland, but those days are over.

WEDNESDAY, FEBRUARY 20—

Today I took my wife and daughter Sherri to Duke, where Sherri is making an unofficial visit. She is being recruited by Duke, Notre Dame, North Carolina, Arizona, UCLA, and Indiana, and she wanted to spend a day with Susan Sommerville, one of Duke's star players, who grew up with Sherri back in Michigan.

Mike Krzyzewski greeted Sherri at the gym at about 2 P.M. Mike is one great salesman, the way he promotes Duke athletics and its academics and way of life. His daughter is a sophomore at the school. Sherri was really impressed. She absolutely loved listening to Coach K. In fact, Sherri told me if she were a guy who was heavily recruited, she would want to play for Coach Krzyzewski. Mike, you've won my whole family over.

Hey, my wife got some pub today. James Brown of CBS, the former Harvard star who played with Kenny Wolfe, one of our award-winning producers at ABC, was in town to do a special on me for a local Washington, D.C., station, and he interviewed Lorraine.

Man, she didn't want to give up the mike. I think she likes being on camera, just like her hubby.

In the evening, we watched Duke play North Carolina State at Cameron Indoor Stadium. There I was, surrounded by Cameron Crazies—it was one of the few times this year I got to sit in the stands at a college game—and it was a wild experience.

Every time Chris Corchiani touched the ball, the students would chant, "CBA, CBA." I said, "Don't bet on it, baby. Don't bet on it." Then they were getting all over the State players, chanting, "If you can't go to college, go to State." The fans were absolutely bananasville.

Duke won, 72–56, in a revenge game. Grant Hill made some big plays, Brian Davis held Monroe to four points in the second half, and Hurley was as steady as can be. He really bothered Corchiani all night, made him work for everything he got. You look at that club, it's just so balanced and deep.

THURSDAY, FEBRUARY 21—

This morning I drove over to Cameron to do a one-on-one with Krzyzewski for Sunday night's "SportsCenter." Mike seems legitimately happy to be at Duke—he told me he turned down the Iowa State job, saying yes to Duke—but there was a time last spring when he seriously considered moving on to the NBA.

Krzyzewski was really upset last year that his three seniors weren't graduating. He felt he wasn't communicating his concepts to them. So, when Dave Gavitt asked him if he would be interested in the Boston Celtics job, he listened. All he had to do was say yes and the job was his. "I thought I could have been a good pro coach," he said. "I just needed time to adjust."

But then Mike talked to Tom Butters, his AD, and Butters told him he was being too tough on himself. Krzyzewski loves Tom Butters, and he said that's when he realized he had done the best he could.

"How many places can you work for somebody who ends up being your best friend?" Krzyzewski said. "I've got a great marriage here. There's no way I'm leaving Duke for any coaching job on the college level. This is where I want to be unless there is a change in the administration."

You can't help but be impressed with Krzyzewski and what he's done here. You should see one of his practices. I mean, it's unbelievable, the organization. Mike breaks each practice into phases. If they've played the night before, the first phase is a review of the game. Next, he shows the players film of the team they're going to play, either game films or highlights. Then he takes them out on the floor, and he explains each different sequence of the practice before they go through it. I mean, this guy is just so detailed and so organized. No wonder our producers love going to watch Duke work out.

During the Big Apple NIT, I went to their practice the day after they beat Marquette. He was going over the stats with the players and he came to Brian Davis, who had started. He said, "Davis, you played twenty-nine minutes, you shot poorly and you had one rebound. Now, I'm not troubled by you shooting poorly, because people can have bad days shooting. But out of twenty-nine minutes, you weren't active, you didn't rebound. That is totally *unacceptable* in a Duke uniform." The next game, against Boston College, Davis was removed from the starting lineup and spent a lot of time on the bench with the assistants, Peter Gaudet, Tommy Amaker, and Mike Brey. Krzyzewski had sent the message loud and clear: You don't do it the Duke way—hustle, scrap, and play with tenacity—you don't play.

Mike does a great job delegating responsibility to his assistants. And Gaudet is one guy I really respect. He's a former head coach at West Point, and he's one guy I'd have to take a long look at if I were an AD. All of these former head coaches who are now assistants want to prove their previous employers made a major error when they let them go.

Right now, if I had to pick the five best coaches in the nation—my All–John Woodens, my All-Rolls-Royce coaching five, based on graduating players, keeping out of trouble with the NCAA, and winning consistently at testing time—Krzyzewski definitely would have to be in there. The others would be Lute "GQ" Olson, Dean "Mr. Michelangelo" Smith, John "The Man" Thompson, and the General, Robert Montgomery Knight. Now, of course, I'll immediately get phone calls from the guys I left out. Please don't call me, Rollie Massimino. You're No. 6, and so is my man Jerry Tarkanian. Obviously, if you're talking pure coaching, Tark would have to be in there, but you can't really do it with all the investigations and everything, not with the criteria we're using.

If there's any rap at all against Krzyzewski, it's his failure to win a national championship. He's been to the Final Four four times now, and he still hasn't won the big dance. Some people are starting to call him the Bud Grant of college coaching. But he's as honest about that as he is about everything else.

"I'm proud of what we've accomplished," he told me as we wrapped up our interview. "Sure I want to win. I want to win just as much as the next guy, but the fact is, I can't look at my program and can't look at my kids and think that we're losers because we've come back with silver instead of gold.

"I want to be remembered as a guy who did it in an honest way, did it with integrity and did it consistently in a positive way, gave people a program they can be proud of. I want my players to get the maximum out of their college education as students and as athletes. If I've achieved all of that, then I'll feel that I've been a winner and will have made a tremendous contribution to the profession."

FRIDAY, FEBRUARY 22—

I got a call today from Roland Lazenby, a contributor to the *Sporting News.* He's doing a piece on the five most powerful people in college basketball, and he wants to put me and Billy Packer in there with Dick Schultz of the NCAA, Neal Pilson of CBS, and Sonny Vaccaro of Nike and Tom Odjakian.

"You two guys have really been very powerful," he said of Packer and me. "People react to whatever you say." I said, "Wow, I can't believe we carry that kind of power, not like the guys who carry the checks."

I told him Tom Odjakian is a great choice. Many basketball fans don't know the name Tom Odjakian, the program director of ESPN. O.J. puts together close to two hundred matchups for cable. He's the guy who brings you all that hoops smorgasbord every winter.

SATURDAY, FEBRUARY 23—

You talk about expectations, you talk about spoiling people. I flew into Tucson for the Duke–Arizona game tomorrow, and I couldn't believe what I saw when I picked up the paper.

I mean, it was incredible. There were several negative letters to the editor about Lute Olson and his team. One guy said Lute's ego was too big, that he's always griping about officials whenever he loses on the road. Another guy tore the team apart in every aspect, saying that the huge front line hasn't dominated, that the guards can't shoot, and that Chris Mills has been a major disappointment.

Wait a minute. Arizona is 21–5, and Lute has won 60 in a row at home, plays a real tough schedule, no cupcakes. I mean, give me a break. What do these people expect? People who complain about that are off the wall. If anything, Lute has spoiled people. Whenever you win, a large number will follow you in a positive way, but other people take shots. If I'm picking my All–Frank Lloyd Wright team architects of programs, Lute has got to be on it, along with guys like Pitino and Cremins.

SUNDAY, FEBRUARY 24—

Another great game, another overtime thriller. Arizona kept its streak alive, 103–96, but needed a great performance from Brian Williams to do it. Williams had only 4 points at halftime and ended up with 26, plus 10 rebounds.

Duke had the game won in regulation, but didn't execute in typical Duke fashion and let it get away. The big mistake was a turnover under the basket on a reverse pass by Christian Laettner to Grant Hill. Then, in overtime, Laettner got fatigued from battling those giants all day and Sean Rooks just took over.

After the game, I jumped in a car and headed for Las Cruces, New Mexico, for UNLV–New Mexico State tomorrow night. It was a five-hour trip through the wild, wild West. It was unreal, the things I learned on that trip. I even saw a coyote run right across the road. Unbelievable, coyotes, man. We were out in the sticks out there. I thought we were going to see Roy Rogers and Trigger come flying through.

MONDAY, FEBRUARY 25—

The front desk woke me up today to tell me the mayor of Las Cruces wanted to present me with a key to the city at a special luncheon. Man, that is the big time. Eat your hearts out, McGuire and Packer. I got a key to the city of Las Cruces. So what if you got a key to the city of New York! This is big-time, man. Aggie land. They even gave me a proclamation:

"Whereas the people in the East better start giving us some publicity. Oh, baby, we need some publicity . . ."

I went from there to watch Vegas practice, and the players were looser than ever. As soon as they saw me, they started chanting, "Dick's a bleep," for picking Arkansas to beat them. Tark wasn't in nearly such great spirits, though. He was concerned about the game. UNLV lost here last year, and Tark says New Mexico State has some great athletes this year.

I'll tell you, the Tark, he worries about everyone. I mean, he would worry if he had to play five guys from an old-age home. But Tark can fool only so many people. Just last weekend, Vegas hosted Cal-Irvine on Senior Night and Tark sent out all six of his seniors for the opening tip. He took the technical, spotted Irvine a four-point lead, and then went on to crush them, 114–86.

Everyone wants to beat Goliath. It was a wild scene here. Before the game, they actually had a Shark dinner, where they served shark meat. And the fans were parading around an artificial shark at the game. But Vegas was Vegas, and they won easily, 86–74. I could tell Jerry's wife, Lois, who was sitting in the stands, loved every minute of it. Lois, a member of my All-Wives team, along with Bobbi Olson of Arizona, Micki Krzyzewski of Duke, Janice Frieder of Arizona State, and Pat Keady of Purdue. Battlin' tooth and nail for their men.

I'm not sure Tark enjoyed it, though. He's got trouble with the NCAA again—on three fronts.

Before their game against Nevada-Reno, Tark said he tried to motivate the team by showing them what had been written in the local paper. He immediately got a letter from the NCAA saying that if he bought papers for the whole team, it was illegal. Tark is really furious about it. He said he had one paper and passed it around to the team. "That's the kind of harassment we're dealing with," he said. "They're out to get us constantly."

Secondly, there's the Greg Anthony situation. The NCAA recently told him he had to give up his share of his T-shirt business or forfeit his eligibility. Tark said Anthony was thinking about seeking an injunction and filing a lawsuit.

I can understand what the NCAA did. Situations such as this could become a major problem across America—kids giving up their scholarships and going to work for alums if they're permitted. But I feel the NCAA should have handled it in the postseason instead of bringing it up now.

On top of all that, the NCAA is investigating Larry Johnson and George Ackles, two of Tark's starters, for room-service bills they ran up during their recruiting visits. Tark said the total was $25 to $30 maximum and that both guys made restitution. But the NCAA is threatening to revoke their eligibility. I think it's time to revise the NCAA rule book. In the case of a recruit who visits the campus, stays in a hotel, and orders room service and a movie for less than $25, that seems reasonable to comprehend.

Some of this stuff is just totally absurd. Maybe, as Tark said, winning 22 straight this season in the face of constant struggling with the NCAA is what makes this team so special. In Vegas' battle with the NCAA, people have to understand that the enforcement staff doesn't make the rules. David Berst and his staff are simply employed to investigate charges and enforce rules placed in front of them.

TUESDAY, FEBRUARY 26—

Today, on the flight home, a guy tried to tell me he feels sorry for Chris Webber because he's under so much pressure. I think by the time I got through with him he might have been sorry he ever brought up the subject.

Chris Webber could pick up the phone today and go anywhere in America. Pressure is when you have to ask yourself: "What am I going to do with my life." "Who wants me?" You want to know about pressure? Just look at me. You had to feel sorry for me, man, when I was back in school in East Rutherford, New Jersey, in 1958. I'm, like, 5-11½, I've got one eye, my other eye goes to the side, I'm messed up like you can't believe academically. I've got, like, a C average. All I wanted to do was go see the Yankees play, go see the Knicks play, go see Seton Hall play basketball games. I mean, I didn't want to study.

All of a sudden it's my senior year and I start realizing I've got to turn it around. But, hey, baby, it's too late. I'm sending applications and I'm getting rejection, rejection, rejection. I finally get into Roanoke College, but I was in love with a girl named Joanne Smith and I missed her so much that I came back home after one week. I begged and pleaded to get into Seton Hall—the Paterson division—and eventually got a degree. So, baby, feel sorry for the Dick Vitales of the world. The zeroes. That's pressure, baby, when you don't know where you're going with your life.

Case closed. If I don't stop now, I'm going to go bananas. Me? I never go bananas, do I? I'm not a wacko, am I?

WEDNESDAY, FEBRUARY 27—

This was one long day in the sky, baby. First I flew into Philadelphia for a speech to the folks at Unisys. Then it was back on a plane to Detroit for Indiana–Michigan State tomorrow night.

The Washington Speakers' Bureau arranged the whole deal in Philly. I came in dressed like a coach, with my sweats and Air Jordans, and laid a pep talk on them. I was Nike, top to bottom. They must have been impressed; Doug Morgan, the head of sales there, invited me back for four more sales meetings.

Whenever I do motivational speeches, I reflect back on my days as a sixth-grade teacher in 1971, dreaming and dreaming and dreaming. Now, I'm standing up there, addressing leading execs. My mom must be proud. She's up in heaven. She and my dad only had an elementary education, but they had a doctorate in love. It just goes to show you, if I can succeed, anybody can.

When I got to the Motor City, I checked into the hotel, turned on the tube, and caught the great news from the Persian Gulf: They laid down the guns. It's over, baby. It was beautiful, listening to General Schwarzkopf, I'll tell you. He reminds me of a football coach, this guy. Bo. Move over, Bobby Knight. This is the real General. This is the real McCoy. Five star.

I'm so happy it's over. This will make it a lot easier to do some promos for MTV, which is running a call-in contest for spring break. They want me to introduce the artists—say things like Mariah Carey and M.C. Hammer are PTP'ers—and comment on the matchups, tell folks that it's an M & M'er when Hammer goes up against Isaac, then invite the kids down to party at Daytona Beach.

Rock and roll, baby.

THURSDAY, FEBRUARY 28—

I read this morning that Michigan State is going to give Bobby Knight a special plaque tonight for making the Basketball Hall of Fame. I hope Bobby can stay awake long enough to accept it. Late starting time, you know.

Hey, I heard a rumor. Tell me it's not true. After Indiana lost to Iowa, they say Knight had the team in the gym until about one in the morning. I wonder how it will affect them academically?

Only teasing, General. I know I shouldn't be joking around with you when you've lost two of your last three. I actually did hear that Knight, whose team is 23–4, kept his assistants on the floor until four in the morning after one of those losses to go over late-game situations.

How bad have things been for the Hoosiers lately?

"I've lost interest right now," Knight said to me at practice today. "I am so disgusted and aggravated. This is not Indiana basketball. I don't want to take anything away from Ohio State or Iowa, but we were so dumb at the end of those games. We made fouls, we stopped the clock . . ."

"Well, Damon Bailey played great against Ohio State," I said, trying to be cheery.

"Great!" Knight shot back. "Dick, he scored, but he made a silly foul, got beat defensively. Those are the things you've got to be able to do if you want to be a complete player, if you want to be a winner."

You talk about pressure. Bailey went scoreless against Iowa. His mind has been preoccupied since he recently learned that his fifteen-year-old sister, Courtney, has leukemia. Could you blame him? It's tough thinking about basketball when you have problems at home. I'm surprised the kid has performed as well as he has.

The big story tonight—it far overshadowed Indiana's 62–56 victory—was a guest appearance at the game by Chris Webber. Chris is really fed up with the whole recruiting process and took shots today in print at the schools still pursuing him. He was quoted as saying that he had narrowed his choices to Michigan, Michigan State, and Detroit, but that "if Michigan and Michigan State keep feuding, I might just shock everyone and go to U of D."

"First, I loved all the attention," he told Mitch Albom in the *Detroit Free Press.* "But now I just wish it would stop. I get fifty letters a week. I never read them anymore. They're so phony. I used to take every phone call, but now I don't even call people back."

Webber has been recruited since eighth grade. Somebody once offered his dad $20,000 to send him to a high school in Indiana. He says he gets calls from coaches who don't even know how to spell his name. One recruiter told him, "Man, I heard you were religious. Well, I was just thinking about you. We sang a hymn in church, and I was thinking how beautiful it would be if the Lord . . . if you would come to our school."

I mean, it's incredible. He said he went to a Michigan State game recently and the students began chanting his name, "Webber, Webber, Webber," at the Breslin Center.

He said, in one article in the *Detroit News,* "The assistant coach sent word out to one of the student trainers to tell the fans, and they started chanting my name. It was so weak, it was incredible. I went there with Jalen Rose, and Jalen tapped me on the shoulder and said, 'Look at the bench.' There's this guy, maybe a student manager, as soon as he saw us, he walked over and whispered something to another student and the next thing you know, they're chanting my name. It's so phony. I hate it."

Webber said they did the same thing at the Michigan game, trying to imitate the Duke fans.

"I feel like a prisoner of basketball," Webber said. "I haven't gone on vacation during the school year in so long. A lot of my friends go to Florida and stuff, but we just have to go to practice. I play in all these leagues, play about two hundred games a year."

Macy Webber, Chris's dad, told the *News* that he really worried about two things—girls and coaches. "The girls, oh they whisper in his ear, say something sweet and then wait for his big NBA money to roll in. But, the coaches—heck, they may be worse. They'll say anything to get my son. It's a dirty business."

"I learned a lot about some of these schools, the ones with so-called clean reputations," Chris said. "One school that everyone thinks is so clean, but I know for a fact that they do the same things that everyone else does. Maybe it's not the coaching staff; maybe it's the alumni or something. But the NCAA won't touch them. They'd rather go after UNLV."

Oooh, those are strong statements from a seventeen-year-old kid. I guess he'll get a call about that one from the NCAA, wanting to know the name of this school. Chrissy, baby, you've just opened up a can of worms by suggesting an unnamed school offered you illegal inducements, then refusing to name that school. We need more kids to come forward. I don't want to hear about situations like Jeff Ruland, where the guy comes out ten years later and claims he was offered illegal inducements at Iona. He put the blast on Jimmy Valvano and his staff, and that really disturbed me, since he didn't come forward when these so-called illegal offers were being made. These high school seniors are not little kids. Stand up at a press conference and name names.

I ran into Chris after the game in the State locker room. "Chris," I said, "all those write-ups today. Unbelievable coverage."

And, he felt kind of bad about it, because he said everybody who read those stories felt he came off like a major attitude problem.

I tried to lay a little advice on him. I said, "You don't gain anything making statements like that. Try to follow guys like Magic and Michael and Mr. Robinson. You're too classy a kid. You come from a classy home where there's love, direction, and you come across in the articles as being spoiled. I've had a number of people tell me that and I've tried to defend you, because I know you a little bit and you're just not that way."

He sort of agreed, and thanked me.

CHAPTER 11

It's March 1—the kickoff to March Madness, baby. It's rock-and-roll time, it's showtime. Eat your heart out, all you football lovers, hockey lovers, baseball lovers. This is the best time of the year—the countdown for high school state championships, the countdown for the collegiate championships. Yes, March Madness is here. I can smell it in the air.

I'm in St. Louis to do some clinics for the "Say No to Drugs" campaign that the Missouri Valley Conference is putting on, and it has been a typically wacky day. I spoke at three different places and in between caught the eight-nine–place game between Drake and Illinois State. By 4 P.M., I was drenched, baby, I was perspiring. I had to run to my room to catch a shower. But I loved it. I loved running into coaches like Tony Barone of Creighton, Rudy Washington of Drake, and Tates Locke of Indiana State.

Talk about a guy who made the most of a second chance. Tates won eight of his last nine to finish 14–13 and was selected Coach of the Year in the Valley. There's never been much doubt about Tates being a good coach. He's the one who gave Bob Knight his start by hiring him as an assistant at West Point. Then Tates moved on and got involved in a recruiting fiasco at Clemson. He even wrote a book about it. But Bobby never forgot what Tates did for him. Knight had enough loyalty to hire him as an assistant at Indiana—the same thing he's doing for Norm Ellenberger now—and then helped him get the job at Indiana State. Locke was clearly at the top of the world.

Then, as I was leaving, I ran into a guy at the opposite end of the spectrum—Bradley coach Stan Albeck. Stan is in the last year of his contract, and he's been taking a lot of heat from the local media. He's a Bradley graduate and he wants to stay, but there are a lot of rumors that the school will make a change if he doesn't make a splash at the postseason tournament.

"People don't realize the pressure we've had trying to recruit because of the NCAA probation we inherited from the previous regime," Albeck said. "We couldn't even leave the office. We have a great player right now in Peoria, a guard named Howard Nathan who's Top 20 in the country, and we couldn't even go out of the office to recruit him. He signed with De Paul. People don't understand how difficult that is."

I hate to see coaches on the bubble like that. Coaching is the greatest job in the world when you're 25–3, 24–4. You're in the NCAA Tournament, the big dance. But, boy, is it the pits when you're, like, 6–20 and you're on the bottom and everybody's at your jugular. In coaching it's "Baby, what have you done for me today?"

SATURDAY, MARCH 2—

All I wanted to do today was hang out in the lobby, man, become All-Lobby. I'm back in Columbus, Ohio, the Michigan State–Ohio State game tomorrow, and they're having a body-building contest here at the hotel. I said to one guy, "Look at these bodies! Is Arnold Schwarzenegger here?" He said, "Dick, are you serious? Is he here? He *is* here." I couldn't believe it. Arnold Schwarzenegger is definitely here, along with Lou Ferrigno, Mr. Incredible Hulk himself. Gregory Hines, the dancer, is here too. His brother's in the competition. I want their autographs. I want to take a picture with Arnold, make like I know him. Forget about Arnold. Why can't Maria Shriver be here? I want to pose for a picture with Maria.

I was joking with Kim Belton, our ABC producer. Talk about hard bodies. I wanted to know if he was going to work our game or enter the contest.

I finally had to leave so I could catch the shootarounds, but I had fun there, too. Ohio State came in first, and I immediately jumped all over Steve Snapp, their SID.

"You're in big trouble, baby," I said. "I have to reveal on the top of the show that Ohio State is going on probation. There's a souvenir store here in town that had 'Jimmy Jackson Day' on its marquee two weeks ago. I got letters from fans in Indiana who remember when their school got all kinds of heat after Steve Alford posed for a sorority calendar for charity. They're sending this to the NCAA. You guys are going to be in big trouble."

Snapp got defensive like you wouldn't believe. He was all shook up. "No, no, no," he told me. "We've got that all cleared. We can't control the store, what they put up on the marquee. We have nothing to do with that." I finally had to tell him I was only teasing.

I don't know why I love to tease guys, but I got on Jimmy Jackson's case. I said, "Jimmy, I'm gonna pick my All-America team tomorrow. Who would you pick?"

Paul Brasseau, the assistant coach, came over and said, "Well, you got to go with Shaquille, Jimmy, Larry Johnson, Kenny Anderson, and Stacey Augmon."

"Wait a minute," I said. "What about a guy from Syracuse named Billy Owens? How do you leave him off at small forward? You got to go Owens, Augmon, and Jackson. Who do you take? C'mon, Jimmy, who do you take?"

Jimmy looked at me with a sheepish grin. He's such a nice, classy kid. He was so embarrassed. I ended up making Augmon my sixth man.

Then Michigan State came in, and Jud Heathcote started breaking down my shot. He was talking about my elbow, flexing my knees, following through as I release the ball. Jud, you're teaching me to shoot? Have you seen your team's shooting percentage this year? They can't shoot the ball, Jud.

As usual, the topic eventually turned to Chris Webber. A lot of Michigan boosters are upset because when the Pistons played the Lakers recently, Webber spent twenty minutes in the Lakers' locker room talking with Magic. "Yeah," Heathcote said. "He also talked to a bunch of other people in that locker room. We have no control over what he does when he walks in a pro locker room."

That's one of the crazy new rules. An alumnus of a school is not allowed to talk to a prospect. You tell me how you're going to legislate that.

I think Jud is losing ground, though, ever since the wife of one of the members of the board of directors snapped a picture of Webber in the skybox at Minnesota and then turned it over to the NCAA.

SUNDAY, MARCH 3—

I picked up the paper today and I felt like a human dart board. All these Ohio State fans were taking shots at me in the letters to the editor. They're tired of hearing about the General, they're upset because I don't give the Buckeyes enough credit. Are they serious? I only picked Randy Ayers as my Coach of the Year, picked Jimmy Jackson as a first-team All-America, put Mark Baker on my first-team All-Big 10.

Even the game couldn't calm these people down. The Buckeyes clinched their first Big 10 title since 1971 this afternoon by a point, 75–74, when Jamal Brown hit a free throw with one second left. Jimmy Jackson did what he had to do—scored 20 points and grabbed 10 rebounds, but the Buckeyes shot only 42 percent and looked flat. All I kept hearing as I left the arena was: "Are we a cupcake now, baby?" "What do you think of us now, Dickie V?" "Bring on UNLV."

Bring on UNLV? You don't want that, baby. There's no way you want a taste of that. It's been struggle city at Ohio State recently even though the Buckeyes are 25–1. Struggle at the buzzer with Minnesota; struggle at the buzzer with Wisconsin; beat Indiana in double overtime; buzzer beater here with Michigan State. Get the paramedics, man.

MONDAY, MARCH 4—

My guy Tom McNeely was due in here this morning. We were going to tape my "Fast Break" series in the backyard, then go over to Bradenton to watch the Pirates work out.

McNeely's plane was delayed out of Boston. Just my luck. I turned on the news and there's bulletins everywhere. Jimmy Leyland got into a big battle with Barry Bonds during photo day. Bonds apparently went berserk with the PR department after they stopped him from taking pictures with a friend because he refused to cooperate with anybody else in the media. Bonds went off, using language that would make Bobby Knight blush, and the cameras filmed it all. Leyland stormed out of left field and let Bonds have it, let him know who was running the show.

It's about time for Barry to sit down and come to grips with himself, because he's blowing away a lot of people and losing a lot of respect in the process. I mean, word is filtering out that the guy's immature, babyish. I've always had a lot of fun with Barry, but I don't like the rumblings I hear. I think he needs to have a long sit-down with my neighbor, Mr. Class, Bobby Bonilla.

TUESDAY, MARCH 5—

McNeely and I really made the rounds today, man. We saw the Pirates in Bradenton, then drove over to Sarasota to see the Orioles and the White Sox.

The highlight was Pirate City, where I got to pick up a glove and warm up on the sideline. I was in heaven, baby. All the coaches said they liked my form. I lost my pop, though. I used to be one heck of a Little League pitcher.

Before that, Jimmy Leyland was trying to sell me on Coastal Carolina as a dark horse in the tournament. "You heard it from me first," he was screaming. "They've got two NBA players. I'm telling you, Dick. They're going to make some noise."

Coastal Carolina, you guys ought to invite Leyland down there as a speaker. I mean, he loves your school. That's all he was talking about. He gave the school more PR than your PR staff. What are they, the Chanticleers? What a nickname.

I wonder if Leyland knows this one: Coastal Carolina is coached by Russ Bergman, who was a backup at LSU in the days of Pistol Pete Maravich. Once, he came into the game for Maravich and the crowd started going bananas. Bergman thought he was getting a standing ovation.

Uh, not quite, Russ, baby. They were cheering for the Pistol.

We visited with Jeff Torborg, the manager of the White Sox, whom I've known since he was an undergrad at Rutgers, then stopped off at the Orioles' camp and talked with Cal Ripken, Jr. He was in the batting cage, taking some cuts. Calvin's a big hoops fanatic. The guy has a full court with two glass backboards in his backyard.

"You ought to come up and see the Ripken Dome," he told

me. It's amazing how many of these guys love their hoops. Especially Ben McDonald, the Orioles' young pitching phenom who once played for Dale Brown at LSU. Today, Ben was all upset over reports that Shaquille O'Neal had suffered a hairline fracture.

All the players were ribbing him, chanting, "Bye, bye, LSU."

All McDonald wanted to know was whether I thought Shaquille would leave for the pros.

"Suppose somebody offered you $25 mill," I asked him, "would you leave?"

Then I told him I heard he was coming back to school.

WEDNESDAY, MARCH 6—

Eat your hearts out, Packer and McGuire. You guys might be big in the Big Apple, but I'm in Monroe, Louisiana, today.

And why am I here? The champions of the six lowest-rated conferences now have go through play-in games to get into the NCAA Tournament, and I'm doing the game tonight between Northeast Louisiana from the Southland Conference and Florida A & M from the Mid-Eastern Atlantic Conference.

This is the first year for the play-ins, and even though each of the teams will receive a full share of tournament revenue, I wish there were a better way. I really think this system stigmatizes a conference, because the NCAA notifies the leagues involved a year in advance and coaches have to carry through recruiting. Why can't the NCAA notify teams prior to the start of the tournament based on what they did this year rather than in the past?

The trip here took forever. I flew from Sarasota to Memphis, then took a puddle jumper that stopped in Greenville, Mississippi, for thirty minutes before arriving in Monroe. It was scary.

I'll tell you something else that was a real trip. I didn't realize this until today, but I used to write all the time to Mike Vining, Northeast Louisiana's coach. "I used to get so much mail from you, Dick," he said when I met him at practice. "When I was coaching in high school and you were at the University of Detroit, I had a player named Calvin Natt." No wonder I wrote to him.

Vining has won 15 in a row and he has a kid I can't wait to

see—Anthony Jones, a 6-3 forward who has been MVP of the
Southland Conference two years running. He got 37 at Arkansas and 32 against Southern Mississippi, so he likes to play
against the big people.

Florida A & M claims it has some stars too. Walter Reed, the
AD, got up at a tip-off luncheon this afternoon and said, "Hey,
you're going to like Kenny Davis. You're going to think Chris
Jackson's out there when he walks in." Later on, A & M's
coach, Willie Booker, told me his big man, Delron Turner, was
a "baby Barkley." Man, everybody's got descriptions. Whew.
If Turner's a baby Barkley and Davis looks like Chris Jackson,
I can't wait to lay eyes on them.

Man, if they have Barkley and Jackson, what are they doing
in the play-in? Unfortunately for A & M, the NBA all-stars
never showed up. Northeast won, 87–63, and Jones, who can
dunk with the best of them, really rocked the house with a 360
slam jam.

I'll go anywhere to see a jam like that. This guy loves the
lights.

THURSDAY, MARCH 7—

The wakeup call came early this morning. I'm going home for
a day before I head to the ACC Tournament, and, man, am I
whipped. Would you believe there was a high school class on
my flight to Atlanta? I was trying to hide in the corner. I didn't
want to be recognized. I just wanted to sleep, baby.

But all those kids came over, and we ended up having a lot
of fun. Boy, to relive those days of being young again. I can't
believe it, fifty-one big ones in and going for fifty-two in June.
I may be heading for fifty-two, but as my girls say, "Dad, you
act about twelve." They couldn't be more right.

I was on my way home through Atlanta when I ran into
Robert McCallum, one of Lon Kruger's assistants at Florida.
He was headed to Bradenton for the Florida State junior col-
lege tournament, which opens tonight.

All those recruiters will be there, searching for an impact
player who can bring them instant credibility. He's got to be a
guy who can contribute immediately, because he's got only two
years of eligibility.

Kruger used to sign a lot of jucos when he was at Kansas

State. He's a believer in the system. Why not? He got a great one out of this state a couple years ago when he signed Mitch Richmond, who has since gone on to become a millionaire with Golden State.

FRIDAY, MARCH 8—

You can tell it's ACC Tournament time. All of the planes heading for Charlotte were packed with fans. I sat next to a couple, Jim and Pat Albright, on the flight up from Sarasota. Jim is a Dukie through and through. He graduated in 1976, then went to grad school there. His wife is a Carolina fan.

"Look at the TV column in *USA Today*," Jim said to me. "You've got Duke going to the Midwest Regional, Carolina to the East. As far as I'm concerned, send that crybaby Dean Smith, whining like he whined last year when he wasn't placed in the East, out west. Yeah, I hope they make him the No. 2 seed, right behind Vegas."

Oh, this guy's cruel, Dean. I mean, is he cruel. He's a Krzy-· zewski guy all the way, Dean. His wife is a little lukewarm. She's not all North Carolina, for some reason. She's not even jumping on him for jumping on you, Dean.

Duke and Carolina have been battling each other all year. Duke won both regular-season games and Carolina would like nothing better than to knock them off in the conference tournament.

It promises to be a wild scene, with 24,000 jammin' their way into the Charlotte Coliseum for the 38th annual ACC Tournament, the granddaddy of them all. Tickets, as usual, are at a premium and require large donations. At Carolina, they tell me you have to donate $45,000 to join the Chapel Hill Rams Club in order to be able to get choice seats.

The pageantry is just unbelievable. The Charlotte Coliseum is packed to capacity. They're committed to play the tournament here again in 1992 and '93, and it looks like they'll be doing it for a lot of years after that. Gene Corrigan, the ACC commissioner, claims there will have to be some special reason for them to change sites.

I did the opening-night doubleheader on ESPN. Carolina dusted off Clemson in the first game, 67–59, to advance to a semifinal matchup with Virginia, which held off Wake Forest,

70–66. Duke, which drew a bye because Maryland is ineligible to participate in the tournament, will play NC State, which knocked off Georgia Tech in the other game.

I felt really bad for Clemson coach Cliff Ellis. You talk about a heavy underdog. His team went from winning the league last year in the regular season to last place—the first time that's ever happened. Cliff needs to get some players. That's why he's been seen all over Florida lately, scouring the junior college ranks. All my buddies tell me they've seen him down there beating the bushes.

Dean's club looked so passive. They were lethargic and didn't play with any kind of desire or hustle even after they fell behind by 12 early in the game. They had to be thinking of round two, because there was no way they were ready for round one.

Or maybe they were thinking even further beyond. I interviewed Carolina's Rick Fox after the game, and when we went off the air, he wanted to know if I thought Carolina had a chance to be the No. 1 seed in the East.

You think these kids don't think about this stuff? You better believe they do.

SATURDAY, MARCH 9—

The newspapers today were filled with surprises. Tennessee and its great guard, Allan Houston, said bye-bye to Mississippi State, the No. 1 seed in the SEC. Rollie Massimino's mystery guys at Villanova upset Syracuse, the No. 1 seed in the Big East. But the big news was down in Roanoke, Virginia, where Louisville, the eighth seed, advanced to the Metro Conference final against Florida State when LaBradford Smith scored on a reverse lay-up with five seconds left to beat Memphis State. What a story it would be if Louisville could battle all the way back from the adversity at the start of the season. Their year looked like it was going to be a throwaway a month ago when the Cardinals—a perennial national power—were 9–14 and still appeared to be reeling from a late-December "Sixty Minutes" report that blasted Denny Crum for his team's poor graduation rate. But now they've won four straight and they have a chance to get to the big dance. That's the beauty of these postseason tournaments. They give teams like Louisville one last shot.

When I got to the arena today, Frank Dascenzo, Bill Brill, John Feinstein, and a bunch of the writers were trying to pick the NCAA field. There is a strong feeling out there that the Big East could end up with eight bids. John Feinstein and I have been known to get into our share of verbal scrapes, but we both agreed that no conference deserves eight bids.

I said on the air later that the NCAA should not take any more than fifty percent of any one conference. I don't think teams like Fordham, Northern Illinois, and Southwest Missouri State should be denied. And I don't want to hear all this stuff about quality wins. In a lot of cases, the big boys won't play these guys. As long as there are automatic bids, the NCAA Tournament is never going to include the best sixty-four teams.

Duke whipped NC State by 21 and Carolina beat Virginia by five to set up a dream matchup in the championship game. Duke is playing exceptionally well right now. Thomas Hill, Brian Davis, and Grant Hill give them so much versatility, Hurley is playing really well, and Laettner, I feel, should be the MVP in the conference. Carolina played better today, too. Chilcutt and Fox were all over the glass, Hubert Davis is really on a roll shooting that jumper, Montross showed tremendous improvement, and late in the game, when Virginia made a tremendous run from 16 down to get within three with nine seconds to go, King Rice forced a turnover and kept Virginia from getting a shot for the tie.

Once the games ended, my personal nightmare began. I took a 7:30 flight to Chicago, then had a four-and-a-half-hour limo ride to Iowa City. Tomorrow I'll do the Ohio State–Iowa game on ABC, drive to Cedar Rapids for the tournament selection show on ESPN, catch a late flight to Florida, and get home about two in the morning. I'll spend a day with my family, then leave Tuesday for Bristol, Connecticut, where Jimmy Valvano and I will be doing studio shows on ESPN through Sunday. Jimmy V. and yours truly, having a little fun in the studio analyzing, dissecting, and making error after error while trying to project what's going to happen out there.

When this is all over, I'm definitely going to need a TO— badly.

SUNDAY, MARCH 10—

"Hey, come on, Tom Davis, do you want to make a big-time statement?" Jim Ecker wrote in today's Cedar Rapids *Times*. "Tell the NCAA and the sporting nation that you're not going to accept the bid to the NCAA Tournament even if you get one. Turn it down because you're going to have your kids go to class, work on term papers, study, stay home. Too much class time is missed."

Wow, wow. Tom Davis has always worked hard to make sure his players attend as many classes as possible. He even arranged for special plane rides during Iowa's last two road trips just so his players could attend morning classes and still play that night. I know graduation is a major concern these days, but there's no way a school will turn down a bid. I mean, an NCAA bid is what coaches and players work for all year long. And besides, if you have the kind of athletes who can't handle it, then you did a poor job recruiting.

Iowa wrapped up its bid this afternoon by upsetting Ohio State, 80–69. I thought Iowa was a lock for the tournament before the game, but this just absolutely seals it, eliminates the judge and jury. They have 20 wins, they've beaten Indiana and Ohio State, plus Michigan State twice, Temple, Creighton, and UCLA. As for the Buckeyes, who are 25–3, they played like they thought they could turn it on and win this game any time they wanted.

We parked way up on a hill so I could make a quick getaway after the game, but I'll tell you something, Dr. Tom Davis, you've got to do something about this traffic pattern. I mean, it's incredible here in Hawkeye land. The game ended at 3 A.M. and we still hadn't budged at 3:50. I was getting worried about making it to Cedar Rapids in time for the selection show. We were moving like two feet every five minutes.

While we were sitting in the traffic jam, I was listening to the Iowa postgame show on radio and Jim Zabel was telling Dr. Tom I probably was blushing because I picked the Hawkeyes ninth in my *Dick Vitale Basketball Yearbook*. Jimmy, I thought you could read. I have nothing to do with the opinions of the respective writers in my annual.

When I did finally get to Cedar Rapids, it was a wild scene. You're hooked up via satellite and you've got all these connections . . . me over here in Cedar Rapids, Jimmy Valvano in Nashville, Bill Cosby and Jerry Tarkanian in Las Vegas, John Saunders in New York, and Rick Pitino in the studio with Chris Fowler.

As for the pairings, I had strong reservations about the Big East getting seven bids and I felt the NCAA had stacked the deck against Vegas by placing them in a Western Regional that also included Georgetown, Michigan State, Seton Hall, and Arizona. I think the West looks like the toughest region, the East the weakest. Carolina, which clocked Duke, 96–74, in the ACC final, is the No. 1 seed there. I think they'll be one of two No. 1 seeds to go to the Final Four, along with UNLV. Ohio State is No. 1 in the Midwest, but I like Duke in that region. In the Southeast, Arkansas is No. 1, but I'm going with Indiana. Hey, I'll even give you four sleepers: North Carolina State in the East, Pittsburgh in the Southeast, Texas in the Midwest, and Michigan State in the West.

I'm a little bit surprised that Ohio State got a No. 1 seed. I know, they're 25–3 and they beat Indiana twice, but look at their QW's, their quality wins, after you take away the wins over those seven cupcakes. I thought that might come back to haunt them. They're also coming into the tournament on a down cycle—two consecutive losses. If I were Randy Ayers, I would be really concerned about that. This is the first time all year they've been faced with adversity.

Two things happened today that bugged me. The first was the Big East getting seven teams in the tournament. That's just not fair. It means that teams like Fordham and Southwest Missouri State, teams that had a hell of a year, don't get the chance they deserve. Heck, who says they're not as good as the others? Remember Ball State last year? Remember Xavier? All some of these teams need is a chance, and they never get it during the regular season because none of the big boys ever give them a chance to play them on their home floor.

The other thing that bugged me was Missouri beating Nebraska to win the Big 8 championship. The reason that bugs me is, Missouri is on probation and shouldn't be allowed to play in the conference tournament. I think that really hurts the image of a league when a team on probation wins the tournament. Who can forget what happened a couple years ago in the Metro when Memphis State, which was then on probation, won the tournament. The conference had to forfeit its automatic bid, and no one from the Metro went to the dance that year.

Kentucky wasn't allowed to play for the SEC championship, so why was it different for Missouri? Even Pitino agreed with me on that one. "I don't think we should have been in the SEC Tournament, and we weren't," Pitino said. "If you're on probation, you shouldn't be allowed to play in the postseason."

By now, you're probably wondering what in the world Bill Cosby was doing on our show. Well, we had Cosby on because he and Valvano had a bet going. Jimmy went on the air last week and said that if the selection committee was only going to take one other team from the Atlantic 10 in addition to tournament champion Penn State, he felt his alma mater, Rutgers, was more deserving of an at-large bid than Temple because Rutgers had won the regular-season championship. Cosby, a big Temple booster, had called the studio with a proposal: If Rutgers got in and Temple didn't, Cosby would have Valvano as a guest on his show. If Temple got in and Rutgers didn't, Cosby would be a guest on the ESPN show.

Well, guess who was right? You got it: yours truly. Temple and Rutgers both got in, just as I thought they would. And because I was right, I think I should be on Cosby's show.

CHAPTER 12

You know how you can tell it's NCAA Tournament time? When Norman Chad calls.

My favorite writer of all time said he wanted to do a story on Brent Musburger and me, on how we weren't going to be part of the tournament for the first time in so many years. CBS has purchased the rights to the tournament for $1 billion dollars. Included in that deal were the rights to televise all first- and second-round games, which had previously been the property of ESPN.

I couldn't believe it. The guy rips me every day and this was the first time we'd spoken all year.

"Norman," I said, "you throw darts at me every day."

Even he had to admit, "Maybe I have gone a little too far. But I have a lot of fun at your expense."

Beautiful. The guy is funny and, I admit, he cracks me up at times, except when my name is in there.

Anyway, if he wanted me to say I was eating my heart out about ESPN losing the first-round games to CBS, I guess he came away disappointed. I told him: "As I've said five million times, I've learned that you can't cry about what you can't have. For example, I don't have hair and there's not a thing I can do about it. I don't have two eyes and there's nothing I can do about it. You learn not to worry about things you can't control."

Speaking of crying, what about the incident yesterday between Bobby Knight and Lou Henson? Come on, guys, you're not little boys. Be big guys. This whole thing sounds like first-grade material.

161

Knight apparently was upset with the Illinois sports information department for distributing material that promoted Andy Kauffman for Big 10 Player of the Year, Deon Thomas for Newcomer of the Year, and Henson for Coach of the Year. So Knight stalked off the court before the game ended—Indiana won by 12—because he didn't want to shake hands with Henson. The two even went head-to-head in the hallway. Then, in the postgame press conference, the General decided to bust some chops by saying he couldn't understand why Illinois hasn't won a Big 10 championship with all that talent and all this coaching success. Then Lou said a few things and the two of them went at it. Lou was absolutely furious. Andy Kauffman of Illinois said it's the maddest he's ever seen Henson.

When Henson entered the press room, he immediately launched into Knight, saying, "Typical Bobby Knight. Always trying to bully, always trying to intimidate, always trying to be king."

It's a shame that recruiting tensions create so much ill will among the coaching fraternity. Knight is too big to be involved in this episode. As for Lou, he's really taken a pounding over the last two years. I would personally love to see all coaches get along, but that will never happen because you're talking W's and L's, intense competitiveness, and a burning desire to be the best.

You know what? I'm going to call up Dennis Swanson and suggest another new soap opera for ABC: "Lou-Doo vs. the General." I could play the role of Lou-Doo. I'll put on my Dickie-do and I'll go head-to-head with the General. Bill Packer can play the General. I think it would be great. I'll get Cosby to give me some tips. You know, I'm in with Cosby now, man. I'm in with Billy C. I'll get him to give me some special training on how to act. Hey, I'll become a male, bald-headed sex symbol. We'll move out "General Hospital."

TUESDAY, MARCH 12—

I got on a flight from Raleigh to Bristol, Connecticut, and who do you think is sitting right next to me? That's right, Jimmy V. What do you think we talked about? Hoops? Forget about hoops. We talked about golf courses. We talked about baseball. We talked about our daughters. Jimmy was telling me he just turned forty-five. Hey, he looks ninety, but that's okay.

He said when he came home from the selection show Sunday, his entire family was there to meet him and they had balloons, ready to sing "Happy Birthday."

This is the first time in twenty-three years Jimmy hasn't had a team. But he's managed to keep busy.

So have I. I picked up a copy of *USA Today,* and I can't believe it. Are you kidding me? They got three pictures of me in the sports section, promoting the fact I'm going to write a column for them throughout the tournament. Me write a column? I can hear writers all over the country throwing up, and I don't blame them. I wonder what my English teachers must think when they see me writing a column. Let's just say that banging the typewriter is not my baby. I'll dictate to guys like John Bannon.

WEDNESDAY, MARCH 13—

Jimmy V. was steamed when I arrived at the ESPN studios today. He was shaking a copy of the *Boston Herald* at me.

"Read this," he said. "Packer ripped us. I mean, I cannot believe this. Here's Billy Packer, a guy who does all kinds of promos and makes all kinds of cash on the side with his Mr. Cash ads. Here's a guy who has an Oldsmobile dealership and has his mug in a full-page ad in *USA Today,* and he's blasting us for self-promotion because we had Cosby on the air."

Jimmy was ticked. "Hey," he said. "I turned down doing Mr. Cash commercials because I didn't think they were right. He's got a lot of nerve. First of all, Bill Cosby called us. He called the station. This is the most popular guy in all of TV. I mean, we're talking about a guy that's like an institution in television. He calls, he's a sports fan. Why not have a little fun?"

Jimmy's right. All we were doing, Billy, was having a little fun. Give us a break. I mean, it is not the Persian Gulf or trying to find a cure for AIDS. We're talking basketball, baby, we're talking hoops. If Bill Cosby wants to talk about Temple, why not?

Tonight, we had a little fun. I wonder if Packer will get on our case for that. John Saunders, yours truly, and Jimmy V. did a live studio show in which we broke down the different regions and interviewed Bill Frieder and P.J. Carlesimo.

Frieder talked about how it felt being in the tournament in just his second year at Arizona State after being so maligned at Michigan. "Well, Dick," he said, "you get labeled as a recruiter and you have to live with that. I don't mind. All I know is, just check out my record. I've been a winner." I'll tell you, the guy's not lying.

I got a kick out of teasing P.J. about all the rumors linking him and Notre Dame. P.J. played for Digger at Fordham. He made my all-pine team, as he sat on the bench on that great 1971 team with Charles Yelverton and company. They had Madison Square Garden rocking and rolling all year long, and then reached the Sweet 16 during the NCAAs.

"What's the deal, man?" I said to P.J. "Is Digger stepping down? Are you stepping in?"

"Hey, I'm staying right here," he said. "It's crazy to even think that. Digger deserves to be at Notre Dame."

When that was over, I went to my room, turned on the TV, and . . . oh, man. Incredible. It was Billy Packer's voice in a little commercial right on ESPN for Oldsmobile. Jimmy V., I hope you weren't watching.

THURSDAY, MARCH 14—

Roy Firestone, one of the all-time Rolls-Roycers in our business, was interviewing Bob Lanier today on his "Up Close" show and they were talking about Lanier playing for me with the Pistons. Suddenly, they flashed a picture of me from back then with my thick glasses, and the entire studio went wild.

"You were ugly," Valvano said. "My God, you were ugly."

"You *were* ugly?" Saunders chimed in. "You *are* ugly."

Come on, Saunders. You're even jumping in with Valvano, two on one in the break. Hey, I remember when you were on my side, Big John.

Well, at least things got better when Lanier described what I was like as a coach. Hey, Bob, I loved your answer.

"Let me tell you something," Lanier said. "This guy knew the X's and O's, knew the game of basketball. But when Dick was there, we couldn't have radios, we couldn't have any music or anything at all on the bus or in the locker room. Unreal. You talk about being firm, tight. Everything was tight. Then I go to Milwaukee and Donnie Nelson and there's music playing, it was loose, relaxed.

"I tried to give Dick advice," Lanier went on. "I told him he had to have somebody from the NBA on his staff, somebody who knew what life in the NBA was about. If he did, I think he would have made it."

No, Bob. I would have made it—maybe—if I'd had a healthy Bob Lanier, a healthy John Shumate. That's the bottom line, what sent me to the showers. It's tough to win in this league when you've got assistant coaches making over $500,000. Lanier and Shumate were sitting on the bench next to me in their $1,000 suits instead of wearing their Rawlings Specials and knocking down jumpers to take me to the promised land.

I always hear about making the transition from college to pro. Who was the last guy to coach college and go right into a head coaching job in the pros? That's right. Dick Vitale. No, not Pitino. He coached as an assistant with the Knicks, then went to Providence before taking over the head coaching job in New York.

I'll tell you where I broke down. I never learned that pro practice sessions are totally different than intense workouts on the collegiate level. I'd put players through intense workouts without taking into consideration that they're playing three to four times in seven days. Lanier tried to tell me that, but I wouldn't listen. I did it my way, and my unwillingness to adjust got me to the firing line.

Notre Dame's in the news again. Their AD, Dick Rosenthal, was not too happy with the comments from Seton Hall AD Larry Keating, who was responding to all those rumors about P.J. going to South Bend.

"I don't know," Keating said. "That was a great job, but not today. Our job's better."

I don't know. Seton Hall's my alma mater. But Notre Dame is national, baby.

THURSDAY, MARCH 14—

The Big Dance began today, and even though we wouldn't be carrying any of the first- or second-round games live as we did in the past, I still had three studio shows to do.

I couldn't believe *The National* this morning. Norman Chad actually gave me some positive PR. At least I think he did. "The NCAA Tournament," he wrote, "became almost a backdrop for two of television's most enduring icons, Vitale and Musburger." What's an icon, man? Come on, Chad. Speaking of Musburger, think about it. What network could come up with a big trio like Al Michaels, Keith Jackson, and Brent Musburger? Pat yourself on the back, Dennis Swanson. That is solid-gold hall of fame all the way.

It was celebration time for the Vitale family. We went out and bought fifty *National*s to frame them, put them in a scrapbook. Hey, your circulation must be up to fifty-one today, Stormin' Norman.

When I reported to the ESPN conference room, they had four monitors hooked up so they could pick up games all over the country. They gave me a telestrator and I broke down Oklahoma State's team defense after their win over New Mexico. Then I got in a debate with Valvano about the strategy in Pitt's overtime win over Georgia. He said Georgia had to foul when Jason Matthews hit the three to send it into OT; I said it was a little too early. It went on like that all afternoon.

And then, what an unbelievable night. Shawn Bradley blocks 10 shots in Brigham Young's 61–48 win over Virginia. Temple beats Purdue by 17. Connecticut knocks off Shaquille and LSU. And, in the biggie, Richmond, the fifteenth seed in the East, upsets Syracuse, 73–69. It's the first time ever that a fifteenth seed has won a game in the tournament—a big, big mega-upset, maybe one of the all-time upsets.

I'll tell you, Dick Tarrant, the Richmond coach, is really something. This guy has worked in the trenches all his life, all the way from Passaic, New Jersey. What a coach. What an X and O man. You talk about a guy who squeezes every ounce out of his players, like Petey Carril. Who can ever forget what Tarrant did in 1988, when he went out and beat Indiana in the first round, then came right back and beat Georgia Tech before eventually losing to Temple.

We had Dick on after the game. Time to celebrate. Dick wants to go out and have a few beers. Then he got serious and explained his game plan.

"Basically, we just tried to shorten the game and really use the clock," he said. "We tried not to allow them to run up and down the floor. We also wanted to try to neutralize Owens. It was just a sensational performance by our kids."

Maybe I shouldn't be so surprised. There's an old theory that suggests teams that are hot coming into the tournament will continue to be hot. Richmond has won 16 of 18. Syracuse came in on a down after that upset loss to Villanova in the Big East quarterfinals.

There was one other big surprise today, although not nearly on the scale of Richmond beating Syracuse. Peter Gillen's Xavier team knocked off Nebraska, the third seed in the Midwest, 89–84. I'll tell you, Gillen's stock just keeps going up and up and up. If there's one guy who would be a leading contender for the Notre Dame job if Digger were to step down, it would be Gillen. He's a former assistant under Digger, and everybody knows he would crawl on his knees from Cincinnati to South Bend for that job. And who can blame him? What an opportunity that would be.

Gillen's team is completely different from the one that upset Georgetown in the tournament last year. The strength of that team was its frontcourt, led by Tyrone Hill, who's now with the Golden State Warriors, and Derek Strong, two outstanding Windex men. This year's team gets it done with perimeter play. The backcourt of Jamal Walker and Jamie Gladden really responded to the challenge against Danny Nee and Nebraska, a team that, even though it went down, still had a sensational year.

I was so excited about everything that happened that I was still talking as we were getting ready to go off the air. I was saying that I wanted to substitute Allan Houston for Harold Miner on my preseason All-America team after seeing the way Miner shot in USC's loss to Florida State. My producer, Dan Stier, whom we nicknamed "Stierdorf" because he went to Michigan just like Dan Dierdorf of ABC, was screaming at me: "Wrap it up, Dick. We've got to go. Wrap it up! But I was in the middle of a two-minute tirade and I never heard him. The reason: My earpiece wasn't plugged in.

Call a T on me, baby. Give me a flat-out technical. I'll take that one.

FRIDAY, MARCH 15—

I was on the radio today with a guy who makes me look like an angel—Chris "Mad Dog" Russo of WFAN in New York. He's a wacky guy, man, but he and his sidekick, Mike Francesa, the CBS analyst, have become the biggest thing in New York. Especially Francesa. You talk about a wide body. Mike's lost a lot of weight, but I'd still hate to see him and Utah coach Rick Majerus go one-on-one at the dinner table. I wouldn't want to pay their expenses for food.

Mad Dog made me feel really great when he said: "Dickie, you wouldn't believe all the calls we're getting from people saying that they miss ESPN coverage of the first two rounds." Hey, like I told him, where else are you going to find somebody who's willing to stand on his head if Austin Peay upsets Illinois?

The big story of the afternoon was Penn State upsetting UCLA, 74–69. James Barnes had a real solid game for Penn State and Bruce Parkhill did a great job on the sideline, but I couldn't believe UCLA down the stretch. Valvano was jumping up and down and screaming, "What are they doing? What are they doing? I can't believe it. They're not even looking for the three. Are you kidding me? You're down six, you've got to think three."

You really have to question the mental toughness of the UCLA kids. A lot of people thought UCLA would be the team to come out of the East, especially after Syracuse went down. But this team has not achieved like it should. The Bruins lost seven games in the PAC-10, and they just have too much talent to do that. You're talking about high school All-Americas in Don MacLean and Darrick Martin, and Tracy Murray is the all-time leading scorer in California history. These guys were just not ready to play today, because they certainly had it all over Penn State in personnel.

But Jim Harrick might have planted the seeds for the upset last week when he told the L.A. media on selection day that he couldn't identify one player on the Penn State roster.

The ironic story of the day had to be Bill Frieder and Arizona State beating Rutgers at the Omni in Atlanta. Two years ago, on the same day and in the exact same arena, Bo Schembechler told Frieder he couldn't coach Michigan in the tournament if he was going to Arizona State. Remember that? Frieder had to sit in the stands and watch his assistant, Steve Fisher, take the Wolverines all the way to the championship.

Another good story today was Tom Penders, whose Texas team beat St. Peter's by eight. I love Tom Penders as a coach. He's one of those guys who always seems to do well in the tournament. Stars are born at tournament time, and this is a guy who's become a hot star. I don't believe, as I said on the air, that Texas is the last stop for Tom Penders. I think some big job is going to pop open and he's going to be on the hot list.

When the night games started, I made one of those crazy deals like I did with Austin Peay. I told Valvano that if Princeton beat Villanova I'd let him tape my mouth shut and I wouldn't say a word the next day on the show.

When he heard that, Mo Davenport, one of my bosses, started laughing his head off.

"Are you kidding me?" he said. "I can just see you. We'll have your mouth taped up, but your hands will be going and you'll be going, 'TO, baby,' trying to get on the air."

"Hey," John Saunders said, "we could also tape your hands."

Well, I got John for that one. As he was talking, I stole his chocolate-chip cookies, man. They bring in the food here about eight o'clock, and you've got to jump in line early because, if you don't, all the technicians will beat you to it and the food will be gone. So I jumped right in there, man. I jumped all over that turkey and mashed potatoes, and I loaded up on those chocolate-chip cookies.

I really sweated out that Princeton–Villanova game, baby. For a while, I thought I was in for a silent Saturday. Villanova fell behind by nine points in the first half, but Rollie Massimino's players clawed back and finally won the game on a drive by Lance Miller in the final two seconds. It was a classic confrontation between two great tactical minds, Massimino and Petey Carril. One of these years, Petey's going to catch a break.

One guy who wasn't catching any breaks today was Billy Packer. We were all over him in the studio for being so serious. Valvano started calling him Gorbachev and then everybody jumped in, saying: "Hey, Gorby's on, baby. Gorby's on."

Whenever Packer's face popped onto the screen from then on, we would all start chanting, "Gorby, Gorby, Gorby."

Don't get mad, Packer. We were just having fun. I'm sure you do the same thing at CBS whenever I'm on. Only then you probably say: "Shut him off. Shut the monitor. Mute that baby." I can hear him now: Vitale is the reason they invented the mute box.

SATURDAY, MARCH 16—

Ooh, was Mad Dog Russo whipping the heck out of CBS this morning for its coverage of the first two days. I thought he was trying to incite a riot. And his buddy, Francesa, wasn't there to defend himself.

Then one guy called in and said, "Hey, I love listening to Vitale and Valvano. They entertain, they analyze." Jimmy and I were listening in the car and we were loving it—until we heard Russo say, "Bye-bye, Art." All of a sudden, Jimmy started screaming in the back of the car, "Wait a minute, wait a minute. That's my agent."

The big story of the day was Temple beating Richmond by 13 and moving into the Sweet 16 against Oklahoma State, which beat NC State by nine. I'm sure John Chaney will get a call. No, not from the president. From Bill Cosby. And do you know what? At Temple, Cosby's more important.

Nobody expected much from Temple in this tournament, but they're playing great defensively and Mark Macon is trying to end his career on a high note. Macon has been so darn maligned throughout his career. Here's a guy 6-5, a big guard who makes a lot of clutch plays. OK, he takes a lot of bad shots, but he hasn't played with a legitimate point guard since Howie Evans back in 1988, when Temple was ranked No. 1 for much of the season. This team's not as good, but they're definitely on a roll now. They've been getting a great effort defensively and now they'll get a chance to play Oklahoma State—which upset NC State, 73–64—in the Eastern Regional semifinals.

Chris Corchiani and Rodney Monroe have finally completed their careers. Corchiani finished with an NCAA record 1,038 assists. Monroe finished as State's all-time leading scorer, but he shot only 4-for-16 in his last game.

The hottest team in the tournament right now just might be Seton Hall. Today they tore up a solid Creighton team, 81–69. Hey, I should call my alma mater and donate a few more bucks, baby. I'm very proud of them. Everywhere I go, I scream, "That's my alma mater." A few years back, I used to whisper it. My guy P.J. Carlesimo is one of hottest guys in coaching.

SUNDAY, MARCH 17—

Hey, maybe there's hope for the rest of the field. UNLV struggled with Georgetown in Tucson today.

John Saunders, who has become a big star on ESPN and ABC, is from Washington, D.C., and is a big Hoya guy, was all over my case at the half when Georgetown was controlling tempo.

"Vitale," he said, "you said blowout."

Vegas went up 15, and all of a sudden Tark starts playing scared basketball. Tark, I picked you as my Coach of the Year. Coach of the Year—you're supposed to be aggressive, you're supposed to go after people. Coach of the Year! I can't believe you're sitting in that amoeba defense, letting them hold the basketball, rather than throwing that Rocky Marciano knock-out punch. Come on, man, hit them with the left hook. Vegas finally escaped, 62–54. If Alonzo Mourning hadn't gotten into foul trouble, who knows what might have happened? Tark probably feels like he had a thousand-pound weight taken off his chest.

By nightfall, the pairings for the regionals were set. Temple will play Oklahoma State and North Carolina will play Eastern Michigan in the Eastern Regionals. Arkansas will play Alabama and Kansas will play Indiana in the Mideast. Duke will play Connecticut and St. John's will play Ohio State in the Midwest, and Vegas will play Utah and Arizona will play Seton Hall in the West.

For our evening show, we used the stock market as the theme: coaches whose stock was going up in the tournament and those whose stock was going down. We had so many guys going up—Ben Braun with Eastern Michigan, Wimp Sanderson with Alabama, Dave Odom with Wake Forest—that producer Stier started screaming at us.

"You guys have got to be a little objective," he said. "Somebody's stock has got to go down."

So I finally settled on Jimmy Harrick of UCLA. "Let's face reality," I said. "I know Jimmy is an intelligent man. He's bright; he did a heck of a job bringing stability back to the UCLA program. But I think he'd be the first to admit, based on their performance against Penn State in the first round, his stock has gone down."

Then Jimmy V. jumped in. "Well," he said, "you look at the tournament, you see Richmond and Syracuse, the biggest upset, maybe, in the history of the NCAA Tournament, and you have to say that Jimmy Boeheim's stock is going down too."

During one of the idle periods today, I caught Jimmy V. in a reflective mood. He was talking about how he had experienced both the best of times and the worst of times in the coaching profession.

The best, of course, came when he won the title with NC State in 1983. I mean, it can't get any better than cutting down the nets in the championship game. V. was so excited afterward, he said he wanted to name his next child "Al B. Querque."

All these coaches in the tournament now are striving for that moment he has experienced. No one can take that away from him, that moment of jubilation.

But then, Jimmy said, he hit the worst of times in his final two years at NC State, the two longest years of his life. He said he was being buried every day in the media, by every writer. Guys he felt were friends turned on him when the going got tough. They just kept throwing dirt. He described how difficult it was to wake up every day, put on a shirt and tie, and face all those people. The only relief, he said, was when he would walk into the gym to be with his players.

"Dick," he said, "there is no way, knowing your sensitivity, that you would have survived that. I tried to stay a fun-loving guy, to have a lot of fun with people, but they just kept going after the jugular. They weren't happy until the day they broke me down to where I had to walk out of NC State, where I loved it dearly."

I'll tell you what, though, the worst was yet to come.

During a break, we were all doing a dance routine, Jimmy

V., John Saunders, and yours truly. Saunders, who won the Rudy Award given by Rudy Martzke of *USA Today* as the outstanding studio anchor, finally got the break he deserves. He's multitalented. Valvano and Saunders can really lay down some steps. I mean, we were doing the ESPN shuffle, baby. We had the cameramen going wild. Everybody loved it, and the producer said, "Why don't you guys dance as we come back to you live?" So, we're all dancing and all of a sudden the camera comes on and those two guys take the cut and I'm left there dancing, man, doing my thing.

They bombed me out, but I let them know, too, on the air. "Those phonies," I said, "they were all dancing, and then they all chickened out when it came time to come on the air." I know I'll get panned by the critics now.

I finally got back to the hotel, and I was getting ready for bed at quarter to one when the phone rang. It was the Garf.

"Did you hear about it?" he said. "Peter Gillen—Notre Dame. Done, finished. And Digger—to Indiana as AD. Digger and Bobby Knight!"

I heard that about three weeks ago, but I just don't believe it, I told him. I don't think Digger's going to step down with the current status. I think he's going to want to go out on top. But I might be wrong. He might be just stepping down sooner than I think. And Gillen sounds logical.

As soon as he hung up, I called V.'s room. "Did you hear it?" I said.

"What?" he asked.

"They want you down at Notre Dame," I said. "They want you to be head coach at Notre Dame. That's the rumor on TV."

"Right," he said, then hung up on me.

Monday, March 18—

Of all the surprises in the tournament so far, the biggest one has to be Eastern Michigan. They're in the Sweet 16 after beating Mississippi State and Penn State, and they were the major topic this morning on my weekly radio show with J.P. McCarthy in Detroit.

"Isn't it ironic?" I said on the show. "Michigan and Michigan State have so many things going for them—TV, the Big 10, prestige, recruiting dollars—and here's Eastern Michigan in the Sweet 16, getting ready to play Dean."

Ben baby, your stock is rising. Get him on the air, J.P. He's got a lot of tough kids from the Detroit area . . . guys like Marcus Kennedy and Lorenzo Neeley. Kennedy's so tough, he's playing with a bullet in his leg after getting hit by a stray gunshot last summer.

TUESDAY, MARCH 19—

Frank Smith, a U of D booster when I was coaching there, called me up today. Thought he had a scoop for me. "Dick," he said, "I'm telling you . . . you won't believe it, but Chris Webber is going to sign with the University of Detroit."

Hated to burst his bubble, but I had to tell him it would be a shock to me if Webber went anywhere but Michigan.

Hey, folks are entitled to their fantasies. I got mine when *Indianapolis Monthly* arrived today, and there I was, right on the cover. I'm wearing an Indianapolis cap and a sweatshirt, and I'm holding a basketball. Can you believe it? A cover boy? Are you kidding me? "A boy, a ball, and a dream," one of the mottos I use in my speeches, became a reality today.

Actually, it doesn't stop there. *USA Today* just picked up some quotes of mine out of *TV Guide* about there being too much boosterism in college athletics. I really do wish the university presidents would step in and do something about the Charley Tunas, the big alums who control the athletic programs and put pressure on administrations to fire coaches if they don't get W after W.

I mean, it has even trickled down to the mid-majors. The Ionas, the Drexels, the Browns, the East Carolinas, the Old Dominions, the North Carolina–Greensboros. And the presidents haven't shown the fortitude to stand up big, strong, and tough and say, "Wait a minute. We're in command. We're not going to allow this to become Jock University, Jockocracy University. We are interested in the student first, the athlete second."

Until that happens, you can have all your Knight Commission reports and analysis.

WEDNESDAY, MARCH 20—

Big day today. My wife and I took our next-door neighbors, Jonathon and Christopher DeGroat, my buddies, to watch the Cardinals play the White Sox in Sarasota. Their dad is a heart specialist and has to put in a lot of hours, and these two guys are sports fanatics. One is five and the other is seven, as cute as can be.

Both guys had their Little League uniforms on. Their mom, Suzanne, told me they went to sleep last night in them. They were knocking at our door early this morning. They were so excited that they were getting to see real major league ballplayers.

We left the house at eleven, trooped out to the ballpark, and got there just as the Cardinals were taking batting practice.

I'll never forget the first time I went to the ballpark. I'm like five or six years old and my uncle Frank Scarpa, a baseball nut, took me to Yankee Stadium. We sat in general admission, I mean way up, but it was just a thrill to be in the ballpark, to see the Yankees, the pinstripes. And, here I am, taking these two guys and I'm fantasizing. I was as excited as they were. I was like a little kid.

As we walked in, they wanted to know where we were going. "Fellas," I said, "we're going right on the field." They said, "What!" We walked on the field and Joe Torre, the Cardinals' manager, greeted us and took the two little guys to the batting cage. Their eyes popped open as they watched guys like Pedro Guerrero, Rich Gedman, Jose Oquendo, Felix Jose—guys they had watched on the tube—take their cuts.

Torre had them running around, getting autographs. My wife had her camera and we were taking pictures galore. Then we walked into the White Sox clubhouse, and what a time we had in there. Robin Ventura showed them around, and they came back with one of his bats. Joe Torre gave them baseballs. Most kids, they get a foul ball, and they're on cloud nine.

These guys walked out—are you ready for this?—they each got two autographed baseballs apiece from the Cardinals and the White Sox, two bats, loads of photos.

We got to sit in the box seats right behind the dugout. Everyone was looking at them. In fact, they gave away a baseball to a little kid who was sitting behind us. They each wanted to know if we could do it again tomorrow. I mean, the whole thing had to be the thrill of a lifetime. Do you think they'll sleep tonight?

Hey, I know I couldn't. I was all set to go to bed when I got a call from Wayne Cody, who does a radio show in Seattle. He said he had Rick Majerus on earlier and Majerus was saying, "I know one thing: I'm better looking than Vitale." You can't be serious, Majerus. Have you looked in the mirror lately? You're the one guy in basketball I know I'm better looking than. I mean, there's no contest, Majerus.

I know one other thing: I don't want to get into an eating contest with big Rick. Seriously, though, Majerus did a great job at Ball State and has Utah on track to be a Top 15 team next year.

THURSDAY, MARCH 21—

They axed us, Packer. They axed us. I mean, the *Sporting News* was supposed to have us in there as part of the five most powerful men in basketball this week. They called me up, they interviewed me. But they got rid of us. They went with the big four—Dick Schultz of the NCAA, Neal Pilson of CBS, Sonny Vaccaro of Nike, and Tom Odjakian, the guy in charge of programming at ESPN. Well, at least I'm happy to see my guy O.J. get some publicity.

Spring is upon us, and in another week it will be Final Four time, baby, party time in Indianapolis. But it's Sweet 16 time starting tonight, and I'm back in Bristol for four more shows on ESPN.

Everyone is still looking for a way to beat Vegas, and Jimmy Valvano said he thought he had found the answer.

"I believe you've got to beat Vegas with dribble penetration," he said. "I played against them, and that's how you beat them. You attack their guards and beat them to the basket. Then set up your inside game with penetration, dumping the ball off."

"Wait a minute, now," I said. "That's their strongest suit. They guard the ball so well."

"Well, we did it," he said.

"Yeah," I countered, "but you had Chris Corchiani. Nobody else has a Corchiani out there who can break down that defense and penetrate."

Utah didn't. Vegas beat Rick Majerus's team, 83–66, with a big second-half spurt.

Final scores can be deceiving, though, and this one was. Tark has a real concern on his hands. His team hasn't been able to blow people away, hasn't been able to take teams out of their offense the way they did in the regular season. And now they have to face Seton Hall, a hot team that is playing its best basketball of the season.

Seton Hall knocked out Arizona, 81–77, behind Terry Dehere's 28 points. I had to eat some crow in that one. I had said Arizona's size was going to be the difference. Naturally, that inspired Valvano and Saunders to jump all over me for picking against my alma mater.

"You guys don't understand." I said. "I graduated from the Paterson division of Seton Hall. They closed that down."

I had my chance for a little revenge when Arkansas whipped Alabama in the Southeast, 93–70. Valvano had picked 'Bama, but I went with Arkansas, baby, and it was blowout city.

Kansas blew out Indiana in the other Southeast game, 83–65. The Jayhawks played like a machine. At one point, it was 26–6. I mean, Dean Smith would have been proud of his disciple, Roy Williams, and the way Kansas moved the ball. I sat there watching what Kansas was doing to Indiana and I couldn't believe my eyes. The guys in the studio—the cameramen, technicians, staff—were all over my case again. These guys are cheering, General. They're going wild. They want you to go down, baby.

They were all over my case, saying, "Vitale, the General's stock—down."

"No, no, no," I said.

FRIDAY, MARCH 22—

Frank Beckman of WJR in Detroit called up this morning, told me they're going crazy out there about Eastern Michigan and Ben Braun. Ben is so calm, cool, and collected. Come on, Ben, make a big name for yourself. Chew on a towel, run up and down, jump off the bench, pop off. Make the most out of this moment in the spotlight. There'll be millions watching on TV when you play Carolina tonight.

Hey, Dean Smith got a little testy tonight. Carolina put on a second-half clinic and ended Eastern Michigan's dream with a 93–67 victory, but Dean wasn't happy. He was offended by a question about Eric Montross, who had been, for one of the few times in an up-and-down freshman season, an absolute monster.

"What do you mean he finally had an outstanding game?" Dean said. "You guys make these kids so big. He's just developing. He's slowly getting better and better, and that's what we look for, for our players to improve."

Dean, relax. The guy was only asking a legitimate question. The kid came in labeled as one of the top players in the country.

I admit there is a lot of pressure on Carolina to get to the Final Four this year. They haven't been there since 1982, and they have the easiest road of any team. I've been calling the Eastern Regional "The Dean Smith Invitational." But Dean, the master psychologist, gets very upset with little comments like that. And he never forgets them.

Admit it, Dean. Admit you got a break in the pairings. Say "We got a great opportunity and it's in our hands now." That's all people want to hear you say, Dean. Are you kidding me? Northeastern, Villanova, Eastern Michigan, and now Temple. Valvano said on the air he wouldn't mind opening up with those four teams if he was still coaching at NC State.

Temple got to the regional final by defeating Oklahoma State in overtime, 72–63. Is John Chaney a riot or what? He described the victory by saying: "You can't win the Dance unless you get off your butt and dance every dance, whether fast or slow."

In the Midwest Regional final, it will be Duke vs. St. John's. Krzyzewski with a big kielbasa on one side and Looie Carnesecca with linguine on the other.

St. John's is playing really well now. They knocked out Texas in the second round and blew out Ohio State tonight, 91–74. What an embarrassing time for the Big 10—Indiana and Ohio State, the two best teams in the conference, getting embarrassed on back-to-back nights. I've been saying it all season, it was not a vintage year in the Big 10. But watch out next year, the Big 10 will be back, big and strong.

Duke beat Connecticut, 81–67, and got great performances out of Greg Koubek and Christian Laettner. Koubek was bleeding, cut, clawing, and he still scored 15 points. John Madden would be in his glory talking about him. As for Laettner, ESPN's Chris Berman, the man with the nicknames, has dubbed him Christian Better Laettner Than Never.

By the way, I got a call this morning from Jim Harrick. I expected him to jump all over me for the things I've been saying about his team, but the exact opposite happened.

"You know what?" he said. "I agree with you. I definitely think we've underachieved. But, you know, you spoil people. Last year we played free and easy. We went out and beat Kansas, and then the expectations for this year were tremendous. We went out and won twenty-three games, yet everybody said it was a bad year and was all over our case. We really did have a heck of a year, but so much is based on the tournament and tournament performance.

"We really haven't been the same since that loss to Arizona when Don MacLean threw the tantrum. I feel bad for him. He took a lot of heat after your comments on ABC about his lack of maturity. I believe he is really gonna learn from this mistake. What we have to do is put everything behind us and look ahead. We've got Ed O'Bannon coming back next year, and we think we're going to have one heck of a team.

"I can stand the heat of being in the preseason Top 10. I definitely can. Heck, you've praised us, you've praised the stability I've brought to the program, so I can take a little bit of heat about underachievement at the end of the year. We did. We flat out underachieved."

All I could say to that was, "The man is honest."

Saturday, March 23—

Billy Cunningham said on CBS today that he felt Jerry Tarkanian belonged in the Basketball Hall of Fame. I have to jump on that bandwagon—especially after seeing the way his team manhandled Seton Hall today in the Western Regional final. The score was 77–65, but it wasn't that close.

Sure, Tark has been involved with two programs—UNLV and Long Beach State—that have gone on probation. Tark built Long Beach into the second-strongest program on the Coast, behind UCLA, then left for Vegas just before the NCAA arrived in 1973. The Infractions Committee hit Lute Olson, Tark's successor, with two years' probation for recruiting transgressions that allegedly occurred during Tarkanian's regime. Olson and Tarkanian have not been close since.

But look at what Tark's achieved on the floor. He's the winningest coach, percentage-wise, of all time, ahead of the legendary John Wooden. He has won playing fast, playing slow. And he's now just two wins from becoming the first coach since Wooden in 1972 and '73 to take back-to-back NCAA championships. With those numbers, he belongs in the Hall of Fame. Case closed.

The big surprise of the day—again—was Kansas, which came back from 12 down at halftime and then took apart Arkansas, 93–81, to win the Southeast Regional. The Jayhawks destroyed Arkansas's press and shot 24-for-30 from the foul line in the second half. Roy Williams had them playing just like they did last year, when they ripped through UNLV, LSU, and St. John's to win the preseason NIT.

Williams really is an amazing story. I heard my guy Billy Packer point out recently—and I agree a hundred percent— that Roy's ten years as an assistant at Carolina are really working in his favor now. Williams had an opportunity at Carolina that a lot of assistants never have—the opportunity to be a game coach. North Carolina is one of the few schools that have a freshman team, and Williams was able to gain valuable experience on the bench by coaching that team. He learned about calling time-outs, working the sideline. It really helped him a great deal when he got the job at Kansas.

What Kansas is doing now ought to tell you all you need to know about the coaching ability of Roy Williams. He lost five key players from last year's team, including pros like Ricky Calloway and Kevin Pritchard, and they're just carving people apart. To beat Indiana and Arkansas within the space of forty-eight hours is absolutely incredible.

Mike Maddox and Mark Randall of Kansas are giving me credit for motivating them against Indiana. That reminds me of the Rony Seikaly–J.R. Reid battle in 1987 when Syracuse played North Carolina in the Eastern Regional finals. Seikaly came out and put a beating on Reid, and then he said, "Well,

Dick Vitale said J.R. Reid was going to lead Carolina to the promised land." I didn't know I had that kind of motivational ability. Maybe I should be compensated by the schools.

SUNDAY, MARCH 24—

Earlier this year, Willis Reed, who runs basketball operations for the New Jersey Nets, told me he really liked Mark Macon. Today I saw why.

Temple lost to North Carolina, 75–72, but Macon was brilliant. He scored 31 points—on the same Meadowlands floor where he shot 6-for-28 in the tournament against Duke in 1988—and nearly sent it into overtime when he missed a three-pointer at the buzzer. Chaney broke down after the game. He said he hated to see Mark Macon go, and you could feel the genuine love he had for his player.

What a bittersweet day for Duke. The Blue Devils earned their fourth consecutive trip to the Final Four with a 78–61 win over St. John's in the Midwest championship game, but now UNLV awaits.

Can the rematch be uglier than last year's 103–73 humiliation in the title game? I'll tell you one thing, baby, I wouldn't ask Bobby Hurley. He spent the entire summer trying to shake dreams of being attacked by sharks. He even went to his teammate Greg Koubek for help. Koubek was taking a dream-interpretation class. By October 15, Hurley had forgotten all about sharks.

Hurley would also like to forget about Carolina. Dean Smith recruited him, but when Carolina could not promise they would not continue recruiting Kenny Anderson, Hurley crossed them off his list. Said, "Bye, bye, baby." Hurley got a chance to watch some of the Carolina game on TV, and, he said he wasn't happy Carolina won. Hey, the kid is honest.

MONDAY, MARCH 25—

It's official: Chris Webber will be wearing the uniform of the Michigan Wolverines next season. Jalen Rose, another All-America from Detroit's Southwestern High, is coming aboard too. Jalen, Jimmy King, Juwan Howard, and Chris Webber. Give me a break.

J.P. McCarthy asked me this morning on his radio show if I thought Webber's signing means Michigan now can challenge in the Big 10. "Can they challenge? They better challenge, baby," I said. "With that kind of talent, the people in Michigan will not expect anything less."

When that was over, Jimmy V. and I hopped on a plane and flew to New Orleans for a national cable TV convention. What a mob scene it was. Hey, guess who else was there? You won't believe it. We're talking Moses, Charlton Heston. Is that big-time or what? Dickie V. and Jimmy V. with Charlton Heston and Dorothy Lamour. They were there for the movie classics, I guess. Then there was the Playboy Channel. My guy Valvano wanted to sneak over to the Playboy Channel booth to take some photos and pictures. Can you blame him? I figured I'd go, right behind him. Don't get mad, hon.

TUESDAY, MARCH 26—

Rick Pitino got a lot of people upset today. He said he thought UNLV could beat the Charlotte Hornets.

I had to change planes in Charlotte on my way home today, and I saw in the local papers that a lot of people are pretty hot over Ricky's comments. Kendall Gill, the Hornets' top draft pick, was really riled. "You've got to be kidding me," he said. "My Illinois team last year, we could beat that team."

How do I think Vegas would do against the weaker NBA teams? My feeling is, if they played the Charlotte Hornets five times, the Hornets would beat them five times. I really believe that. The depth factor would be just too much. Vegas would get killed from the sixth guy through the twelfth.

CHAPTER 13

WEDNESDAY, MARCH 27—

Greetings from Hoosier land. I flew into Indianapolis this morning, and the place already was jumping. Scalpers are running wild around here, and it's still three days before the games. It's legal to scalp tickets here. One guy even tried to sell me three. Can you believe it? I was really humbled. I said, "I don't think I need them," and everybody around me started laughing.

I checked into the Ramada—Lorraine and Sherri were flying in later from Miami, where Sherri was competing in a tournament—and then took a walk to the Hyatt Regency, where all the coaches are staying. As soon as I entered the lobby, I heard this voice screaming out, "Dick Vitale, sex symbol, sex symbol." I looked up, and it was George Raveling at the top of the escalator.

"George," I yelled, "you used to call me when you were at the bottom of the valley. Now you're at the top of the mountain. Harold Miner takes you to the tournament and I don't hear from you."

"C'mon," he said. "Let's go upstairs. The Coaches Association is holding a board of directors meeting. All the guys are there—Gene Keady, Digger Phelps, Lou Carnesecca, Johnny Orr, Big House Gaines."

We entered the room, and the first person I saw was Digger.

"Dick," he said to me, "did you hear the latest? Mark Asher of the *Washington Post* just came in and said I'm going to the Department of Education as an executive. All these rumors. Everybody says I'm gone and Pete Gillen's in, that it's going to happen in a week. They must know something I don't, because I'm not leaving."

I said my hellos to the other guys and then I made my way down to the lobby. Man, I was in my glory. I love running into all the coaches.

Tonight I went to dinner at St. Elmo's Steak House with Lorraine, Sherri, Bob Ley of ESPN, IMG's Peter Goldberg, and Rudy Martzke. All of a sudden, Billy Packer appeared, along with the rest of the CBS Rolls-Royces like Ted Shaker, Jim Nantz, and Bob Fishman.

"Billy," I said, "this meal is on Cosby, baby." He waved and we laughed at each other.

As soon as I sat down, people started coming over to our table, wanting to know whether I thought Duke could beat Vegas. "Don't ask me," I said. "Ask Packer. He's the multimillion-dollar expert."

After a few minutes, I went over to visit with the CBS guys. Billy wanted to know how I would play Vegas. "I'd play probably a gimmick defense," I said. "You have a week to prepare, to do something special."

Then Packer started diagramming X's and O's on napkins. "This is what I would do," he said. "I'd play a triangle, then I would take my worst offensive player and I'd put him right in the face of Anderson Hunt, wherever he goes. Follow him. And then I'd have my little guy, Hurley, play Larry Johnson like Jimmy Valvano used to do when he had Corchiani at NC State. Just to mess up their minds, to try to do something special and unique, because you're not going to run up and down the floor with them."

Everybody has a theory, but I think Krzyzewski believes in his system, believes you've got to take it at them, play your normal game, try to attack their defense and get good shots by driving the ball at them.

A little while later, I saw Pete Gillen at the restaurant. He said three things about the Notre Dame rumors: he hasn't been contacted, he'd certainly have to listen if approached, and he feels embarrassed for Digger.

"Give me a break," Peter said. "Why is everybody doing this to me? I don't understand it. They should be patient. Digger's done a great job."

At one point in the evening, the CBS people sent us over an expensive bottle of wine. Boy, it was really nice of Ted Shaker and his people. I know Packer didn't pay for it, I'll guarantee you that.

Thursday, March 28—

What a wild day. I went over to Q95 with Peter Goldberg this morning and I did the "Bob and Tom Show" live. We took calls about the tournament and did a segment in which we asked the people to call in or fax in a title for my book. Some of the names were unbelievable. Two of my favorites were *Vitale Statistics* and *A Season on the Blink*. John Feinstein would probably love that one, if we did a takeoff on the title of his best-selling book.

Q95 gave me the free use of a big stretch limo for the day, so I drove to a restaurant for lunch and then over to the Hyatt. There, Tark and his wife Lois were holding court out front. "I can't believe it," Tark said when he saw me. "My guy Vitale, I can't believe it. I remember he used to take taxis, and now he's in stretch limos."

Tark told me he was going to be on Ted Koppel tonight. "Jerry," I said, "you better hope and pray that I interview you on ABC, not Ted Koppel. He's not going to be talking about jump-shot city." Let me tell you something about the Ted Koppels of broadcasting. We are talking genuine PTP'ers. He is a genuine Prime Time Performer.

"I'm gonna blow this nation apart tonight," he said.

"Calm down, Jerry," I said. "We don't need any real wild scenes. We're here to play basketball."

Tarkanian's latest beef with the NCAA involves what he feels is selective enforcement. After Vegas signed Lloyd Daniels in 1986, one of Tark's assistants became his legal guardian and there is some question about whether that allowed him to provide the player with so-called extra benefits.

Tark pointed to another parallel. He claims Arkansas coach Nolan Richardson did the same thing when he became the guardian of Davor Rimac in 1988, when Rimac was a junior in high school. Rimac, a Yugoslav exchange student, eventually signed with the Razorbacks and has been cleared to play by the NCAA.

"Where's the recruiting edge, when a guy's a junior in high school or after he signs a letter of intent," Tark said. "We didn't gain any recruiting advantage. And they made that kid eligible, so I don't see how they can turn against us on that."

Tark told me he was worried about Duke. "I know I worry about everybody, but they're going to play like you can't believe," he said. "They were embarrassed last year, humiliated, and I know we've got ourself a war on our hands."

From there, it was inside for an afternoon of hanging out in the lobby. McGuire, you would be proud of me. I was shooting the breeze big-time, playing the role, strutting around like you can't believe. Is this work? Are you kidding me? I love every minute of it. Get out the hot dog, get out the mustard, get out the sauerkraut, because I'm in hot-dog form now, baby.

I was shooting the breeze with P.J. Carlesimo at the Nike hospitality room and I asked him about his buddy Boeheim. "How's he handling all this?" I said. "Is he in town?"

"Turn around, Dick," P.J. said. "He's right there, coming off the elevator."

Sure enough, it was Jimmy B. And he seemed to be holding up well under the pressure of an internal investigation and an NCAA probe into his program, which has been under the microscope ever since the Syracuse *Post-Standard* printed accusations that boosters were allegedly supplying the players cash and free meals and arranging for greatly reduced rental-car rates. The *Post-Standard*'s series also claimed that LeRon Ellis's father, LeRoy, was hired as a real estate agent on the West Coast by a former Syracuse player nine days after LeRon had transferred to Syracuse from Kentucky.

In addition, Joseph Giannuzzi was forced to resign as president of the school's Hardwood Club after the in-house investigation confirmed the fact he had housed David Johnson and Mike Hopkins rent-free at his house the summer before they enrolled at Syracuse and that Johnson had engaged in sexual practices with an underage girl at the home.

"As far as I'm concerned, people in Syracuse have been okay," Boeheim said. "Guys in the media want to make a lot of big things out of everything, but things are going OK. We'll be all right. I'll survive it. Hey, Norm Stewart and Lou Henson survived—why won't I?"

The first part of the evening was spent at a popular sports bar at Union Square at something called "The Big Southern Comfort Nerf Ball Shooting Regional Championships." We had all these guys shooting bricks like you can't believe. I had to go out and demonstrate how to shoot the rock.

The event was hosted by Tim Brando, who just told me he was once runner-up to be the host on "Wheel of Fortune." I wish he had gotten the job. Then he could invite me on as a guest and I could get a kiss from Vanna.

I hustled from there over to the Radisson, where UNLV was staying and Tark was getting ready to go on "Nightline." John Thompson and I were there watching Tark's advisers running back and forth giving him tips. Tark's wife, Lois, was whispering words of advice in his ear.

"Hey, I've got it under control," Jerry finally said. "I'm not worried. I know what to do."

Tark was right. He did handle it well.

"Why subject yourself to this kind of pressure, being interviewed?" Thompson wondered afterward. "You've got the tournament to worry about."

The answer is simple: Tark doesn't duck interviews. He's got a message he wants to send loud and clear—that he's a battler and that he's not going to give in to the NCAA. He will battle and battle and battle. He's obsessed. In fact, Tark believes he shouldn't even be on probation. He firmly believes probation ended with the penalty his program suffered in 1978. That leads me to the theory proposed by John Feinstein. Feinstein's theory is that the reason Vegas was allowed to play in the tournament was that the NCAA sold out. They sold out because of CBS.

Here it is. Blame it on TV. His theory is that CBS gave the NCAA $1 billion dollars for the rights to the tournament and that they wanted Vegas in the deal no matter what. He believes people love David vs. Goliath, and no way did CBS want Vegas sitting on the sidelines.

His feeling is that if Vegas weren't part of the tournament, it would be a fraud in the eyes of the CBS execs. He said every time Dick Schultz denies this, it just furthers his belief that the theory is valid.

I totally disagree. No way in the world did CBS place any pressure on the NCAA for Vegas to be part of the big dance. Why can't it simply be a scenario where some human feelings entered the picture and the NCAA showed some compassion for guys like Johnson and Augmon after they bypassed the

NBA and millions to return to college for their senior year? My feeling is that the NCAA, under the solid leadership of Dick Schultz and first lieutenants like Dave Cawood and Tom Jernstadt, will take more of a commonsense approach to the problems of college athletics in the future.

Sonny Vaccaro is another one of John's pet peeves. John feels he buys and sells players, that he delivered Alonzo Mourning to Georgetown. Can't it just be the kid wanted to play for John Thompson and go to a quality school where players graduate? Besides, can you imagine how Lute Olson, Bill Frieder, Bobby Cremins, Randy Ayers, John Thompson, and every other coach under contract to Nike would feel if they discovered Vaccaro were actually delivering players to a specific school?

FRIDAY, MARCH 29—

Tonight we're doing the NABC All-Star Game on ESPN, so the morning was taken up with a production meeting. These All-Star games can get a little boring, because there is so much one-on-one play. I proposed to our producer, Jay Rothman, that we try to make the broadcast more interesting by picking a preseason Top 20 for next year.

"No way," he said. "I'll give you five."

"What about the All-Rolls-Royce team for next year?" I asked.

"Lay that on us," he said.

My Top 5 for next year is Indiana, Duke, Arkansas, Arizona, and Kentucky. And my All-Rolls-Royce team is Shaquille O'Neal in the middle, Jimmy Jackson and Christian Laettner at the forwards, and Alan Houston and Lee Mayberry at the guards.

I'm picking them by position. I'm always amazed by guys who pick simply five best players. If you pick a baseball team or football team, you do it by position. Do you hear me, Packer and Al?

After the meeting, I ran into Jack O'Hara, a hoops freak who attended Marquette during the halcyon days of Al McGuire and is our VP in charge of programming at ABC. He just told me we no longer have ties to any specific conference like the Big 10. "We're going to cherry-pick," he said. "Pick some great games, do more national games in January, February, and March instead of going head-to-head with football the first month of the college season.

Later on, I had to go over to Union Station to tape our segment for "SportsCenter." The place was jammed. I mean, chaos. Trying to get through the crowds was panicsville. But it was loads of fun. I was having a blast with the Indiana fans, saying, "Where's your Hoosiers, baby? Where's your Hoosiers?" They were having fun too. A lot of them wanted to know who I thought was going to be No. 1 next year, so I grabbed the mike and said, "Hey, my No. 1 team for next year, I'm going to tell you, baby, it's the Indiana Hoosiers with Alan Henderson, Damon Bailey, and Calbert Cheaney."

The place roared like you can't believe. Take down the Union Station building. Hey, I'm no dummy. If I was down in Durham, I've got to yell, "It's the Duke Blue Devils, with Christian Laettner and Cherokee Parks."

Jimmy V. and I did our bit with John Saunders, and then it was off for a brief interview at the local ABC affiliate before driving over to Market Square Arena to broadcast the NABC game for ESPN and to tape my All-Windex team—you know, for the guys who clean the glass. I chose Shaquille O'Neal, Anthony Avent of Seton Hall, Brian Williams of Arizona, Perry Carter of Ohio State, and Harold Miner of USC (I've got to have a guard on the team).

The game was lots of fun. It was three men in a booth—Jimmy, myself, and Timmy Brando—and it went well. We didn't really step on each other at all. Poor Timmy. He didn't get many words in edgewise.

We were just trying to imitate the legendary trio of Dick Enberg, Al McGuire, and Billy Packer, who did such a beautiful job for NBC all those years. That's right. I know I kid around with Packer. But he really has set the tone for what I'm doing. He's passed the test of time. That's the sign of stardom in any profession. Yes, I have to flat out admit it. Mr. P., you have been Mr. Consistency.

I was impressed by several players in the game—LeRon Ellis of Syracuse, Greg Sutton of Oral Roberts, and Elliott Perry, the guard with the goggles from Memphis State. Ellis—who was one of the most maligned players in the senior class—was really aggressive, really went to the glass. Jimmy Boeheim would have been happy. Sutton was drilling the jumper. He can really shoot the rock. He's not a great ball handler, but he can really stroke it. Perry was doing a good job locking up Corchiani. He was right in Corchiani's face, quick as a cat. Jimmy and I were saying at one point that we didn't know whether he could shoot the rock, then he came down and drilled a three on the next possession.

I was going hysterical on the air. "Lock it up, Elliott," I was screaming. "Don't shoot anymore. You've shown the scouts enough. Your liabilities will come out and you'll lose some cash."

All the NBA scouts were there, charting, evaluating, watching every move. They can't make any mistakes, since the draft has only two rounds.

Two guys getting a lot of scrutiny were Perry Carter of Ohio State and Marcus Kennedy of Eastern Michigan. Carter is Brick City U.S.A. anywhere beyond seven feet from the basket, but he can rebound. He showed again tonight that rebounding's his strength. But is it enough? Kennedy had a great tournament and has a lot of power around the basket, but the scouts wanted to see if he's big enough, if he has the range to go out to the corners. Those are the kinds of things the NBA people were here to evaluate.

We finished up, then drove right back to do the 11:30 "SportsCenter." Krzyzewski was our guest, and he immediately started getting on me for saying on the air that last year's Duke team was better than this year's.

"I thought I coached Duke," he said.

"Come on, Mike," I said. "You told me that yourself that the team last year had better size and strength."

Hey, I understand what Mike's doing now. It's a psychological thing. He's got to say this team's better to get the kids really believing in themselves. But the truth is, even though this team does have better versatility and quickness than last year, they miss having another big guy like Alaa Abdelnaby to complement Laettner up front.

But then again, look where they are. Krzyzewski's really done an amazing job. I don't think Mike ever could have believed at the beginning of the season that this team could be where it's at now.

When we went on the air, I asked Mike if he thought he

would have a problem matching up with Larry Johnson and whether he was thinking about using any gimmick defenses. He said there would be no gimmicks, that they would rotate three different guys on him and that he felt his kids were ready physically.

"Hey," I said, "I was talking with Nolan Richardson over at the All-Star Game and he said he thinks you'll play Vegas tougher this time because you were exhausted against them last year from having to battle Arkansas in the semifinals."

"He's right," Krzyzewski said. "I like my chances better coming in rested." Coming in rested and with a week to prepare.

SATURDAY, MARCH 30—

You could just feel the excitement today. The town was wired. It's like I wrote in *USA Today*. Eat your hearts out, Tommy Lasorda and Sparky Anderson. This is where it's at. I walked to the Hoosier Dome, and the fans were all over me every step of the way. All I kept hearing was: "Dick, you've got to walk in with us." "Dick, you've got to stand in line here." I was out there with the real people, man, the real people, and I was loving every minute of it.

Inside, it was even wilder. I had Kansas fans in my face telling me they were going to beat Carolina. I had strangers coming up to me, familiar faces, buddies I hadn't seen in a long time. It was wall-to-wall people.

Roger Valdiseri, Notre Dame's assistant AD, spotted me and made his way through the crowd to say hello. Roger, the Notre Dame flash. He uses the same barber I do. He exchanged hugs and kisses with my wife and daughter—we're part of the Notre Dame family now—and then we got down to the serious business. What about Digger?

"Digger's going nowhere," Roger said. "What's he done to go anywhere? If Digger wants to leave, that will be his decision, but we're not doing anything in terms of firing him."

Then David Berst, Jerry Tarkanian's best friend, came by. Berst is the NCAA's director of enforcement. There is no love lost between him and Tark.

"Dick, if you really want some info, call me up sometime,"

Berst said. "Give me a buzz so you guys in TV know what you're talking about."

"Don't be so defensive, David," I said.

Berst came back ten minutes later and apologized. David's OK. He's got his job to do. He doesn't make the rules. He just tries to enforce them. I guess he was just a little upset about my defending Tarkanian when the NCAA started harassing him this season over what I felt were trivial matters such as hotel incidentals of less than $30 for recruits making official visits and the fact that Tarkanian once bought a newspaper for his players to motivate them.

"Hey," I said, "if they've done something major and they're definitely guilty of it, then nail them. Nail them big-time. But all this trivial stuff that's coming up now . . . I mean, are you kidding me? Enough is enough."

At that point, it was game time, time to head to the stands and watch Kansas go at it against North Carolina. Time to watch Roy Williams go up against his former teacher, the guy who recommended him for the job. Roy played freshman ball at Carolina, worked for Dean Smith and recruited a lot of kids on this team—flew over to West Germany to recruit Henrick Rodl, in fact. If Rodl beats him with a three today, he'll probably wish he left him overseas.

The Kansas fans to my right were going berserk right from the start, and they got even crazier when it became clear that the Jayhawks were going to win the game. But the biggest explosion came from the Carolina fans when referee Pete Pavia ejected Dean Smith with 35 seconds left. It was the climax to a frustrating evening for Michelangelo. His three seniors—King Rice, Rick Fox, and Pete Chilcutt—shot a combined 8-for-36. His heralded freshmen—Eric Montross, who had come home to play in his backyard, and Cliff Rozier—were not effective. The final was Kansas 79, North Carolina 73. Roy Williams, the longtime Carolina assistant, had beaten his mentor.

After the game, Carolina assistant Bill Guthridge ran after the officials in the hallway and had to be restrained. It never should have come to that. A ref has got to swallow the whistle at times and understand what's going on in the game.

I'll tell you, Pavia's really got the quick trigger, baby. He got rid of Billy Tubbs earlier this week in the NIT and he sent

Marquette's Hank Raymond to the showers in an NCAA game in 1978. Hey, Pete's a great guy and a good official, and he's got far bigger things to worry about than blowing a whistle. You talk about adversity, this guy's battling cancer of the lungs. He's an amazing story. Mr. Courage. Runs a banquet every summer to raise money to send kids with terminal illnesses to camp. But I think he was way out of line in nailing Dean. I guess he felt Packer and I were out of line questioning him, too. I heard he called us a bunch of idiots in one story.

Between games, I was talking to Freddie Barakat, the ACC's director of officials, and I told him I thought the entire grading and selection process needed to be reevaluated. "There's too much politics, too much jealousy in the evaluation process," I said. I also told him there was no reason why Dick Paparo, Tim Higgins, and Jody Silvester—three of the ten best officials in the country—shouldn't have been working in a game of that magnitude. Freddie really couldn't say much, other than to tell me that Paparo was absolutely crushed about not being selected.

It's a shame, but the Pavia business really overshadowed an incredible defensive performance by Kansas. Adonis Jordan totally outplayed King Rice. And how about the Jayhawks' freshmen? Boy, did they make contributions, especially Richard Scott. He was on the offensive boards like you can't believe. He also gave them 14 big points off the bench.

This game was proof that all those preseason recruiting ratings are really subjective. Most of the year Carolina was ranked in the Top 10 nationally, and Bob Gibbons of "All-Star Sports" scouting service rated Carolina's freshman class of Montross, Rozier, Pat Sullivan, Brian Reese, and Derrick Phelps the best of all time. In all fairness, he did that based on their high school performance. The Kansas freshmen were rated nowhere near them. And look what happened.

In the second game, Duke made it clear right from the opening tap that it wasn't going to be blown out again. The Blue Devils started out attacking the defense, taking the ball inside. Laettner set the tone early, and Hurley showed immediately that he was not going to be intimidated.

From beginning to end, it was one of the best college basketball games I've been able to witness. There was just such intensity and emotion. Hurley hit a huge three-pointer down the stretch and Laettner scored 28 points and knocked down the game-winning free throws with eight seconds left. Vegas still had a chance to force an overtime with a two-pointer or win it with a three, but they were in complete chaos at the end of the game without Anthony, who had fouled out with 3:45 to go. Vegas threw up a prayer on the last possession and Duke came away with the upset of the season, 79–77.

I said all year that Anthony was the one player Vegas couldn't replace, and they clearly were rattled without him. Without him at point guard, the Rebels let a five-point lead slip away in the last minute and a half. It was the first time all season that they had been tested in the final five minutes, and they came up short. The 45-game winning streak was history.

Strangely, Larry Johnson and Stacey Augmon, Tark's two main stars, seemed very passive. Johnson passed up an open jumper on the last possession and rarely touched the ball inside. Augmon was nowhere to be found.

You've got to believe the higher-ups in the NCAA were smiling after this one. In fact, Bob Ley, who really took me under his wing when I first came on the air, reported on ESPN that sources had told him David Berst supposedly said, "The drinks are on me" after the game. Tell me that's not true, David.

Guess Duke's win shoots holes in the theory that Vegas was the best team of all time. In my mind, that distinction still belongs to the 1976 Indiana Hoosiers. I really believe if Vegas had played in the Big East, Big 10, or ACC, they would not have been unbeaten. As it turns out, they were really tested only four times—once against Arkansas, once against Michigan State, and twice against New Mexico State—before the tournament started. They weren't tested enough during the course of the season in the Big West.

You've also got to wonder if a couple of tough games along the way would have helped Vegas. All season long, they always gave off the feeling that they could just hit a button and turn it up a notch.

As for Duke, the question now becomes whether they will have anything left for Kansas. As Krzyzewski said after the game, "We've used every physical investment that we possibly had in this game." I'll tell you, though, kids are resilient. They're not playing UNLV after Arkansas. They're playing against somebody they definitely can compete with. They also have an advantage, I think, playing a team that uses North Carolina's system. Duke, don't forget, played Carolina three times this season. But then again, Kansas didn't have nearly the physical and emotional test that Duke did.

From the Hoosier Dome, we rushed right over to the "SportsCenter" set to do a wrap, but we didn't get on the air until one in the morning because the NCAA hockey championship went three overtimes. Williams was gracious enough to go on the air with us. I mean, this guy's going to the final game in just his third year as a head coach, and he seemed just so relaxed. He was sitting there in our version of the green room eating a sandwich and reading the newspaper like it was nothing.

The Kansas fans, though, were a different story. They went nuts on me after the game because I had picked Carolina.

"Hey," I kept telling them, "you guys just won a game, but you lost a coach. In my mind, this seals it, locks it, puts it away. When Dean Smith steps aside, Mr. Roy Williams will be the man down at North Carolina."

They didn't want to hear it.

But I believe Roy Williams has the edge over another one of Dean's former assistants, Eddie Fogler of Vanderbilt, if and when Dean ever decides to step down. My gut feeling is, he'll be around long enough to challenge Adolph Rupp's all-time record for career wins—875. The man has won 20 or more games in 22 straight seasons, and I don't see him slowing down. People wonder why I get carried away speaking about Dean, but the guy has been an amazing story in basketball. But it should be a heck of a horse race between those two—Williams and Fogler, with Larry Brown also in the picture. It's the Carolina Derby: neck and neck as they near the finish, with Williams nipping Fogler at the wire.

SUNDAY, MARCH 31—

I can't believe my schedule for these next two days. I've been shaking just thinking about it.

Today I went to Easter Mass with my family, and then it was off to the races. I did a "SportsCenter" with Dick Schaap, dictated my column for *USA Today*, did the Mercedes Player of the Year show and a Windex sound-alike contest at Union Station, went back to "SportsCenter" to tape a segment for the 7 P.M. show, shook hands with some advertisers, and finally did the introduction at a John Wooden tribute. Phew. Get me a TO, baby.

By the time I got to the Mercedes show, I was in high gear. I had to be. I had to be careful not to say All-Rolls-Royce.

I walked in and John Saunders said to me: "How'd you like to coach this five?" And he ticked off Kenny Anderson, Jimmy Jackson, Shaquille O'Neal, Billy Owens, and Larry Johnson. They're the finalists for the Mercedes Player of the Year Award.

"You kidding me?" I said. "That's my All-R— Oops. That's my All-Mercedes team."

You'd think the suckers would throw me a Mercedes. I mean, I get some Windex when I mention their product.

I was glad to see Larry Johnson show up after that heart-break-hotel scene against Duke. All things considered, he was in good spirits. He told me he was looking forward to going into the NBA.

"I'd really like to play for the Dallas Mavericks," he said. "That's where I grew up." My guy Richie Adubato would love that, but he's got no chance. No way will Johnson slip past the fourth pick.

Johnson was there with Tark and Lois. Jerry looked really down.

"Tark," I said, "I know it's got to be tough on you."

"It hurts like crazy," he said. "We just didn't play well. Stacey wasn't to be found."

Tark was really second-guessing himself. For one thing, he thought he should have had Ackles shoot the ball more, because Duke was leaving him wide open and double-teaming Johnson. Tark also was upset about his defensive strategy down the stretch. He thought he should have played more amoeba zone instead of man-to-man. I told him I totally disagreed. In fact, Jimmy V. and I were talking about that yesterday. We said they should have been playing man so they could have come out in Hurley's face and eliminated that three-pointer. Vegas was up five when Hurley got the open look. He hit the three and got it down to a deuce.

After only a few minutes there, I had a pretty good handle

on the NBA draft. O'Neal has already announced that he's staying in school, but I'm more convinced than ever now that Owens and Anderson aren't coming back.

I ran into Owens out in the hall, and he told me his mind was pretty well made up. "I'm probably going to go into the draft," he said. "We don't know what's happening at Syracuse with the investigation and everything. We could wind up on probation. I don't want to get caught in a bind."

Cremins told me Anderson was all but gone. His main reason for leaving, Bobby said, was to provide financial help for his ailing mother.

"There's no doubt he's going to go," Cremins said. "All that's really up in the air is trying to get a feel for where he's going to be drafted. Some guys say anywhere from five to six, some guys are saying nine to ten. As far as I'm concerned, he certainly deserves higher than nine to ten."

We did the show—Johnson won the award—and then it was off to the Windex sound-alike contest. The place was jammed and the contest was wild. Listening to these guys imitate me was very flattering. Some of their lines just blew my mind. As I told a lot of them, "Man, if I sound that bad, I must have done an amazing job conning the nation for twelve years."

The first prize was $500, the second prize $300. The guy who finished second was Spook Daves, the assistant sports information director at Notre Dame.

"Daves," I said, "you better give my daughter some PR now that you got your $300."

He came back with the best line of the night: "They don't have Billy Packer sound-alike contests." I didn't say that, Packer.

The Wooden affair was like a dream. I mean, this is one special man. I was writing letters to him back in the sixth grade. I remember how excited I was when he sent me his "Pyramid of Success" in the mail.

He's eighty-one now and he's still just so sharp.

Wooden hasn't been to a Final Four in a while, not since the death of his wife a few years ago, but this was like a homecoming for him. He's from Martinsville, which is just a little bit south of Indianapolis, so he had all his family with him, and it was just an unbelievable setting. Bill Walton was on the dais and so was Denny Crum, who coached under Wooden before going to Louisville. Sven Nater, another former UCLA center, was there, too, and he sang the great Bette Midler song "Wind Beneath My Wings." And Willie Naulls, who grew up in Watts, played for the Knicks, and has gone on to become a prominent businessman in L.A., told the audience how Wooden played a great role in his development.

After dinner, the lights went out and we watched a twenty-minute film tribute to Wooden put together by NFL Films. It was really beautiful. I can't tell you how touched I was. My wife had tears streaming down her face when coach Wooden finally got up to speak.

Oh, yeah. Almost forgot. I've got tomorrow night's winner.

Three years ago, after Kansas won the national championship, I said I would scrub the floor of Allen Field House if Larry Brown returned as coach. Larry even sent me a brush, which I still have in the house. If I had to go I probably would have lined up a good sponsor, made some cash by following the Larry Brown school of economics. Anyway, I never had to make good on that deal, because he split for the pros.

This time, I've promised I'll do the same thing if Kansas beats Duke. I'm not worried, though. I think this is the year Duke is finally going to do it.

MONDAY, APRIL 1—

Here it is, the final day. The countdown. These last four weeks have been four of the most hectic weeks ever, but I'm not ready for this all to end. We've worked around the clock out here, but you know, I wouldn't trade this for anything.

The first stop today was the Convention Center, where I did a special guest appearance at the Mohinder booth. When I arrived, I ran into two coaching legends—Ray Meyer and Clarence "Big House" Gaines.

Ray told me a great story about Wooden. "Nobody knows this, Dick," he said, "but when I was coaching De Paul in the early seventies and we were struggling, coach Wooden offered to schedule us so we could use the game as a draw. That game really helped us. I've always been indebted since then. You talk about a guy that's a legend."

Then "Big House," who won 816 games at Winston-Salem

and coached Earl "The Pearl" Monroe, brought over his ten-year-old grandson, Loren, to meet me.

"Do a Dickie V. for him," he said. And, I mean, he did. The little guy was unbelievable. He had the whole place going crazy.

As if that wasn't enough, Bill Walton brought over two of his four sons, Chris and Luke, and asked me to autograph two basketballs. Bill said Luke is named after Maurice Lucas, Walton's former teammate on the Portland Trail Blazers. He's divorced and he's raising the four boys by himself. If I told you back in '71, when I was teaching sixth grade, that Bill Walton would be sharing time with me . . . It just blew my mind. I still can't believe I'm hanging out with guys like this.

The day's next major mindblower came a few hours later, when I read in *The National* that Tarkanian was in trouble at Vegas. I talked with Jerry after I saw the story, and he totally denied it. He said he got a three-year extension on his contract that kicked in in February.

"The president's never been nicer," he told me.

Tark also said he thinks Duke will beat Kansas. He loves Bobby Hurley. "He's a winner," Tark said. "He's a tough kid. I've always believed in him, even after he had that bad game against us last year. I've always thought he was special."

Baby, the man knows what he's talking about. I thought, just like Tark, that Hurley would be the difference in this game, and he was. He played flawlessly.

Duke won, 72–65, and got great performances from Laettner, Hurley, and Billy McCaffrey. Laettner was selected as the MVP, but I can't say enough about Hurley. In fact, I feel he should have won the award. He played 40 flawless minutes against both UNLV and Kansas.

His daddy, Bobby Hurley, Sr., has to be so proud. Bobby was MVP of the Midwest Regional and Danny, his youngest, was voted MVP of the New Jersey state playoffs. This has got to be a dream come true for a guy who's a part-time parole officer and coaches St. Anthony's in the afternoon. In my mind, he's the Mike Krzyzewski of high school basketball.

Kansas was just as gallant as could be, fighting back after Duke jumped out to a 14-point lead, but they had a lot of trouble converting their shots and Duke just had a great defensive effort. And the Blue Devils made every big shot that had to be made.

Krzyzewski cut down the nets with poise and dignity. I mean, if I had won, I would have been ripping them out, going bananas, being a wacko.

What a coaching clinic Michael K. put on. I mean, it was incredible. He did it all. He did a tremendous job of substituting. He protected Laettner after Christian picked up a couple of quick fouls. And he adjusted to every situation, particularly when he went to a zone after seeing how easily Kansas was getting the ball inside at the beginning of the game. I mean, that's an incredible adjustment in philosophy right there. This is a guy, remember, who's a disciple of Bobby Knight, a man who hates zones with a passion.

The one thing I would like to have seen was Knight hugging his guy Mike at the end of the game. Knight coached Krzyzewski at West Point, took him on as a graduate assistant, got him the job at West Point, and helped him get the job at Duke. Bobby wanted to stay out of the limelight this weekend and flew out to Arizona to catch some baseball with his guy Tony LaRussa of the Oakland A's, but I'll bet he'll be the first guy on the phone with Mike tonight.

The other really special story to come out of this game was Greg Koubek, a senior in his fourth Final Four. This is a guy who was playing so little earlier in the season—he never even got in against Oklahoma—that he started to question himself and his value to the team. But Mike simply explained to him that guys were playing better and that he had to step up his level of play to get more minutes. By the middle of the season, Koubek was starting at forward. And now here he was tonight, finally with a championship to savor after three years of trying.

When we got back to Union Station to do our bit for "SportsCenter," the place was rocking. Duke students were going crazy, chanting at the Kansas students, "Get the tractors out. Get the tractors out." Then, when they saw me, they started chanting, "Dick needs a haircut."

Hey, I didn't mind. I even put on a Duke hat and was leading some of the cheers. In fact, I think I'm going to change my mind and pick Duke as my preseason No. 1 ahead of Indiana.

TUESDAY, APRIL 2—

Well, here it is, the end of the line, baby. It's been a fantasy trip, it's been Disney World, it's been an absolutely unbelievable journey.

This whole year has been one tremendous trip from Day 1, from the Big Apple to the Hoosier Dome, with all of the stops in between. Oh, baby, it has been awesome with a capital *A,* a four-and-a-half-month journey with a basketball junkie who has loved every moment. There isn't a job in America I would take in place of this one.

Hey, I don't even mind what happened this morning. We left for the airport at 7:30, got halfway there in a taxi, and then— are you ready for this turnover?—we forget we had a rental car. Luckily, we left early enough. The driver dropped Sherri and me off at the terminal so we could get in line, and my wife went back for the car.

And then—can you believe this?—the guy at the U.S. Air counter wanted to talk about next season already.

"Watch Indiana next year," he said. "They're going unbeaten, baby."

Give me a break. Take a TO, baby. It's six months until Midnight Madness.

TUESDAY, MAY 7—

The college basketball season has been over for more than a month, and I still haven't come down to earth.

Do you know what? It's starting to seem like maybe I never will. Forget about Alcoholics Anonymous. I need Basketball Anonymous. Got to see some hoops.

So much has happened since the end of the season—and keeps happening. Just today, I was wandering through the Philadelphia airport on the way back from a speaking engagement with the folks at Unisys when I ran into a bunch of soldiers who had just returned from the Persian Gulf. They were still in their fatigues—the Fort McClellan Chemical Corps from the 318th Division of the Army—and they had just spent eight and a half months in Saudi Arabia.

Well, when they saw me in the men's room, they went nuts. They wanted to know everything they had missed during the college basketball season. So I laid some Duke on them, told them how the Blue Devils finally won the gold ring at the NCAA Tournament and how all those Cameron Crazies, lawyers and doctors, were dancing in the streets of Durham.

I'm doing play-by-play: "Hurley drops off a pass to Laettner to the deuce. Get a TO, Tark." Guys were going crazy.

But I told guys like Lieutenant Marcus Culiver, Sergeant George Zimmerman, and Sergeant Reggie Giles that they were the real PTP'ers of this season, that they were just awesome, baby. Then I played the role of the General, Stormin' Norman Schwartzkopf. I told them, "I'm going to motivate you guys."

The news hadn't stopped, either. Here are some of the things that have happened since Michael K. and the Blue Devils cut down the nets in Indianapolis:

Jerry Tarkanian, who has been constantly catching heat by the NCAA, announced he would coach only one more year at Vegas, then step down, bringing the soap opera there to an end. There are three reasons why Tark is not leaving immediately. One, he feels a sense of loyalty to his assistant, Tim Grugrich. Two, he doesn't want to give any credibility to the theory that the pictures of three of his players with Richard "The Fixer" Perry that ran in the Las Vegas papers did him in. And, three, he wants to see the NCAA investigation through.

Shaquille O'Neal stayed at LSU. Billy Owens and Kenny Anderson made it official and left school for the pros. So did Anderson Hunt of UNLV, joining the other four starters in the draft. Charlotte won the NBA lottery, and guess who Alan Bristow is gonna take? That's right. The big guy from Georgetown, Dikembe Mutombo. They need any star, but I don't think he'll be the major star that Billy Owens and Kenny Anderson are going to be. As for Larry Johnson, who won many of the Player of the Year honors, I think he'll be a solid ten-year pro, but I don't think he'll have the same impact on the game as Owens.

Digger Phelps resigned at Notre Dame and was replaced by John MacLeod of the New York Knicks after Pete Gillen, Bobby Cremins, and a bunch of others withdrew their names from consideration. Shock city. I thought Gillen would crawl all the way to South Bend for that job. But Notre Dame's AD, Dick Rosenthal, may have the last laugh. I think MacLeod, who has almost twenty years' experience in the NBA, will get it done.

I went to the Dapper Dan Roundball Classic and got a chance to see some of Michigan's recruits—guys like Chris Webber and Juwan Howard. I don't want to put any heat on Steve Fisher, but I think the freshman class of Webber, Howard, Jalen Rose, Jimmy King, and Ray Jackson is the best I've ever seen in terms of pure athletic ability. Bob Gibbons had four of them ranked in his Top 12.

I see Perry Watson of Detroit Southwestern finally made it official and signed on to become an assistant at Michigan. I have a feeling that was a done deal a long time ago, and I certainly think Watson, who coached Rose and is good friends with Webber, played a major role behind the scenes in helping put together this group.

I also notice North Carolina lost forward Cliff Rozier, who left the program and transferred to Louisville after considering Florida State and Kentucky. I think he would have gone to Kentucky if Sean Woods, one of Pitino's guards, hadn't unknowingly committed a violation by taking him to a party in Louisville—670 miles away from campus—when the kid visited during Derby week. The NCAA only allows you to go thirty.

Tobacco Road was filled with news. Billy McCaffrey, who played such a big role in Duke's national championship drive, left school and will transfer to Vanderbilt. The word I get is that McCaffrey's father wanted him to go somewhere where he could play lead guard.

I spoke at BC's dinner, and they gave out special awards to all three of their seniors, who are on target to graduate. This is what basketball should be all about. Not just W's and L's. But throughout the night I kept hearing murmurs that Jimmy O'Brien's future might be in jeopardy after next season. Wouldn't *that* be contrary to the Knight Commission preachings. Here's a guy whose players graduate, whose team competes in an outstanding league, and who has never had a hint of controversy connected with his program. It never ceases to amaze me. This has not been an easy time for Jimmy, who recently lost his beautiful wife, Chris. Here's wishing him the best.

EPILOGUE

The National folded unexpectedly and I'm gonna miss it. It provided me with a lot of in-depth material. Frank Deford should be commended for putting together an All-Star staff of guys like Dave Kindred, Scott Ostler, John Feinstein, Charles Pierce, Mike Lupica, and even my guy Norman Chad. The question I have now is, when will Norman pop up again to pop me? I'm checking the transactions every day.

Jim Boeheim and I are going to hook up later this summer in a one-on-one game that will be the prelim for a three-on-three tournament in Rochester. All of the funds raised there will go to Camp Good Times, a charity for youngsters in need, and they are expecting thousands for the event.

On a personal level, my wife, Lorraine, and I just celebrated our twentieth anniversary. My oldest daughter, Terri, just completed her first year at Notre Dame. Played on the first Notre Dame tennis team to be ranked in the Top 25. My youngest, Sherri, who will be a rising senior at St. Stephen's High in Bradenton, won the Florida State high school No. 1 singles championship and made the National Honor Society. I'm really lucky. They definitely get their intellect and their looks from my wife. And my neighbor, my tennis buddy Hal McRae, was just named manager of the Kansas City Royals. He'll be united with his son Brian, who's the center fielder for the Royals. It couldn't happen to a nicer family.

But the ultimate compliment came when I was nominated for the Notre Dame job by Bobby Cremins after he pulled out of the running. He wants to get me off the air, baby, so he doesn't have me second-guessing him.

He's not stupid. He's a New Yorker. He knows what it's all about. Hey, I haven't lost a game in twelve years. Billy Packer and I have been unbeaten over the last decade. We should be candidates for every job in the nation.

Index